ADVANCE PRAISE FOR
THE LETTUCE DIARIES

"In this astonishing, soulful, moving, and often funny memoir-cum-business-primer, Xavier Naville tells the story of how he traded the boardrooms of Paris for the agricultural fields of China, along the way building the country's largest fresh-food company. Word by word and acre by acre, Naville learned how to speak, and to operate, in Chinese. The Lettuce Diaries traces Naville's journey from the industrial kitchens of Shanghai to the red-baked earth of the Inner Mongolian plateau as he encounters hostage-takings and an attempted coup, food-safety scandals, fraudulent suppliers, cutthroat rivals, loyal colleagues, and spends many hours in the vegetable fields of China with the farmers whose traditions and practices shape the food we eat every day. The Lettuce Diaries is a story of where China has been, where it's going, and why it matters to all of us."

— Leslie T. Chang, author of *Factory Girls: From Village to City in a Changing China*

"Xavier Naville's account of how he built a successful company buying vegetables from Chinese farmers and selling them to a huge new market of fast food outlets and supermarkets is sure to become a classic. This is a fast-paced story of diving into China business and almost drowning multiple times, but not quite."

— Yun Rou, author of *Turtle Planet*

"The Lettuce Diaries is an informative and well-written story of entrepreneurship in China. Few international business leaders have more insight about the skills and strategies required to grow a business in China than Xavier. This fascinating book successfully convey the complexities and nuances of founding, scaling and operating a company in the country that is soon to become the world's biggest economy. His style is straightforward and fun to read and his message is clear. It's not easy to run a company in China, but if you do it properly the rewards are significant."

— Agust Gudmundsson, CEO, Bakkavor Group plc

THE
LETTUCE
DIARIES

**HOW A FRENCHMAN FOUND GOLD
GROWING VEGETABLES IN CHINA**

XAVIER NAVILLE

The Lettuce Diaries

By Xavier Naville

ISBN-13: 978-988-8552-89-4

BUSINESS & ECONOMICS / General

EB143

Published by Earnshaw Books Ltd. (Hong Kong)

To my Orchid

Author's Note

This is a work of nonfiction. Most of the events described in this book were witnessed firsthand or documented through interviews. The names of certain characters featured in the book have been changed to protect their privacy.

Contents

Contents

PREFACE

HOSTAGE TO BROCCOLI

WHEN SUN GUOQIANG climbed into the front seat of the black Volkswagen Santana on a drizzly day in January 2001, the last thing he expected was to be taken hostage over a shipment of broccoli. He was wrapping up a business trip to Linhai, amid the flat rural expanse of eastern China, on a mission to find the best broccoli for my fledgling vegetable company, Creative Food. His day had begun in the usual way: awakening in a cold local hotel room, washing his face and hands with water from a thermos (the hotel turned on hot water for only two hours each evening) and slurping rice porridge with other hotel guests in the common room.

Sun was no stranger to the rough countryside. Like hundreds of millions of Chinese, he had grown up on a family farm of less than a half-acre, where his parents planted rice, corn, and some vegetables. A young man in his twenties, he had the dark skin and small stature of many people from rural Anhui, a landlocked province whose harsh continental climate forced many of its population to migrate to larger cities like Shanghai in search of a decent income. But Sun had studied hard and graduated from the prestigious Shanghai Agriculture Institute before joining the city's Agriculture Research Center. His courteous smile masked a scrupulous mind and fierce ambition. I had hired him away as an agronomist for Creative Food only a few weeks before. He was looking forward to a visit home with his parents now that his two-week trip was ending.

After breakfast, he went outside looking for a ride to the packing house where Wang Jinzhuang, our company's local supplier, sorted the harvested broccoli. But Wang was already waiting for him in a car. Once he saw Sun, he got out of the car.

"Get your things," Wang said. "I'm moving you to my house."

Wang had picked Sun up at the guesthouse before. But Sun could feel today was different. Wang usually told stories in the staccato of the local dialect, punctuating an uninterrupted flow of words with jokes and laughs. Now he was short and cold. Sun decided it was probably better to do as Wang said. The two men drove in silence to Wang's home, a five-story building with bare concrete walls a few minutes away. Once there, Wang settled Sun in a room on the second floor.

Sun eventually asked why he had been moved.

"Your company owes me money, and you're not leaving until I get what I want," Wang said. "Don't try to escape. I know everyone here: the police, the government. Everyone here depends on me. So, stay put until the people at Creative Food pay me what they owe me."

Sun's first call was to Yang Zhongcheng, his manager at Creative Food and the man I had running the company's agriculture operations. When I learnt about Sun's predicament, I tried to hide my astonishment and anxiety. I wanted him freed, but I also didn't want to fold. Giving in would set a precedent for other suppliers to whom I owed money. It was true that I hadn't paid Wang for a certain container of broccoli that his company had shipped to Japan a week before. I had taken a gamble on it, because the broccoli heads were smaller than usual and my Japanese customers were picky. The market had recently been tight, and these customers had indicated they might relax their standards for the same price. But in the end, they turned it down. I knew Wang had pressured my company's executives into accepting the low-quality broccoli, and so I wanted him to share the hit with us. He had refused, arguing that we owed him the full amount. I learned later that he himself was worried that he wouldn't be able to pay the hundreds of farmers who had sold him the broccoli, carrying it on tricycles to the little corrugated-iron shed where his twenty workers put it in boxes.

So, he had taken a hostage. I winced as I imagined myself picking up the phone with an interpreter to tell Sun's mother and father, "Your son is being held against his will by a farmer in the countryside."

"Why?" they would ask.

And I would have to tell them the truth: "Because I've failed to do my job."

I was less than a year into the start of my company. I was running out of cash. Every business I had started was losing money. And now, eight hours' drive away from our Shanghai headquarters, a hard-nosed local entrepreneur had imprisoned a decent young man I had hired away from a safe government job. Watching employees pace the corridor outside my office, I realized that no amount of analysis and blame would make up for my failure. I was alone. I had to decide what to do. I wished I could lie down on the carpet of my office, just for a minute or two. But the glass door let everyone see inside.

Some Westerners come to China in the hope of creating a new identity. Moving to China for me was a calculated choice, one that involved no dreams or passions. I didn't have an urge to start a business, either, but I had always felt an urgency to see the world. For a large part of my childhood in France, I grew up in the hotels my parents managed for a government-owned chain that only accepted sailors. I remember accompanying my dad on board cargo ships stationed in the port of Le Havre, ships with dangerously steep corroded stairs, an overwhelming smell of fuel oil, watertight metal doors that clanged behind us, and the Filipino sailors' family pictures next to their bunk beds. This was my playground. The sailors, missing their own kids back home, gave me candies and soft drinks. These rough men were poorly shaved, their tight T-shirts tainted with grease, and they spoke abstruse languages. I could have been intimidated, but their faces brightened when they watched me roaming around, and I knew instinctively I had nothing to fear. Better, I felt special. On the bows of those ships, flags transported me to exotic ports of origin: Panama, Malta, the Bahamas, Taiwan. I didn't know they were just flags of convenience.

And though my parents brought me up in restaurants—my dad was a chef—I meandered through the hot kitchen madhouse during lunch service without really paying attention to what was happening there. Later, I studied business with the vague idea that it was the best path, practically, and I decided to major in finance after a partner at a prestigious accounting firm challenged me with basic questions I couldn't answer.

My decision, years later, to move to China was equally pragmatic. Shanghai was where I was needed in a business sense, so that is where I went. I had no particular sense of the Chinese people, no detailed knowledge of Chinese agriculture or food processing or any of the things that in just a few short years would become my life's work. I spoke no Chinese and, after seeing the mysterious neon characters flashing over mom-and-pop shops on the wet Shanghai streets on my first visit, had little hope that I would ever be proficient at it. It was simply another unsentimental step in my career.

At first, I saw the Chinese as a uniform group of people. Their reserve, their indirect way of expressing opinions, led me initially to overlook a lot that was important. I remember observing the staff at my company at lunch, watching as they chewed their food, rolling tiny bones in their mouth and spitting them polished and bare of meat directly onto their stainless-steel trays. Always smiling or joking in the Shanghai dialect, they looked relaxed, happy to be squeezed against each other. I sat apart, a little envious of their rapport, but also a little appalled at the spitting of tiny bones onto the common table.

Over time, though, I learned what was at stake in these individuals' lives and livelihoods. I came to understand not only my own company's workers, who struggled to comprehend why anyone would buy lettuce, much less the lettuce in a bag we were trying to sell, but also farmers like those broccoli growers who carted their crop to the packing shed, and calculating middlemen like Wang, trying to placate overseas buyers with finicky and incomprehensible tastes.

In the same way their lunchtime habits mystified me, the things ordinary Chinese did as they struggled to lead a better life made them seem cunning, ruthless and inflexible in my eyes. Their history and their values were vastly different from mine. But eventually I began to see them as individuals and their real struggles. My own workers, I discovered in many cases, had left families and children back in the village and shared tiny rooms where they piled into bunk beds at night. Office staff usually came from Shanghai, but they also dealt with their own challenges. One of my accountants' daily commute took up to four hours. At home, she took care of her child—she monitored homework for three hours after school—and also her parents who lived with her. Working in a company with Westerners who had expectations of certain behavior—we wanted her to be resourceful and self-driven—added to the burden of her home life. Once I realized this, even the behavior at lunch began to make sense. Around the table, pressed against each other on a bench, my Chinese co-workers enjoyed the feeling of being part of a group. Bonding, they re-created their village communities and family networks with their colleagues. I will never be Chinese and I won't pretend to be a China hand. But I learned to enjoy those moments too.

My story is a patchwork of mistakes and chance encounters leading to success against great odds. I built a business from nothing into the largest fresh-food company in China. I struggled with near-bankruptcy and treacherous managers. I discovered that my Western education had to be blended with an entirely new set of principles guiding relationships between people. In the end, I sold Creative Food to a European company, along the way becoming one of the rare foreigners in China who built a business by buying crops grown by Chinese farmers and selling the resulting products to Chinese consumers.

Food safety in China, now the world's largest producer and consumer of food, is a global problem. One food scandal after another has erupted in recent years, despite repeated assurances by the authorities that they are tackling the issue. The country is now America's third-largest food supplier, accounting for most of its cod, a third of its processed mushrooms, and a third of its garlic. Large quantities of imported Chinese dried and frozen ingredients go into many of the processed foods that Americans eat. In 2019 China exported around $65 billion worth of food to the rest of the world, so it is not a surprise that anxiety spreads around the globe each time a new Chinese food scandal flares up. But the Chinese themselves care just as much about food safety, and they respond by often preferring to buy foods that aren't made in China. In 2019 China imported more food than it exported—$133 billion—three times as much as a decade ago. This trend will not stop, simply because China's agriculture cannot keep up with the needs of a fast-changing population. As more Chinese buy the imported meats, fruits or fish they need for their families, more farmers, producers and consumers around the world will feel the impact.

If you struggle to comprehend the scope of it, think of the vast American food market.

Then multiply it by four.

Too often, media reports lump the Chinese government and the companies caught in a new scandal together in scathing commentaries. Even those who try to repair the damage are accused of being evildoers, incompetents or both. But understanding how this can change starts with learning who is behind it all: hundreds of millions of Chinese farmers, their lives, their aspirations, their struggles.

For a week, Sun stayed in Wang Jinzhuang's house in Linhai. At night, Wang came down and slept in the same room on an adjoining bed.

"I want you to eat good meals," Wang said, "but don't try to escape."

Once he had gotten over his initial fear, Sun took the measure of his captor. "Wang is not a bad guy," he said later to his boss. "Like many farmers, he reasons in very simple terms and focuses on the cash he feels he is owed."

When Sun was tired of watching TV alone in his room, Wang took him out for walks along the seashore a few minutes away. There, they sat at a small temple, looking over the horizon in silence. Sun even felt secure enough to argue openly with Wang, raising his voice in anger, explaining that Wang's behavior was illegal. At times, Wang nodded, but then caught himself and added, "*Mei banfa*—I have no choice."

Eventually I sent Yang out to rescue Sun with some cash toward the amount we owed. I had come to understand the situation: Wang was trapped between my company and the farmers. But I also explained that he had to bear some of the cost, and in the end, he agreed to swallow a good portion of what our company owed him. I continued buying from him for the rest of the season at a reduced price. When I finally saw Sun, I gave him a hug, and he traveled at last to see his family.

As a Westerner, I thought Wang's actions were morally wrong. But Wang, who was accustomed to cramming bad broccoli into a box and hoping customers didn't notice its poor quality, had not grown up in a society steeped in two thousand years of Judeo-Christian values. He had been shaped by forces just as powerful and just as heavy with tradition—and in many cases opposed to the values I thought were fundamental to every business negotiation. It wasn't necessarily Wang and his fellows who needed to learn from me. In order to run a business in China, I needed to learn from them.

And learn I did: over and over again, as China transformed before my eyes from a purely practical career choice into the defining adventure of my life.

1

SELLING RICE TO THE CHINESE

THE VIEW FROM the window of my ancient Volkswagen taxi was not inspiring. The buildings of Shanghai resembled sad gray giants, with air-conditioning units covering them like warts. Heavy clouds leaking an incessant drizzle draped the tower tops. Rugged men in drab navy-blue suits that were too big for them shambled along busy roads, their hands in their trouser pockets and their jacket forearms shiny with wear. On that day in June 1997, it all looked particularly dreary to my ignorant eyes. But I had only two days to decide whether it was worth leaving my company's plush headquarters in Paris and moving to Shanghai.

At twenty-seven years old, I was no stranger to uncomfortable foreign locales. In my four years at Compass Group, a London company managing canteens in seventy countries, I had traveled across Asia and Eastern Europe, preaching the gospel of disciplined financial management to newly-acquired companies. In Moscow, I had faced Kalashnikov-bearing militiamen paid by the mafia to control access to the airport, where we produced ready-made meals for airlines. I had spent a lot of time in India training a new joint venture's finance staff in Mumbai's damp basements. In my narrow view of the world, finance was at the center of everything; keep it in order, I believed, and everything else would be fine. Cleaning up the books of a money-losing

Chinese venture seemed like a natural next step.

But on that first day, something bothered me. Didn't I need to be passionate about China to move here? India felt like a technicolor movie in comparison. When I saw the passersby in their sad-looking blue and gray clothes, my mind kept going back to the Indian people wrapped in bright fabrics. Despite much misery — rank odors, stomach bugs — Mumbai felt real, joyous even. In Shanghai, I smelled nothing, felt nothing. I hoped that something brighter was hidden behind the bland faces and incomprehensible language, which sounded to me like the chuff of a steam engine sometimes punctuated by *wows* and *wahs*.

The second day didn't go much better. Asiafoods, the company Compass had invested in, operated a factory located on the outskirts of Shanghai, near the airport. The large compound included an office building and a large U-shaped factory hosting a central kitchen and several preparation workshops. In the back, there was an empty lot overgrown with weeds. In the large poorly insulated office, the American founder, Mike DeNoma, gave me the sterile pep talk I guessed he had given a hundred times before: "We're going to serve safe, hygienic meals to the largest population in the world." I had seen his books. He had been working on that lofty mission for three years already and had run out of cash trying — China's government-run schools had too little money to buy lunches made by expatriates with imported equipment. Once Compass bought a twenty percent stake with an option to buy the whole company five years later, it was understood that Asiafoods would focus on staff canteens in offices and factories, something the British caterer already did successfully in thousands of locations around the world.

But even though he theoretically wanted me here, it was clear that he and his tight team of founding managers saw me, in my impeccably-tailored suit, as an outsider. After hearing his talk, I visited the vast and empty food-processing plant next to the office, following a Chinese-American manager roughly my age, tasked with the chore of showing me around. He pointed at empty rooms and idle equipment as fast as possible, explaining their functions in English words I didn't understand. The only part of the building that seemed alive was a workshop with a dozen lady workers dressed in white lab coats and wearing disposable masks, cutting vegetables on stainless steel tables. Once in a while, he paused to address the local staff in Chinese, leaving me in awe of his language skills—and conflicted about whether I could do any good there at all, for Asiafoods, for these foreign people, for myself.

In the end, as always, I made the practical choice. For all its bleakness, Shanghai's infrastructure was decades ahead of Mumbai's. The Chinese economy was growing by more than eight percent every year, attracting the attention of businesspeople everywhere. Newspapers claimed that one-third of the world's construction cranes were stationed there. If I succeeded in this job, I could write my ticket to the next one, I thought. So I signed a two-year contract with Asiafoods, packed my things and left Paris for good, just three months after that short first visit to Shanghai. I would just have to live without colors for a while.

My new home was in the gloomy town of Xujing on the outskirts of Shanghai, not far from the airport. The area would one day become a prime residential district covered with multi-million-dollar villas, but when I arrived in September 1997, it was just a large industrial zone surrounded by rice paddies. I lived in a modest pink-tiled walk-up in a gated community that overlooked the one and only store in a one-mile radius. It was stocked with instant noodles, biscuits, sodas and other staples, but no fresh produce, fish or meat. For all its drabness, the place was an oasis alongside a high-traffic highway, a few minutes away by car from Asiafoods' plant and my office. I would go for my morning runs out among the paddies, trying to ignore the smell of manure — human and animal — that farmers spread over the crop to save on fertilizer.

Every morning, I would phone the local taxi company's call center. "Hoo Tching Ping Loo, Yi Tchien Babaihao," I would say hesitatingly, reciting Asiafoods' address on Huqingping Road, using the only words of Mandarin Chinese I knew, and dreading the times when the operator asked for clarification. When that happened, I either repeated the same sentence or hung up, hoping to try again with another less chatty operator. But *Huqingping Road #1800* and the number I called from were enough most of the time for them to figure out where I was and where I was going. My colleagues — Americans, Austrians, Frenchmen and others — would be standing on the sidewalk, also waiting for taxis. We never coordinated with one another to share the five-minute ride, even though we all lived in the same compound. Maybe that was the first sign that something was wrong at my new employer. A blend of mainly European and American managers, we clearly were not communicating well, not managing expenses properly, and not working as a team.

Every evening I took a taxi back. I cooked most of my meals at home or ate quickly in the cavernous, nearly empty restaurant across the block. Alone, staring at a molding carpet covered with cigarette burns, I quickly consumed the handful of Chinese dishes I had learned to recognize — stir-fried broccoli and dumplings mainly — before heading home. Socializing was rare; I had a reputation among my colleagues for falling asleep at the dinner table.

At my new job, I had the impressive-sounding title of vice

president of Finance. "You'll sit on the purse," my boss back in Paris had said with a wink when I left. But I quickly realized that the crisis at my new employer ran much deeper than any finance director could solve.

Asiafoods had been set up three years earlier by Mike, a high-level corporate executive turned entrepreneur whose ambition was to supply good clean food for the largest population in the world. Initially hired to investigate the possibility of starting a Western fast-food brand in China by Hutchinson Whampoa, a sprawling Hong Kong-based conglomerate, DeNoma became convinced that the real opportunity lay instead in making safe Chinese, rather than Western, fast food at a time when the country's food supply was still early in its modernization.

When the conglomerate decided not to pursue the investment, he raised private equity and started Asiafoods. Endorsed by Yu Roumu, China's head nutritionist and the widow of Chen Yun, a high-profile Communist leader, he received a license for what was at the time a rare wholly foreign-owned food-production business. The license gave his venture much greater room to maneuver than a joint-venture with a local state-owned company would have had.

Asiafoods built its first plant in Beijing and cut its teeth by serving meals to two schools there. When it won the contract to serve a giant theme park set to start operations in Shanghai, DeNoma moved quickly to build a second plant there. "We tried across many, many meetings to have the theme park company to let us finish the Beijing factory and ship the food chilled to Shanghai," he said to me later. "They refused ......so we built a factory in record time, rerouting all the equipment from Beijing, setting up the 17 different hot food restaurants in the park."

By the time I arrived, the theme park had failed. "The park had been forecasting 10,000 visitors a day, but it is getting only

100," Mike said in an article written at the time. After that, he shifted again, opening ten restaurants inside nearby factories run by multinationals to feed their Chinese workers, setting up the platform for what would eventually attract Compass' s interest.

Mike never stopped coming up with new ideas to rekindle the company or accelerate growth. When the goal of "feed the factory workers of China" wasn't achieved quickly enough, it morphed again, into "feed the train passengers of China" and "feed the plane passengers of China."

There was merit in Mike's persistence to reinvent the company rather than simply abandon the field. But every pivot caused the Asiafoods ship to creak and groan. A born salesman, Mike would return from prospective clients' meetings asking everyone to drop what they were doing and work instead on the next big thing. Some of us questioned the reason for such haste, but most Chinese employees simply fell in line, dutifully obeying instructions. Nobody asked them what they thought, anyway.

A man in a hurry, the Ohio native had been Procter & Gamble's youngest brand manager. Then he went on to run strategic planning for Pepsico in Europe. And soon after that, he was running 2,000 restaurants for one of KFC's largest operating regions in the U.S. A few years later, in the early 1990s, he jumped to banking and became Senior vice president for Citibank Asia. That's when Hutchison Whampoa hired him to explore investments in China's food sector.

The day I met Mike, he was wearing a blue sleeveless puffer vest over a white open collar shirt and crisp blue cotton slacks. Bad insulation made for freezing winters inside the office, so he had adopted this Casual Friday look. The tall square-jawed middle-aged American was still in amazing shape two decades after his days as a Golden Glove-winning amateur boxer. His blond crew cut and blue eyes radiated a buzzing energy that could turn fierce in a blink if things didn't go his way. But most mornings, Mike bounced around the office with a bright smile, coffee mug in hand, exhorting staffers with brash and loud encouragement.

"Hey Xeiiiivieur, Goooood Mooorning!" he would call to me in the deep confident voice of a coach shouting from the sidelines, slapping me on the shoulder.

I didn't know how to respond in the same casual tone. The whole thing left my inner French snob a little aghast and embarrassed by such familiarity. In contrast to Mike, I had kept my gray suits, silk ties and smart leather shoes.

Even his comments on my memos sounded over-the-top: "Excellent!" "Fantastic!" "Amazing!" he would write in big round red letters. Instead of being happy, I wondered whether something was wrong with my work, that he thought I needed so much praise.

For all his exuberance, Mike could also be stubbornly dismissive. In fact, when I confronted him with problems he didn't want to acknowledge, he reasoned and spoke so fast in rejecting my case that I couldn't keep up.

"It's a moot issue," he would say, an introductory phrase that meant he was about to destroy the argument I was planning to make. I often emerged from his office dazed and confused, kicking myself for not making my point more convincingly.

Nevertheless, it was hard not to like and respect him. Despite traveling monthly to visit his wife and five young children in Ohio, he never seemed tired. He exuded positive energy, powering ahead with pep talks and always ready with a quote from one of the many self-help books he speed-read every week. Though I disliked his rushed decisions, I appreciated his personal rigor; he spent most evenings at the gym or on the phone with his family while other expats hung out in bars.

Like so many businesspeople in the 1990s and the early aughts, Mike had been seduced by the allure of 1.3 billion potential customers without figuring out the proper strategy to reach them. Observing China from his own experience in the U.S. and Southeast Asia, Mike brought strategies that worked well elsewhere but did not apply to China. It worked like this: A Chinese-American chef trained in the U.S. led workers in Asiafoods' central kitchen in cooking meals that they then chilled and packed into vacuum-sealed plastic bags to be transported to clients' canteens. In the canteens, patrons watched in disbelief as staffers — none of whom were cooks — dumped the bags' contents into stainless steel pans, often spilling in the process.

By the time I arrived, Asiafoods was quickly burning through Compass's cash. The canteens were operating profitably but aside from the daily meal deliveries, the plant in Shanghai was nearly empty. Meanwhile construction had stopped in Beijing. Thinking he wouldn't get more money to finish the work, Mike decided to sell a stake in the Beijing plant to raise funds. One possible buyer was Sara Lee, which was looking for ways to make its eponymous cheesecake in China.

"This is for all effective purposes a turnkey operation; you can start to manufacture as soon as you outfit the factory with your equipment," Mike told the Sara Lee executive at our meeting in a five-star hotel in Beijing.

Anyone who had walked the plant would know that was an exaggeration. It looked more like a storage facility for all of the unused equipment that Asiafoods had bought for various projects. In his efforts to reinvent the company's model, Mike had moved equipment from one plant to another, not always able to make good use of what had been purchased. The "turnkey" factory that Mike described was a labyrinthine warehouse of half-opened wooden crates. Each time I visited, I felt a pinch in my stomach at the sight of so much money laying idle.

But Mike believed Asiafood's rare business license was what made it stand apart. In the meeting with Sara Lee, he stuck to his mantra: always begin on a positive note to set the tone of the conversation.

"The value is in two parts," he said. "First, you start with a completed factory envelope and infrastucture, both to Western standards, with all electrical, water, gas approvals. Second, you can operate under a Wholly Foreign-Owned (WOFE) business license in the most senior jurisdiction in the country. A WOFE license allows you to effectively branch your operations nationally."

The Australian CEO of Sara Lee's Asian operations wasn't very impressed. "Well, there is a lot of work to be done based on what I've seen," he said calmly.

"Look," Mike replied, "if you want to enter China's food business through Beijing, we are your only option other than going into a joint venture partnership with a Chinese company."

He then detailed horror stories about the challenges of working with Chinese joint-venture partners that had little experience with Western business practices. "China doesn't believe it needs foreigners to teach it how to make food, and they're probably right," Mike concluded. "The only reason we were approved for a wholly-owned license, is because of our commitment to help the country protect its children by making school lunches hygienic and safe."

I could see the Australian taking in the point. China was very strict about the kinds of businesses in which it allowed foreign companies to invest. Unlike the auto industry, food was considered a traditional sector that didn't need foreign knowledge to grow. So, the Chinese usually tried to protect local players by restricting the issuance of business licenses to foreign food companies.

"It's going to be nearly impossible for you to obtain a license like that," Mike explained, staring at the executive with intensity. He added that someone else would probably grab the chance if Sara Lee didn't: "It's your choice!"

I watched this exchange, thinking about the plant's half-finished concrete work that would need to be undone anyway and how I had no idea where half of the equipment that would be included in any deal actually was. But Mike got what he wanted. A few months later, Sara Lee bought 51% of the Beijing plant, bringing badly needed cash into Asiafoods' coffers.

The arrival of myself and other executives from Compass unintentionally added to the dysfunction of Asiafoods; we brought a culture of managerial discipline that didn't mesh well with its more entrepreneurial approach. It was a company that had never turned a profit and whose founders had just spent a year without salaries. I argued vocally we had to change old ways. In their eyes, I was probably a spoiled corporate brat.

I did what I could to right the ship. I set up a budget system, started to monitor cash flows and created procedures forcing everyone to follow orderly steps before spending money. The biggest challenge was boiling our business activities down to numbers, the heart of a finance director's job. Part of this was the chaotic nature of the company's books: I tried to make sense of the millions of dollars' worth of kitchen equipment that had been ordered and was now spread between our Shanghai and Beijing operations, but no one had a clear idea of what was where. Some had been cannibalized for spare parts; some had been damaged or had disappeared, presumed stolen. Even more challenging was figuring out the profitability of the food we processed.

When you cook food, when you slice a cabbage or clean a trout, you end up with less than you started. The more you lose in the process, the more it costs to make a dish. I calculated standard rates for our recipes in order to have a reference against which to measure a cook's ability to control food costs. That reference is also the base to calculate how many raw ingredients the chef needs. If your rates aren't reliable, you either buy too much or you buy too little, causing either waste or shortages. And both mean trouble in the kitchen.

None of the ingredients we received came in standard weights or sizes, and the quality was often compromised, causing the rate of waste to fluctuate haphazardly. One common trick we had to contend with was the injection of frozen meat with water to increase its weight. This caused the meat to shrink dramatically in the pan, creating heartburn for Harry Schreiner, the new Austrian chef sent by Compass to run the plant. And that was just one of the complications. Harry created new recipes all the time under pressure from the canteens to provide daily variety. When he found a good supplier for a new ingredient, he might suddenly change his recipes, leaving us scrambling to understand the shrinking rates in the new dish.

It didn't help that the ingredients themselves sounded exotic even in English. Chinese people consume vegetables with unfamiliar—and sometimes unappetizing—names like winter melon, taro, black-eared fungus, and water chestnuts. Even common produce names and cooking procedures sounded foreign to me when translated into English. I had to learn the difference between dicing, shredding and slicing. My English was good enough to use "goodwill," "amortization," and "discounted cash flows" in the same sentence, but "snow peas," "bamboo shoots" and "pomelo" didn't register.

For all its problems, Harry's kitchen had a welcoming feel. I came up with elaborate ideas that Harry diligently implemented with mediocre results. But elsewhere in the company, despite my nominal hold on the purse strings, I was often the last person to know about decisions made by Mike and his team. The first management meeting I attended – a few weeks after I arrived – was about an event called Family Day at the Johnson & Johnson factory nearby. The festivities were a test. For one day, we would serve hundreds of lunch boxes prepared in our plant for Johnson & Johnson employees and their families. If we did well, we had a good shot at winning the business of managing their staff canteen with its two thousand daily meals.

No one had told me I would need to bill Johnson & Johnson for this event. I had no idea what the per-meal price was. For all I knew, we could be losing money on every dish we served. I heard about Family Day for the first time at that management meeting – exactly one day before the event was scheduled to take place. The blackboard in the room was covered with a list of detailed tasks with a name assigned to each. I was glad to see mine up there, though my assignment had nothing to do with finance: I was supposed to come help serve the meals.

Mike went through every line in this list at a fast tempo, as if everyone was familiar with it. I struggled to keep up.

"Charles! Do you have any questions?" he asked.

"No sir!" I heard Charles reply, all gung-ho.

It looked as if Mike and his team had done some serious preparation. The tone of the questions and the speed of the answers seemed to be aimed at making a point to the newly-landed Compass managers: Asiafoods' founders were in control. It was all reminiscent of high-octane exchanges between a football coach and his players before a match – except that half the team, the Compass half, was benched.

"Steve, are you on it?" said Mike, still moving through the list.

"YES, SIR, no problem," I heard from my right.

At the end, Mike wrapped up the session with a hearty "Let's go!" I remained silent, trying to digest what I had just seen. Everyone else left the room. I was so taken aback that I had had no time to ask about meal costs or pricing. But I wasn't the only one hearing about this project for the first time. I had noticed that none of the Chinese managers spoke at all, even though I suspected most of the detail work would have to be done by them.

Language was also an issue at work. All day long, my foreign colleagues complained when puzzled Chinese staffers fumbled answers or misunderstood instructions. We were all speaking in English and expecting Chinese people in China to keep up. And watching someone criticized for his bad English always made me feel uneasy. I myself often struggled to make sense of the American slang and idioms that Mike used in meetings. So, I hired a tutor, deciding that I would learn Mandarin Chinese instead of expecting staffers to get better at speaking English.

I didn't worry too much about being able to learn Chinese. I already spoke English and German on top of my native French, and I figured, arrogantly, that it would be easy to add one more language to the list. Chinese was slow to come, though. Farmers watching me jogging made comments I didn't grasp. Taxi drivers' attempts at small talk usually devolved into hand-gestures: the driver hopelessly trying to draw the word he had in mind on the palm of his hand, me looking into the palm with a dumb stare. I was far from being able to read any characters, and further still from guessing their meanings from a mid-air sketch. Each day after dinner, I went to sleep with fragments of Chinese words in my mind, and woke up in the morning repeating the same words written on little notes that I stuck to the bathroom mirror. The morning's teeth brushing took place standing as I scrutinized vocabulary. But unlike English or German, there was no commonality with French. I had to relearn everything.

I was in awe of foreigners who had come armed with East Asian studies degrees. They spoke with what sounded like a flawless accent in long debates punctuated with laughs. I was sure they grasped something I didn't, not just about Mandarin but about China itself.

If coming to China was a choice devoid of passion, the quest to move beyond the superficial caused soul-aches I had not expected. After a while, I could grasp some of the immense diversity of landscapes, foods, languages and people. But it was like looking at the world through a periscope, and that wasn't enough. I beat myself up for not trying harder with the language, second-guessing my every condescending thought about filthy streets or waitresses' empty stares, disgusted by my fickleness and inability to feel a deeper connection. When my morale was low, I felt like a fraud: the guy who came to China to straighten everyone out but who couldn't get the simplest things done.

I joined an evening language class that met several days a week, but eighteen months in, I still couldn't order from a menu. The dense list of dishes common to most Chinese restaurants looked like an encrypted script, something like "(...) (...) (...) (...) rice." Sometimes I got a quick burst of satisfaction when I recognized an ingredient's name. Mostly, I crumbled and ended up pointing at pictures, always feeling guilty for not trying harder.

After a while, I gave up on learning how to write Chinese characters entirely. It took too much time to practice, and left me with a limited vocabulary despite long hours of solitary work. I focused instead on learning the sounds of the words, which I wrote in a small notebook in a transliteration system called "pinyin." I carried the wrinkled booklet everywhere, always ready to pull out my pen and write a new word down with the help of a waitress or whoever was around at that time. Even that was often wrong: few Chinese master the pinyin spelling. It is taught in grade one but largely abandoned by grade three. Back at work, I would proudly use my new words, leaving my interlocutor clueless, trying to find a polite way to tell me that my Chinese stunk. And still, each time I dropped my books in frustration and stepped out for a walk, every sign in the streets screamed at me, reminding me I was illiterate in this country.

Serving Chinese food to the Chinese isn't simple. The companies we served ranged from big multinationals like Johnson & Johnson (our Family Day feast won them over) to a small stand-alone factory making hearing aids destined for the Japanese and U.S. markets. All of them employed some of the tens of millions of migrants from the interior of the country who had poured into cities seeking work—Chinese villagers from as far away as the foothills of the Himalayas in Western Sichuan province or as close as the poor soils of Anhui province, four hours' drive away from Shanghai. They worked hard—salaries were calculated by piece and not by hour—and slept in bunk beds in dormitory rooms that could hold twelve people, or twenty, or more. With spouses who were usually required to sleep in separate dorms, they came in search of a better life, often leaving their young children back in their home villages to the care of grandparents. Mealtimes in the canteen were their only chance to relax during their otherwise arduous days.

There isn't really any such thing as "Chinese food." Asiafoods' clients in Shanghai, where the cuisine tastes sweeter than in other parts of the country, demanded fiery spicy dishes because most of their workers came from Sichuan. Near Ningbo, four hours from Shanghai, workers were locals who expected more seafood on their menu. No matter where they were from, workers eating every day in the same bare-bones industrial-looking staff canteen expected the food to be diverse and interesting. There was no such thing as a standard menu. They also wanted to see a chef tossing his wok under a jet engine-strength flame. In their eyes, seeing it prepared meant trusting the dishes they were being served.... That was one of the first surprises to me: no matter how poor or deprived these workers seemed to be, they had high standards about the food they ate.

At Asiafoods, we tried to replicate in our central kitchen the flavors and textures that the workers wanted. Our meals consisted of a meat dish with a flavorful sauce — sweet-and-sour pork or steamed chicken feet with black beans, for example — with a dish of stir-fried greens, a serving of noodles or rice, a soup and some fruit.

Shortly after he arrived, Harry stopped producing chilled food in plastic bags and instead started shipping food hot, hoping for a fresher look and taste. The cooked food was poured into stainless-steel pans at a sizzling temperature of 170 degrees. Adding to the ambient chaos, Harry, a heavyset middle-aged man with a fiery temper, shouted invectives to exhort his troops to up the tempo. It wasn't just that the man was raucous and bawdy. On any one day, his kitchen had to produce up to four thousand meals in a few hours. If things didn't move fast enough, food temperatures would drop below 140 degrees Fahrenheit and bacteria would develop inside, potentially causing food poisoning. Workers hastily slid pans into insulated plastic containers. Once the food was loaded onto a truck for transport to the various work-sites, we would tell the drivers (who would ignore us) to avoid bumps and sudden jerking motions, which pounded the food into glop. The drivers could not go too slowly either, because the high temperature inside the containers would keep cooking the dishes, turning crispy vegetables into mush. Once on site, the containers had to be emptied fast and guests served in an orderly way, avoiding swarming around the staff person holding the ladle.

If any part of the process broke down, the reaction from our clients wasn't pretty.

One day a few weeks after we expanded our business with Johnson & Johnson, Denis, a Frenchman from Compass in charge of the work-site canteens, received a call from the manager there. Sitting in front of me, he quickly put the speaker on. I heard the manager explaining in panicked broken English that workers were turning on him.

"Boss, they want to hit me!" he said in a shrill voice.

In the background, I could hear people shouting and stainless trays pounding against tabletops. Dissatisfied with the rice cooked in the plant, the workers had concluded that the manager was running a scam, buying cheap rice and pocketing a kickback.

Denis had studied in the best hotel schools in Switzerland, and for twenty years, he had run catering operations all over the world. Mike had won the Johnson & Johnson contract, but Denis' skilled client development now helped Asiafoods operate a fast-growing number of restaurants in schools and supermarkets. With experience managing much larger operations in Africa, Turkey and the Middle East, Denis pondered the problem for a minute but didn't panic. Showing up was essential in such situations, he said to me. He rushed out of the office and drove to the plant. While he calmed the restless crowd, he sent the still-shaking manager to every greasy hole-in-the-wall restaurant around the plant to buy all the rice he could find. There was no scam. The rice we had prepared was good quality—certainly better than the restaurant rice we were replacing it with—but it had been cooked by Harry in German-imported steam ovens, and somehow it did not taste right to them.

That was a big deal. Rice was at the core of all our menus. We precisely portioned other dishes to save money, but we offered unlimited rice. Rice is at the center of everything Chinese. Eating—Chinese say *chifan*—translates as *eating rice*. It is more than a staple, rice is a symbol: the starch that links all other dishes. When they ate, workers filled a bowl with rice, formed a small mound and then placed vegetables or meats on top of it. As they munched, they eroded the mound bit by bit with their chopsticks, one clump of rice at a time. Talk to Chinese people and you won't find out any one unique way of cooking rice. All claim to wash the grains to clean away the milky starch, but the number of rinsings differs. Some add lots of water, others add a little only. And the question of when to lift the lid on the rice pot is a matter of controversy. But all take their rice seriously. Once cooked, it needs to be fluffy but sticky enough to hold between chopsticks, soft but not soggy, dense but not gummy or mushy when pressed gently between the fingers. Thousands of years after agriculture appeared in China, the sorting, washing and cooking of rice remains a ritual that goes back to village life—a doorway into what it means to be Chinese.

What happened that day at the factory? Did Harry open the oven door too early, releasing the steam that normally completes the cooking process? Did he fail to let a Chinese cook taste it before shipping it? In any case, it didn't taste at all authentic to the workers.

After more disturbances, complaints and endless head-scratching sessions with Harry and the production team, I learned that cooking in the central kitchen and shipping the food in those insulated containers made our vegetables soft and soggy. I also discovered that our meats were saturated with oil, lacking the chewiness that even poor Sichuan villagers considered non-negotiable.

One afternoon amid our investigations, Harry and Denis stood in front of my flimsy aluminum desk, gesturing at each other, arguing about yet another food quality complaint.

Harry exploded, his German-accented voice shaking: "You fucking guys act like children!"

That was intimidating. He stared straight at Denis, face flushed, his entire body tense and shaking, as if a thousand kilowatts were flowing through his veins. He ranted on in an incomprehensible mix of German and English: "You complain about the food instead of keeping an eye on your useless monkeys!"

Harry was used to getting his way. He barked, and everyone did his bidding. But today was different. Denis had had enough. He made an imperceptible move forward. For a second, I thought he was about to hit him. Harry's eyes widened.

Instead, Denis stared back at him and said with contempt, "The food you cook is Western food with Chinese colors. No one likes it—it's expensive—and it costs me new clients every day. If I had my own cooks, I'd do a better job for less money."

Harry was working from a database of recipes created a few months before by a Chinese-American chef. He had started to work with his local cooks to adjust many of them, but creating a new range of dishes with so many different regional flavors slowed down the preparation of the five thousand meals he had to make every day. His compromise was a simpler daily menu that didn't meet anyone's expectations.

I was partly responsible for the tension too. In my attempt to better understand the performance of each part of the business, I had set up a system that treated the canteens as clients of the plant. The plant produced meals and sold them to the canteens. The canteens bought the meals for a cost I had calculated and negotiated with both sides. With this in place, both Denis and Harry could manage their respective business's profitability, even though they were both Asiafoods operations. Denis's main supplier was the plant, and Harry's main customers were the canteens.

It was all a bit tortuous, and it forced issues to flare up. Uncooked rice, expensive vegetables, and water-injected meat all had an impact on Denis's costs, and he would challenge Harry about them. Then they would both turn to me for a solution.

I enjoyed the world of plants and canteens. It was tangible, real, a far cry from my privileged professional life in Paris. Harry's blowups didn't bother me either. My dad's cooks were equally loud-mouthed. I knew that his tantrums meant he cared. But it was clear that our system didn't work.

So, as Denis suggested, we started cooking more and more inside our clients' kitchens rather than at our central kitchen. This solved the problem. We quickly grew, eventually serving 10,000 meals per day to satisfied workers. But this solution also created a new issue. Because we had transferred the cooking of meals to the kitchens attached to the workers' canteens, Harry's factory lost most of its business, forcing us to think of new business models to fill it. We looked at serving meals on Chinese trains or airlines, but none of these ideas took off.

Still, I was proud that we were opening new staff restaurants every week, each with its own chef. In a few months, we had learned to make money selling Chinese food to Chinese workers for an average price of less than one dollar per meal. Mike recognized the effort but was still on the lookout for yet another project that could help Asiafoods grow faster. Nevertheless, despite the millions of dollars invested in the huge central kitchen, the profits churned out by the small, humble canteens scattered around Shanghai were what offset some of the losses in the largely idle factory.

Most of my interactions with my Chinese co-workers served to remind me that I was an outsider, both in the company and in China. Of course, I learned more from them about the way things happened at Asiafoods than I did from my fellow foreigners.

One morning, Director Qin, a Chinese woman in her late fifties who was in charge of the company's government relationships (we called her *Director Qin* as a sign of respect for her position and age), entered my office with a squad of assistants and one interpreter. Rumor had it that she had been close to China's power circles for many years before being purged during the Cultural Revolution. Though her figure had thickened with age, her round face and wide eyes had retained some of the shine that once would have made her pretty. But whenever I saw her, surrounded by her cohort, it was always with some apprehension. She was haughty and demanding, always coming to me with some seemingly unsolvable problem. And her army of assistants and extensive travels dug a hole every month in our cash.

That morning, she greeted me with her usual pasted-on smile, and I quickly exhausted the narrow range of polite salutations I knew.

"*Qin zong, zenme yang*? Director Qin, how are you?" I said, avoiding a direct question as a way to show respect.

"*Hao, ni ne*? I'm fine, how are you?"

"*Wo hao*. I am fine."

She then launched into a long harangue. I could grasp only a few words, including *shebei*, which means equipment, and *haiguan*, customs. After several minutes of speaking at high volume, she stopped.

I turned to her translator, a young man just out of college who looked about sixteen. "Director Qin is worried about the equipment," he informed me.

Silence.

Slowly, after much back and forth with the interpreter, who summarized her long remarks with a frustrating lack of detail, I pieced together the chain of events. Qin had spent weeks schmoozing customs officials to help clear the delivery of some imported equipment. Now, it was out of customs in record time, but sitting at the factory gate. She was there to ask me what to do with it.

I had no idea what it was for. I had never heard anything about it. But I did know that its purchase required the payment of hundreds of thousands of dollars we didn't have. When I angrily confronted Mike about it, he looked at me as if I was over-reacting. He said it was the equipment for a new kitchen destined to serve meals on board the Shanghai-Beijing trains. I asked how I was supposed to know this or pay for it, but he turned his back on me with a dismissive gesture.

"It's a moot issue; we're going to get long overdue funds from one of our shareholders," he said.

That too was news to me.

I wondered when I would have found out about this major purchase if Qin hadn't visited me. That day, I wrote to all our equipment suppliers in the U.S. to tell them I wouldn't pay any invoice if it wasn't attached to a purchase order signed by me. From then on, when called to order a new piece of equipment, vendors politely sent him back to me.

At first, Mike liked the idea of bringing this kind of discipline to the company. For a while, he would come and ask me to sign purchase orders, giving me a chance to check that we had the cash and a plan for the investment. But after a few weeks, he felt it was slowing him down. He showed up at the door of my office.

"Hey Xavier, can you give me ten blank purchase orders?" he asked.

Before I had time to tell him I would never do that, he added: "And can you sign them first so we can save time?"

In later conversations looking back on that time at Asiafoods, Mike disagreed with my recollection of the situation, feeling that it misrepresented his commitment to financial discipline. He says that his requests for getting purchase orders in advance was connected to getting import licenses to get equipment through customs. He says he never meant to flout company rules, but though I agree his intentions were good, I have confirmed with other executives at Asiafoods that in his rush to get things done he could by-pass several steps, viewing procedures as guidelines only.

In my day-to-day work, I could not function without our finance manager Fang Yijie, one of the three accountants I supervised. She was my main conduit for communicating with the two other employees because she spoke good English. A young woman with a cheerful manner and pimpled cheeks that made her look even younger than she was, Fang was also laser-sharp with figures, something she took great pride in.

Once, I asked her to drill into the pricing of a dish for a large restaurant chain. The buyer, a supercilious older woman with a disingenuous smile, had a reputation for niggling about trifling details if it served her agenda. She had already worn out the sales people, who came begging for help to hold off a price decrease for a vegetable salad we made for her. Fang wasn't intimidated. She called up the woman on the phone. Over the next hour, I watched as she spoke in the staccato Shanghainese dialect. Fang and the buyer were from the same city, and I had half-expected that she would just go through the motions of negotiating, avoiding escalation to preserve the relationship. But Fang charged hard. Her biting comments and exasperated sighs—this could not be staged. From time to time during the call, she would hand me notes to let me know the progress of the negotiation. I realized, during that phone conversation, that Fang had chosen to break through commonalities of culture, language, and nationality she shared with the other woman to draw a new circle that included me.

After an hour on the phone, she hung up, turned to me, and said, "She's like a watchdog; she doesn't let go. But she's not very smart." Fang normally used her thirty-minute lunch break to hang out with the other young women at the long canteen tables, dealing with me only on work details without sharing much personally. But on that day, I felt part of things for the first time. Fang had my back. And we did not lower our price for the salad dish.

As I got to know and trust my Chinese colleagues, I decided I needed to crank up my efforts to learn Mandarin. I dropped the night class and found a private teacher. Professor Cai Huaixin taught French at the prestigious Fudan University in Shanghai. A small animated man with a mane of white hair, he explained to me in perfect French that his method could shape up a Chinese engineering student in a few months, readying him to attend classes at the elite Ecole Polytechnique in Paris. "Of course, my students are incredibly smart," he repeated frequently. The message was clear. "And," he added, rubbing it in, "they're

Chinese students, so they're committed."

Professor Cai was conceited, intense, and expensive. And he didn't take amateurs. My suggestion that we start with pinyin instead of characters was immediately dismissed. "It's out of the question; Pinyin is not Chinese," he said. "If you don't want to work hard, you can get a tutor." He meant someone not as qualified as he was. He was ready to fire me as a student.

"A successful student is one who falls sick after a few weeks," he said.

I booked him for two weeks in early 1999 during the long Chinese New Year holidays, when my foreign colleagues departed for Southeast Asia's beaches. Professor Cai's method was relatively simple. He made me write a long passage of text in characters on a subject of my choice. That took hours because I had to search the dictionary for every word. The next day, he went through the text with me, commenting on the use of words, adding more vocabulary and teaching fine nuances. He usually left me with more than a hundred new words each time. By the next day, I was expected to learn the corrected text by heart, re-write it in characters from memory and recite it to him. And there was a new text to prepare for that day's lesson. It built up pretty fast into sixteen-hour days. His view was that languages must be internalized. Formulas, expressions, syntax: all need to be learned by heart so they eventually flow out naturally.

By the end of the two weeks, as my tanned and rested colleagues returned from their vacations, I caught a bad cold. Professor Cai brought me tea infused with medicinal herbs. But he never ceased his chatter and he chuckled while he poured out the tea, taking pride in the fact that he had laid low one more student.

Two years into my Chinese adventure, I was realizing that paying attention to people like Qin and Fang, my young accountant, could be Asiafoods' path out of dysfunction, but nobody else in management—Harry and Denis were exceptions—really listened to Chinese managers. It wasn't that the other foreigners in the company were fools. Chinese employees simply wouldn't openly share a view unless they felt secure enough to do so. I had gained my Chinese Finance team's trust; Harry and Denis had done the same with their teams. But it was harder to create the same culture across the organization. Instead, the company continued to shift strategic direction regularly. I knew nothing could be changed from my perch in Finance and that my next career step had to be to a position of leadership. But I envisioned that happening back at my company's headquarters, somewhere outside of China.

By the end of 1999, the giant plant with the central kitchen in Shanghai was essentially empty. Only a small section there continued to function, a sterile white room full of stainless-steel work tables. There, a dozen or so middle-aged women in hairnets shredded lettuce and mixed coleslaw for KFC, the fast-food chain that was expanding rapidly in China. I had no idea that in that chilly dark space, my future awaited me.

2

AMERICAN DREAM PARK

IN THE BEGINNING, I didn't consider working with KFC a major achievement. I didn't know what *coleslaw* was. The fast-food chain had less than five restaurants in France at the time; its name evoked fluorescent-lit dining rooms selling greasy chicken in Paris' seedy districts.

But by the time I arrived in China, KFC was already in its tenth year here. Though it wasn't yet considered the trailblazing success it would later become, it was already running more than three hundred restaurants across China. Unlike the French, Chinese people appeared to like the food. In its early years, KFC had produced coleslaw and shredded lettuce in small white-tiled rooms outside its own restaurants. It had recently started to transfer everything to professional suppliers like Asiafoods.

Nobody seemed happy with the arrangement. I did not initially see KFC's business as an activity that could fill our empty processing plants. It was just a sideshow, muddling along but making only a little money. My lack of enthusiasm showed, and KFC began looking for other suppliers. The company's overseers wanted a slick partner, one with conveyor belts and processing lines, packaging machines and farms. In April 1999, we received an ultimatum: if we didn't make a serious investment in their business, KFC would find someone else to process its lettuce.

I was upset by KFC's blatant disdain despite my lack of enthusiasm for their cuisine. But Mike, Asiafoods' ever-optimistic founder, was unruffled. As usual, he had a new and brilliant idea: he would transform our ten or so older women cutting vegetables at the plant into a twenty-first century vegetable processor, spin it off as its own company and list it on the New York Stock Exchange — or Nasdaq, or wherever he was dreaming.

A few weeks after we received KFC's ultimatum, a successful Taiwanese entrepreneur, an energetic woman in her fifties with a pixie haircut, came to visit our Shanghai plant. Anita Wang's company served ready-made meals to four thousand 7-Eleven convenience stores in Taiwan. I figured she could partner with Asiafoods to start the same business in mainland China. She arrived one afternoon as night was falling. Our talk in my office was brief. She listened to my presentation about the company and asked questions in the tone of someone who already knows the answers. Then we went together to our processing plant.

We entered a deserted changing room, lit with bright white fluorescent lights. Mrs. Wang didn't need much guidance. She slipped into white boots that were too large for her while I put on a white coat and covered my bald head with a food-grade net. Once dressed, we pulled open the heavy sliding doors, crossed a ten-inch deep bath of chlorinated water and washed our hands under an icy cold tap. Then we entered the long empty corridor to the processing rooms. We said little. She didn't seem interested in social niceties.

Inside, silence reigned. The squish of our rubber soles echoed across the cavernous space. Arriving at KFC's lettuce and coleslaw operations, we found the room dark and empty. Everyone had been off work since noon. I groped around, looking for the light switch.

Suddenly Wang spoke sharply to me.

"You own plants, but you don't know where the switch is? I can tell you that I know every little corner of every plant I own," she said.

"Well, you know, there is normally a production manager here," I replied feebly.

She sighed.

The white-tiled room brightened when I finally flicked the switch, revealing the stainless-steel tables and some salad spinners. Mrs. Wang shook her head and moved on to the next room. I anxiously looked for the switch there, hoping I would find it quickly. When I finally spotted and flipped it, the resulting light showed a room filled with state-of-the-art stoves, ovens, kettles, all slowly rusting since Harry stopped producing for the canteens. I was embarrassed. Mrs. Wang turned back toward the changing rooms.

Her criticism hurt, but she had a point. China's operating environment requires intimacy with details – like knowing where the light switch is – that we did not have at Asiafoods. I saw the empty plant as a drag on the company's finances and KFC as a difficult, prickly client. The small vegetable cutting business was a temporary solution until we could afford to replace it with something better, bigger, more profitable. All it did was pay part of the bill for an otherwise unused space.

KFC was not wrong in its assessment of Asiafoods as a lackluster partner. Nor was Wang. She did not make us an offer.

When I arrived in the late 1990s, China was experiencing phenomenal growth—and unlike in the U.S. and Europe, it wasn't just dot-com companies exploring new frontiers. Everything in China was changing: the economy was growing, and the relationships between city and countryside were being transformed. Villagers left home to work in factories and eat in canteens like ours. Motorways, railways and airports were expanding, allowing Asiafoods to buy meat, fish and vegetables from more and more distant regions. Back when I visited Shanghai for the first time, I sensed this vitality, even if I didn't yet understand it, focusing instead on the surface drabness.

In the roughly two decades following the death of Mao Zedong in 1976, Deng Xiaoping's reforms had transformed China's command economy into one where markets played a larger role, while turning a mainly rural agricultural society into a modern urban one. Eyeing this developing middle-class, foreign companies started to invest heavily. Investors from around the world rushed to China.

But mistakes multiplied. Multinationals often saw China as a way to expand the reach of their global brands, adding one more flag to the map of their world coverage. Few made a conscious effort to understand what this new Chinese middle class wanted to see, do or eat or to consider the long-term implications of the terms on which they were allowed entry. At best, they sent a bunch of adventurous but largely ignorant managers to work out the details. Many of us working at Asiafoods fitted the description.

One notorious failure in our neighborhood was a place called Shanghai American Dream Park. When it opened in 1996, the theme park's executives made grandiose pronouncements about bringing the best of America to China. The park had thirty-one rides, including a surround-vision theater. Every day, it staged seventeen costumed performances and street theatrics across five themed areas ranging from "Wild West" to "Miami Beach". American Dream Park's creators assumed that the Chinese would pay to see "great American sites." But next door, "Global Paradise" offered 150 acres of attractions featuring great monuments around the world – for half the price. Closer to where people lived downtown, another attraction called Jinjiang Park drew 600,000 visitors a year for an investment of only $3 million. Altogether, there were eighty other amusement parks in Shanghai at the time. For local residents, American Dream Park was only one choice among many, and not the best one.

American Dream Park had been an early cornerstone of Mike's plan for Asiafoods. The park's founders had assembled a group of high-profile investors who promised to invest up to $600 million in this project and several others around China. Mike's idea was to serve meals to the millions of visitors these parks were expected to attract. American Dream Park, he believed, would merely be the first step. But a few months after opening, the expensive tickets and the lack of transportation to its relatively remote location translated into only a trickle of visitors. Soon the park ran into financial difficulties and even stopped paying salaries, causing widespread worker unrest. By the time I arrived, the founders' grand promises echoed over the deserted grounds of what looked less like Disney World and more like urban blight.

I saw for myself what was left of the Dream Park in December 1999 on an off-road bike ride with a friend through the rice paddies extending behind Asiafoods' plant. We were riding toward what looked like mysterious ruins when I recognized the interlaced crimson "AD" over the front gate. A lone guard wearing a scruffy uniform was trying to warm up in a small booth made of corrugated iron sheets. The guard hailed my friend and me in a lame effort to stop us.

"Hey!" he shouted from the tiny window.

We looked and gestured back to show we didn't understand.

Recognizing we were foreigners, he didn't insist on pursuing us, opting to stay warm.

He was all that was left of the 2,000 employees who had once worked there. When the company that owned the park failed to pay them compensation for terminating their employment contracts, employees raided the facilities in a surge of repressed frustration, smashing windows and stealing computers, fax machines, phones, and anything else they deemed valuable. In the walls of the derelict buildings my friend and I explored, naked electric cables poked out, evidence of this final wave of destruction. *Main Street* was deserted. *Miami Beach*'s colorful row houses were unoccupied near a dried-up twenty-five-acre lake. A decaying Ferris wheel stood idle.

Just as the park's backers had been drunk with the potential of the Chinese market, Asiafoods' investors had poured millions of dollars into state-of-the-art facilities filled with expensive imported equipment that proved useless—because they didn't produce what Chinese consumers were looking for. Bringing the best of the West was not a recipe for success in China. I had seen first-hand how fancy German steam-ovens had failed to cook rice the way a twenty-dollar plastic cooker could.

Foreign companies tended to focus only on the high-end part of the market. International beer makers, for example, all entered China at the same time. They built astonishingly modern factories by Chinese standards. But they produced global brands that didn't appeal to the average Chinese beer lover, who remained loyal to historic local brewers. The result was disastrous. By the end of the 1990s, foreign beer manufacturers produced one third of the beer in China but sold it to less than five percent of the consumers and in only a handful of cities where most foreigners lived. Their prices were five to six times higher than those of local beer makers'. Most of these big international companies ended up selling their Chinese operations to savvy local companies like Tsingtao and were out of China by the end of the decade.

Asian companies, especially Taiwanese ones like Anita Wang's ready-meal business, were better at serving the Chinese consumer. They shared common values with the consumers and dealt with China as their main market, not just as one of many. They knew how to design products that could appeal to millions of average Chinese people. Starting in 1992, Taiwan's Master Kang's Noodle tested a new concept of instant noodles with thousands of consumers, trying to find the right taste. Then it priced each bowl of instant noodles at 20 cents, pitching it between the ultra-cheap local instant noodles which sold for seven cents and the expensive imported noodles priced at 90 cents. Almost overnight, Master Kang took over a third of the gigantic Chinese market thanks to its locally-appropriate flavor, folksy-sounding name and careful market research.

Native Chinese firms, which learned from foreign companies' mistakes, were even faster to adapt. Often run by aggressive individuals, they made quick decisions, unimpaired by overseas home offices and free of joint venture partners with conflicting agendas. They improved their products' quality, they made big bets on markets outside the main cities, and reacted quickly when competition arrived. Unlike Western rivals, they understood how to get around government red tape but also how to take advantage of government programs to build plants in developing areas with cheap financing. And they hired local employees who did not need to speak English.

KFC was one of the few international companies whose bosses in China understood all of this. The company built larger stores with air conditioning, which invited people to linger and snack for hours during the sweltering summers. It tailored its menu to meet Chinese tastes, introducing new dishes like spicy chicken burgers or wraps filled with plum sauce and scallions. As it grew larger, the brand even introduced Hong Kong milk tea, chicken congee and seafood soups. When KFC China launched shrimp burgers, Colonel Sanders must have turned over in his grave. It built its own logistics company and centralized purchasing in order to avoid corruption and improve quality. And it was not a coincidence that many of the company's key managers were originally from Taiwan. Under its Taiwanese leader, Sam Su, KFC China embraced a Chinese version of its corporate culture, training thousands of employees a year to manage its new stores and rewarding them in lavish recognition events. At one celebration I attended, the company hosted its restaurant managers for a banquet in the Great Hall of the People in Beijing—the equivalent of the House of Representatives—and had its entire China leadership team serve them dinner. When the executives entered the stage balancing trays filled with Chinese dishes on their shoulders, the hundreds of twenty-something managers roared with joy and pride. KFC expanded fast across the country while retaining ownership of all its stores and built a confident culture centered around the Mandarin language and respect for Chinese consumers. For nearly three decades, Yum Brands in the U.S. retained full ownership of the China business. Sam Su built a leadership team that was mostly from Taiwan and therefore intimate with the Chinese environment. KFC's wholly-owned China stores represented a large investment compared to a franchise model. But it guaranteed tight control over execution, a key part of building the brand. In the end, China became so big that it made up only 10% of the group stores worldwide but accounted for 40% of the profits. In 2016, its 6,000 restaurants in China were spun off and listed separately on the NYSE.

Anita Wang's comments at our plant were my first inkling of the difference between a company like Asiafoods and one like

KFC. After her visit, I became aware of the foolish assumption among foreign companies, especially in the food sector, that the Chinese would one day graduate to a higher level of refinement — meaning they would eat the food we Westerners preferred. This was easier, and lazier, than working to understand what kind of food the Sichuan worker in the canteen liked.

Mike now started to work on every manager, hoping to convince one of us to take the lead at the amazing new vegetable-processing venture he wanted to spin off. For weeks, he paced the alleys of our offices, feeling out his core team of founding managers.

"This is an amazing opportunity. We have an existing business at break-even, a fast-growing client," he said with his usual coach-like enthusiasm, standing in his puffer vest, the aroma of coffee wafting from his mug as he made the morning rounds.

But we all knew about the challenges with vegetable sourcing and growing in China — in both supply and hygiene — and we also knew that KFC was a demanding and exacting customer, ready to abandon us at the first opportunity if we underperformed. Who would be mad enough to start a business on such slippery ground?

By the time he had worked his way down the list to me, every young and ambitious manager at the company had turned him down. Many of them were leaving for more promising industries. He himself already had announced his plans to depart for a new job at a leading global emerging-markets bank. He had lived apart from his family for almost four years. Now that both Compass and Sara Lee were likely to acquire Asiafoods, he wanted to get his family back together. I also could tell he felt an urgent need to find a new use for the empty plant to prove that although many projects related to it had failed, his entrepreneurial grit had created pathways to solid returns for his shareholders. He was good at appearing confident, dismissing critics, brushing off setbacks. But as his departure date neared, his face showed strain and bags formed under his eyes.

When he broached the subject of the vegetable spin-off with me, he caught me at the right moment. I was becoming restless in my role as a financial watchdog. Along with businesspeople the world over, I had also been absorbing the hype of the Internet boom and found the whole idea of scrappy companies exploring new frontiers exciting. So, surprising even myself, I agreed to put together the plan for the salad business, reasoning that I would at least learn something in the process.

I wasn't sure where to start. I didn't know anything about vegetables, and while I liked the term "business plan" — it sounded cutting-edge — I had no idea how to write one. But I had no time to worry. One of Asiafoods' investors, intrigued by the project (and perhaps also smitten by the promise of feeding the Chinese millions), offered to fly me to California to meet a couple of Internet ventures as well as an expert in the vegetable processing sector.

What did dot-com have to do with coleslaw? The answer should have been.... nothing. But the year was 1999, and the energy in Silicon Valley was contagious. It seemed like every corporate big-shot was resigning to join a start-up. For two fast-paced days, thanks to the investor's offer, I toured the Silicon Valley area and found myself gawking like a boy among heroes. I met the founders of a Palo Alto-based Internet venture, who were toying with bringing their business to China. They granted us only fifteen minutes. That impressed me. I also met Sand Hill Road venture capitalists in immaculate offices decorated with modern art and oozing studied power and sophistication. It would have taken someone more clear-eyed than I was not to get swept up in it.

In comparison, Steve Wolfe, the vegetable expert, was underwhelming. In a shabby meeting room in a Sheraton hotel near San Francisco airport on the third day of my visit, Wolfe put his two hands together, imitating the movement of a bellows. "Heads of lettuce, like all vegetables, breathe. They consume oxygen and release carbon dioxide," he said. "Each time core temperature increases by one degree, the breathing rate doubles, and so does the rate of damage inside the leaves." At that, he accelerated the pace of his hands, pumping as if the imaginary lettuce were the heart of a runner.

His eyes then rose from his hands, watching the group of potential investors in front of him. "And each time the leaves are damaged, the lettuce ages faster. It looks wilted. Even if you put it back into cold storage, it continues to breathe for hours." Within two hours of harvest, he said, fresh lettuce needs to be cooled to 33 degrees and kept there so this breathing process slows to a minimum. It's like putting the vegetable into a state of hibernation.

As I sat at the table, I was listening, but distracted. I was busy fabricating an Internet strategy for Asiafoods' spin-off and fantasizing about a global role for myself back at Compass Paris headquarters. Steve's ramblings about vegetables breathing bored me.

I was certainly not the only one drunk on dot-com. When Steve finished, the others in the meeting started to discuss opportunities of bringing more Internet start-ups to China. I listened intently, but Steve sat in silence. Eventually he slowly stood up, gathering his things. People turned to look at him, puzzled. The creases on his face became more pronounced and turned red. "I didn't drive two hours to come here to be kept waiting on the side," he said. "This is a waste of my time."

We all stared at him, taken aback. Nobody thought of apologizing, though. After all, he was the one who didn't understand that we were going to change Asia's ways of doing business. I had known before the meeting that I would meet a vegetable expert, but I hadn't bothered to learn any more about him. He seemed to have quite a temper. The Asiafoods investor who had invited me calmly took a pen, pulled a yellow page from a notebook, and started to write out the terms of a consulting agreement, reading aloud as he wrote and checking from time to time with Steve to ask if he agreed. He then turned to me and asked if I was comfortable with it. I hadn't known I would have a say in it and had no opinion anyway. Steve sat back and signed the page without a smile.

Steve Wolfe, I later learned, was a lettuce pioneer. The biological process he described in that first meeting was at the root of an entirely new industry that had emerged in the U.S. in the past ten years. Steve, who had earned a PhD in chemistry and worked at a detergent multinational for a while, advised entrepreneurs who would later go on to build fresh salad businesses for Fresh Express and Dole, the largest fresh salads brands in the U.S., teaching them what it took to keep clean, cut salads inside bags for up to fourteen days. Sales of these bagged salads now brought in more than $10 billion per year in the U.S. alone. Once Steve arrived in China and I got to know him better, I learned that he hadn't really profited from his role as a pioneer. When I asked why he would consider uprooting himself from California to China, he flatly answered that he needed a job to pay the mortgage. I asked more questions. He reluctantly explained how he had been fleeced, listing names of industry players, unaware that none of those names meant anything to me, though I did understand that he felt hurt.

I came to like Steve a lot. Restless and impulsive, I was pushing for fast results, but Steve didn't rush. "Let me plod on," he told me. "That's what I do best." He soon gathered around him a group of bright young Chinese agronomists, bringing them a sense of continuity amid our flailing start-up's incessant changes of direction. Though he stood well over 6'5", he never used his height to intimidate. Instead, he leaned over his laptop, shoulders bent, more keen on making his case in writing than on doing so face to face. When we talked, he was intelligent, honest and straightforward to the point of bluntness. Disdain, conceit or lack of moral courage in others occasionally caused him to blow up, as he had in the initial meeting. Otherwise he was a peaceful giant.

Back in China, we started to discuss our strategy for the new vegetable-processing company. The goal was for Steve to write the business plan and for me to support him with a financial model. Steve spent hours patiently teaching me the intricacies of vegetable growing and processing. I grasped only fragments. But it turned out that Steve's idea for the business was a good one.

When I first heard about his background, I was not convinced the successful American bagged-salads model could be replicated in China. Pre-washed pre-cut greens were expensive, and I couldn't envision my frugal accountants paying for them. Also, the Chinese rarely ate raw vegetables. I knew from our canteen menus that to them, raw food was not food, period. But the opportunity as Steve pictured it wasn't about Chinese consumers at all.

In 1999, Japanese companies imported close to $1 billion worth of fresh vegetables from California. McDonald's in Japan even air-freighted processed lettuce from California when none was available locally. It made sense that money could be made cutting and cleaning vegetables in China and shipping them to fast food chains in Japan. Unlike the Chinese, the Japanese would be willing to pay the higher prices, and China was only a three days' journey from Japan by boat, not weeks like California. We figured Japanese buyers would jump at that time- and cost-saving opportunity if we could replicate the quality standards their U.S. suppliers offered.

When I learned all this, it started to come together. KFC China would only be a stepping stone, bringing credibility and income while we ramped up with new customers in Japan. I didn't think we would have to rely on it for very long. The volumes of orders that we expected from Japan would quickly dwarf the most optimistic sales growth I had projected for China. With Steve coaching me, we centered the business plan on Japan first, then envisioned a domestic expansion once we deemed the Chinese market ready for bagged salads.

Still expecting to depart once the new company was off the ground, I focused my energy on turning Steve's idea into reality. I christened the business Creative Food. Asiafoods had a subsidiary called Creative Food Technologies, and KFC knew it as "创造" or *Creative* in Chinese. Since Asiafoods and its group of companies were trusted by KFC as part of Compass, I reasoned that using "Creative" for our new company would deflect attention from the fact that it was actually a start-up. I also acquired equipment and sub-leased the space in Shanghai which Asiafoods used to package KFC's vegetables. The corps of ladies in hairnets and white coats was now ours, and I had at least learned where the light switches were.

My plan was to place Steve at the head of Creative Food and then make a swift exit for greener pastures. But I couldn't leave before getting some more funding, a process I believed would be another good thing for me to experience firsthand. Compass was not interested. One executive told me, "We won't tell the stock exchange in London that we're the king of vegetables in China." So I started knocking on the doors of investors in Hong Kong, Europe and the U.S.

Steve and I held a few meetings with these potential investors. Steve brought credibility to the project because of his background and knowledge, so initially he led the meetings. But his presentations were heavy with technical details, and his monotone voice caused our audience's eyes (and my own) to glaze over. We were getting nowhere.

In two years at Asiafoods, I had dealt with several private equity investors, and I had learned the hard way what they wanted. At my first Asiafoods board meeting in 1998, I had proudly put together a budget for the next year that showed us breaking even for the first time in the company's five-year history. I figured our investors would be impressed that at last we were on solid ground. Instead, one of them turned an angry red and said, "I am a *venture* capital investor. I want you to show me where the blue sky is. I know I can lose my investment if you don't get there. But I will blame you forever if you don't try to shoot for it."

Investors weren't interested in Steve's scientific explanations. So, one morning in the middle of February 2000, when Steve and I met with two wealthy businessmen from the U.S. and Canada in Hong Kong, I took the lead.

"California ships $780 million of vegetables every year to Japan, and that takes fifteen days by boat," I said, showing the investors a slide quoting the figures Steve had told me when we were crafting our business plan. "At Creative, we will replicate California quality, but we are only three days away by boat from Japan."

I could see the businessmen's eyes spark as they did calculations. *Three days by boat…*

I went on: "Of course, the Chinese don't eat salads, but neither did they drink milk or eat burgers ten years ago. They will eat our salads, not because they like raw vegetables, but because it is healthy and convenient. This will come naturally as the population urbanizes and the middle class graduates to more convenient foods."

The Chinese middle-class was the group of consumers every company wanted to reach. Again, I could see the numbers turning in their heads: *150 million salad-eaters…*

The two businessmen, successful entrepreneurs themselves, asked if I had plans to build something connected with the Internet. That's where the real value was, they said. I agreed. I didn't need more encouragement. It was what I had wanted anyway; Steve had held me back. I went back to Shanghai and drew up an internet strategy. Steve helped a little, but most of the idea was my own. A few days later, I returned to Hong Kong with a plan to add a vegetable-trading platform online, connecting buyers and sellers in China and in Japan. I called it I-Veg.com.

That did it. Creative Food as I portrayed it was a real business with factories and a tremendous market with an Internet piece. I knew only a fraction of what Steve knew about farming and processing—one day he had to sit down and explain to me why seasons and temperatures prevented us from growing all our lettuce in a single place—but I was the one on the team who could sell our message. As for the Internet part, everyone was so blindly gung-ho I didn't need to know anything.

After I returned to China, the two businessmen said they were interested in investing $1 million. But there was one catch: they wanted me to lead the business, not Steve. Steve said he was content to take a more technical role in charge of operations.

I was flattered.

A few weeks later, the two businessmen signed on as investors along with some of Asiafoods' old shareholders. I had raised close to $2 million and was convinced that the hardest work was over. One of my new backers told me, "We decided to invest in you because it looked like you had carefully thought about every risk. You had an answer for every question."

More or less by accident, I decided to stay at Creative Food and become an entrepreneur and a CEO. And almost nothing I said in those early meetings turned out to be true.

43

3

OLD HUNDRED NAMES

WITH THE DECISION to commit to China came a sort of peace. Life found its pace. I moved to a flat downtown and built a steady group of friends—what Shanghai lacked in bright colors and blue sky, I realized, it made up for in vitality and energy. By spring 2000, returning from trips now felt like coming home.

Part of my attitude shift came during the months I dated Yang Yang. I met her at a small cafe downtown where I normally reviewed my Chinese lessons. Three times a week after my evening classes, I took a cab to the former French concession, the old part of town. The owner—a Shanghainese globe-trotter in her late twenties named Tina—had opened the place a few weeks before I started to visit. She had tried hard to replicate the West Coast coffee culture she had loved back in Vancouver, Canada.

But brick exposed walls, vintage lights and iron guard rails weren't enough to bring good business. Most nights, the place was empty. Her friends sat at one table while I huddled over my books a few steps away, looking up occasionally to observe them. The men wore trim leather jackets with worn-out jeans. Chic discreet leather purses enhanced the women's classic black dresses. They chatted quietly without the liquor-induced effusions I had seen at banquets I attended for business.

Watching them felt like a peek into what Shanghai would one day look like. But I was too shy to engage. I assumed my Chinese was too weak and I didn't know whether they spoke English or Mandarin because they mostly interacted in Shanghai dialect.

Then one night, Tina glided toward my table and invited me to come and join her friends. She introduced everyone, and I forgot every Chinese name as soon as she said it.

"And this is Yang Yang," she finally said, pointing at an attractive young woman with long hair reaching down her back. I was sure I would remember that name—and not just because it repeated itself.

"I've known Yang Yang for years," Tina continued, "she's a very good friend and you should talk." Then she withdrew to the other side of the table, forcing us to engage while the group sat separately. Yang Yang invited me to sit across the table and explained in simple English that she and Tina had known each other since they were minor celebrities on Shanghai TV's singing contests for children. Unlike my group of diverse but foreign friends, she was born and bred in Shanghai.

I found her hesitations and silences when she searched for English words charming, but it felt selfish to let her struggle on for my own pleasure. So, I asked her to speak in Mandarin. After all, I was the one who should adapt, I thought. When she switched languages, her tone changed. Gone were the hesitations. As a TV host at the local station, she had the assurance of someone used to an audience. When I shared that I wanted to know the city better, she volunteered to show me what made Shanghai so special in her eyes.

In restaurants across the city, I watched her order from the fog of menus written in characters only, uncovering flavors and textures beyond my usual fare of dumplings and broccoli. There was eggplant braised in soy sauce and sugar—something far more appealing than the pulpy and watery aubergine I tasted back home—and squirrel-shaped mandarin fish deep-fried in a caramelized tomato sauce and sprinkled with pine nuts and bamboo shoots. With her, Shanghai showed me its true flavors.

The urgency I had felt to formally study the language faded. Daily conversations with Yang Yang helped make my Mandarin more vivid, and my newfound interest in the city made my morning tooth-brushing vocabulary routines seem less interesting that talking to shop owners in their language. My intensive lessons with Professor Cai also reached a milestone. After making myself sick working for so long on the text translations he required, I finally began to find it easier to communicate at work and when I traveled. I wasn't ignorant enough to think I spoke fluent Chinese, and I was far from understanding the still-inscrutable signs on the streets. But I was proficient enough to say what I wanted. It happened slowly as I chipped away at the grammar, and it was mostly one-way. I could instruct my staff, a taxi driver or a clerk at a hotel. I still often lost track when they replied, but I now had a strategy that allowed me to cope: learning common conversation routines so that a single word could help me guess what to say in response, even if I didn't understand the full sentence.

Professor Cai's program was too intensive to continue beyond short bursts during holidays. For lessons during most of the year, I hired my former teacher from the evening school. Her Chinese name, *Heping,* translated as "harmony and peace." I studied with her for a few hours every weekend, adding new words to the same type of old wrinkled notebook I had carried around since I had arrived.

In the maze of red brick townhouses of old Shanghai, what had previously been enigmatic gradually became approachable. Greasy food stalls produced hand-made noodle soups in sweet-

and-sour stocks. Out of grubby neighborhoods marred by clothes hung out of windows on lance-like brooms emerged smiling shop owners and vibrant markets. As we walked back to her home one evening, Yang Yang pulled me into a small basement restaurant into which I would never have set foot without her. The decor wasn't fancy and the time was past normal dining hours. She peeked inside, begged our way in with the owner, and then waited for him to finish removing polyethylene tablecloths covered with previous guests' leftovers. As we ate, I watched them talk in the incomprehensible Shanghainese dialect in the easy, relaxed way that only two people from the same community can share. It recalled my childhood and my own granddad as he poured a tumbler of red wine for neighbors stopping by our farm on their way back from the village's weekly market. I could still hear the cows' hooves next to our kitchen. My grandfather, too, spoke in dialect, in his case Provençal.

Deep into the Inner Mongolia plateau at 3,600 feet in altitude, five hours north of Beijing, lay the village of Qipanshan, essentially a group of isolated courtyard houses built with rammed-earth walls. It didn't rain much there. The soil was so dry that clouds of dust rose up after each step. A couple of tin-glazed buckets near a stone sink in the yard indicated the lack of indoor bathrooms. Past the houses, the vast Mongolian plain extended beyond sight, capped by a range of mountains. There were no trees, just grass already brown under the scorching sun of June. Even animals found it hard-going; a dead rat lay decaying by the side of a house, and an undernourished cow stood lonely inside a concrete yard, a chain attached to the wall, painfully twisting her neck.

Yang Zhongcheng, the man I had recruited to run Creative Food's farms, the same man who would later help to resolve

Sun's hostage situation, stood beside of a nearby field, watching the first seedlings of lettuce creep out of the baked reddish soil. Six months into his new job as Creative Food's agriculture manager, he had led the China-wide search for the right growing climate outside of Shanghai's hot and humid summers. Yang had joined Creative Food because he felt his work as a professor at Shanghai Agriculture Institute was too disconnected from local farmers' livelihoods. Now, walking the village's dusty paths, he felt some apprehension. He had spent the last five months instructing around a hundred farmers, whom we had essentially hired as employees, in our California methods. It had not been easy.

He spotted a villager skipping a row of lettuce while spraying pesticide. Yang walked toward him, pointing his finger nervously at the neglected range of lettuce heads.

"You need to spray uniformly or we'll have trouble with these heads," Yang shouted at the farmer.

The man, with a straw hat and a flimsy plastic container strapped on his back, barely acknowledged him, continuing to action the lever in his right hand while walking away.

After a few steps, he finally stopped and turned toward Yang, speaking through yellow and black teeth.

"*Tai gui!* — Too expensive!" he snapped in the loud argumentative voice villagers often used with each other. "*Tai langfei le* — It's such a waste!"

Then, he walked on to prove that he wouldn't listen to what he considered nonsense.

Yang told me later that he saw the writing on the wall. "There won't be a crop to harvest if pests or diseases descend in such brutal climate," he thought. Yang knew that this farmer and others like him would continue to skip rows of lettuce when spraying. He also knew that if aphids, a sort of plant lice, swarmed his field just before harvest, the same man would panic and spray willy-nilly. Farmers like him refused to consider potential problems until they were urgent. What they didn't know was that aphids were basically impossible to eradicate once they surfaced—and since pesticides take two weeks to evaporate, they could leave potentially dangerous residues on the leaves even after the harvest.

Still rattled by the interaction, Yang moved into the field to inspect a new batch of recently transplanted lettuce seedlings. He walked slowly and stepped carefully over the planting beds to check that his seedlings were separated by the twelve inches he had requested. That had been another battle. Yang had explained to the villagers that when heads of lettuce are too close to each other, they compete for nutrients and light, resulting in smaller heads and a smaller harvest volume overall. But even though the locals didn't have to pay for it, they felt it was a waste of space.

"The beds aren't elevated enough," he noted as he continued his inspection. Villagers kept the same raised beds on which they planted crops from one season to another—it saved time and energy. The problem was that when it was time to irrigate, a lot of the water rushing between the rows—sprinklers weren't common—spilled over into beds that were too low, washing dirt and fungus onto the fragile leaves. That meant diseases and rot a few weeks later.

As he marched on through the rows of feeble plants, clues that Qipanshan farmers weren't following instructions continued to accumulate. In a ditch, he spotted an empty container. Yang saw from the label it was a cheap pesticide bought from Weichang's convenient store. He made a mental note to remind his farm manager that villagers probably sold the more expensive stuff Creative Food had bought and delivered to them and cashed in the difference. This meant also that his men on the farm weren't catching such practices. In a country where the government itself acknowledged that half of the pesticides sold on the market were fakes or toxic, this could have even more harmful implications.

The villagers seemed to see the more expensive seeds, fertilizers and pesticides we brought to them as a form of extravagance. In their view of the world, there was a single, non-negotiable price for anything that came from Qipanshan. The only way to extract some profit for themselves was to reduce what they put in — and that habit was so deeply rooted that it didn't matter that they were just employees. If we weren't smart enough to understand that, they believed we deserved to be fleeced.

In the end, none of this would matter if the drought wiped out the crop. The cracked earth indicated that the precipitation information Yang had been given about the area was horribly off. "The weather bureau guy was wrong," Yang told me, remembering how he had convinced the local civil servant to share his weather data in exchange for a good meal. On paper, Qipanshan had come out ahead as the best combination of dry weather, easy access to irrigation, bright daylight and cool nights — exactly the California environment lettuce needed to prosper. He worried that now the only thing that would thrive in the reality of the climate would be crop-destroying insects.

Yang was not like many of the young and inexperienced managers from my Asiafoods days. His English was near-perfect and he held a doctorate in plant biology. But the fact that he had grown up in rural Anhui, one of China's poorest agricultural regions, helping his parents extract a living from the province's notoriously poor soils, gave him a grasp of rural realities others lacked. "With Creative Food," he said to me during his job interview, "I can make a difference and improve the livelihood of Chinese peasants like my parents." His dream felt both idealistic and refreshing compared to other candidates I had interviewed.

"My parents' tomatoes sell for ten cents a pound to local traders," he continued. "Three hundred kilometers away, in a Shanghai supermarket, the same tomatoes sell for five times that amount."

I liked that he was a believer, that he saw Creative Food as the chance for remote farmers like his parents to by-pass the traditional mesh of intermediaries that kept them isolated from those lucrative markets. He genuinely believed he could bring a better life to the commoners. "*Lao Baixing* – the Old Hundred Names," he called them respectfully.

At five feet six or so, he didn't strike an imposing figure. What set him apart from his more conventional colleagues was a quick wit and a sense of irony. One day over lunch, I asked innocently how husbands and wives referred to each other in Chinese. He ploughed his chopsticks into his rice bowl, and said, looking down:

"My wife calls me *Hei*."

I searched for vocabulary I may have missed in my morning routines – "hei" can translate as "black" in Mandarin. Was it because he had the brown skin of people who toil outdoors? I didn't ask aloud for fear of hurting his feelings – being tanned isn't fashionable in China. Judging that he had paused long enough to attain the desired effect, he continued in English without the trace of a smile: "You know, like '*Hey*, you – come here!"

I had approved Yang's recommendation to plant in Qipanshan, not because I understood anything of his technical data, but because since the days of Asiafoods, I had been buying summer lettuce from Yunnan province, on the opposite side of the country near the Vietnamese border. Yunnan's temperatures were so mild that lettuce could grow there almost all the year round; in fact, it was the only place in the country where the climate could remotely compare to California. But it took four days by truck to haul it to Shanghai, and transportation costs weren't even the biggest problem. I was convinced growers in Yunnan had formed a cartel to gouge their customers. In Yunnan, I paid more than double what I paid in the winter near Shanghai—and even more when my suppliers there knew Creative Food was stuck with a bad crop elsewhere. I needed an alternative to Yunnan, and Yang seemed to have found it in a range of hilly locations north of Beijing.

Diversifying away from Yunnan meant that Yang had to manage more than one growing base. He was organized—he had to be. We needed fresh lettuce every day in Beijing, Shanghai and Shenzhen where we had just started a small workshop to serve KFC in the south. The plants were separated by thousands of miles; storing bags of shredded lettuce wasn't an option because once cut, the leaves turn brown after a few days. From our sales forecasts, he derived what he needed to harvest and planted accordingly. Unpredictable weather patterns could wreak havoc during the twelve-week growing phase; that meant either a wasted crop or a scramble to buy from another region. He hedged the risks by staggering the growing season so that some of our locations would be ready to begin harvesting while others were about to finish.

The weekly planting plan he had designed was mindboggling. Starting at the end of May, our growing locations in Beijing and Shanghai would move to 1,200 feet in elevation an hour's drive outside Beijing for three weeks, then to 2,400 feet in elevation after that. This meant that by the time we learned about new growing conditions in one place, we already had to move to a new location; each time it meant new soils, new varieties of pests, and new villagers to train. Qipanshan was the final step in our race to avoid the heat and the Yunnan cartel. Up in Inner Mongolia, soils remained frozen until May, but summer temperatures didn't exceed 86 degrees.

At least, that's what the data said.

Since Yang needed to keep an eye on so many farms, I hired a company that had formerly competed with us to help manage the multiple locations in North China. I felt this was a canny move on my part. Creative Food would buy only from this company, China Green Concept Ltd, thus avoiding the complications of dealing directly with village politics. This meant relying on the company's two employees: Leo, a young graduate student from Tianjin, and Jimmy, a rugged Australian grower. Jimmy knew how to grow lettuce, and Leo bridged the language and cultural gaps.

The plan was for China Green Concepts to lease a 50-acre piece of land from Qipanshan's government. To make sure we would get local support, Yang hired the village leader as field manager and employed local farmers as day-workers. Leo and Jimmy supervised daily matters. At the time of the harvest, Creative Food would buy the crop for a fixed price. If they managed their costs well, the two fellows and their partners could earn a sizeable profit. But I didn't give too much thought to what would happen if they failed. Yunnan was there for me in the worst case—and I saw the details of Qipanshan as their problem.

Leo, Jimmy and, Yang—who visited every other week—slept in a bare four-bedroom apartment in the nearby town of Weichang, a thirty-minute drive away. Up at six in the morning, they worked non-stop until dusk set in. Together they taught locals how to irrigate and apply pesticides and fertilizers. The farmers there had never planted lettuce before. For them, such a crop was as exotic as growing mangoes would be for a Virginia farmer. Their traditional staples—corn and sweet potatoes—didn't require much attention. Lettuce, in contrast, needed daily scrutiny due to its large leaves, which expose it to dirt, insects and diseases. Furthermore, a complex wrapping process allowed the leaves to turn into a ball roughly half-way into the growing process. If the plant lacked water, or nutrients, or if temperature was too hot, the plant would by-pass the slow and energy-consuming wrapping stage, sprouting vertically in a process called "bolting". If lettuce "bolted," it was essentially a total loss for me.

Almost all of China's countryside looked like Qipanshan. For all its industrial progress, the country at the turn of the 21st century hadn't developed a modern agriculture. Even in the wealthier regions around Shanghai, the landscapes were bare, almost medieval, with hundreds of small plots, each farmed by an individual. The tiny parcels of land were separated by small roads delimiting one field from another and giving access to irrigation water, usually a river or a well. A few ponds, covered in gooey green algae, were scattered around, filled with fat yellow carp often plagued with diseases. If farmers used machinery at all, it was small gardening equipment like mini-tractors that could move around between small pieces of land and plow under plastic greenhouses. In poorer areas, the vehicle of choice was still the water buffalo. Dressed in blue Mao suits, farmers plowed the land by standing on flimsy frames of white wood to let the chisel penetrate the soil better while the animal pulled them forward. In Qipanshan, they didn't even have water buffaloes. Spades, shovels and pickaxes were the common tools. Such backyard operations provided most of the food consumed in major cities like Shanghai and Beijing, and they provided a large part of the produce shipped overseas.

For most of recorded history, the majority of Chinese people lived on such plots. Unlike Europe or America, most of China is desert and mountains, leaving only a quarter of its territory suitable for agriculture. The little plots people farmed when I arrived were the product of both this unfavorable geography and a population explosion. After hovering around sixty million people for a thousand years, the number of Chinese increased sevenfold from the Ming dynasty, which stretched from the mid-14th to the mid-17th centuries, to the beginning of the 20th Century. This was due to a long period of peace; the arrival of new, more nutritious crops from the New World, including tomatoes, sweet potatoes, corn and peanuts; and the settlement of new parts of the country, mainly in the west. By the end of the 19th Century, China's population exceeded 400 million; it is now 1.4 billion. The population grew so fast that it forced families to split land into ever-smaller plots, one generation after another.

Incredibly, China managed to keep feeding its people. But the average size of a parcel of farmed land at the beginning of the 20th Century had fallen to a half-acre per household, 1/400th the size of a typical American farm, and just a fifth of the 2.5 acres that had been standard during the early Ming.

Historically, China's farming families worked the same pieces of land for generations, but they often didn't own their plots, instead working for absentee landlords and borrowing funds from one season to another to buy seeds as needed. They sold their crops to the very merchants who had lent them money or collected the rent on behalf of the landlords. It wasn't an easy life. But resilient and creative farmers not only brought in New-World crops but also new fertilizing methods—for example, soybean cakes resulting from oil production in the north were sent to the south as fertilizer. Technical improvements such as flood control systems improved irrigation. Faster-growing rice varieties allowed farmers to harvest two or three crops per year instead of just one.

But all that wasn't enough to fundamentally improve their condition. The ever-surging population kept eroding the benefits. While America and Europe invested in mechanization to allow farmers to handle larger areas, Chinese farmers focused on getting the best from what little land they had, neglecting any technical innovations that didn't make sense on small parcels.

In most regions of China, for example, letting land lie fallow to restore itself for a growing season was out of the question; every square inch of arable land needed to be fully productive. And when crop rotation existed, it was limited to those essential grains that could be consumed by humans. Compare this to English farmers in the 19th Century, who could rotate clover and turnips in between grain crops to provide feed for animals. English farmers were then able to rely on those animals to reap greater financial returns with less human labor. In China, grain was too important as a basic food source for humans to allow for setting aside any land for animal fodder. So, the Chinese focused on extracting more value from their plot without much consideration for how much labor it would require; labor was so plentiful that it wasn't an issue.

The historian Philip C. C. Huang was the first scholar to articulate why increasingly intensive farming did not lead to better living standards for Chinese farmers. In his classic book *Peasant Families in the Yangzi Delta 1350-1988*, he described how farmers might switch from growing rice to cotton, which required eighteen times' the labor input (including spinning and weaving) but did not bring anything comparable in terms of economic returns. Or they might change from growing rice to cultivating mulberries for silk production, which required nine times' the labor input for about four times the returns. These

changes brought about an increased degree of commercialization
to the Yangtze Delta, but at the cost of reduced returns per laborer.

Huang called this process "involution." In his view, the
concentration of labor on increasingly small plots of farmland —
husband working the fields; wife, children and elders spinning
the cotton into thread — prevented the emergence of a surplus
worker population that could have been productively used in
village-based industries such as weaving, which was the root
of the industrial revolution in Europe. Worse, the involution
process stymied the development of larger modern managerial
farms. In the highly commercialized regions around Shanghai,
farmers and their families were so busy working their land that
they couldn't hire themselves out as wage-earning laborers any
more than they could abandon their farms to become weavers.

Huang explains how involution also prevented adoption
of new technologies. Quoting the work of Xu Xinwu, another
researcher who studied cotton industries, he explains:

"Xu shows that the three-spindle spinning wheel
operated by a foot pedal was readily available in the
Yangzi Delta by the 18th century. That technologically
superior spinning wheel was able to produce at nearly
two times the rate of the one-spindle wheel. But it
didn't gain real currency in the delta. The logic was
once again a simple one: the cheap auxiliary household
labor used for such production made the installation of
a higher price multi-spindle wheel uneconomical. The
three-spindle wheel had to be operated by an adult in
her or his prime, while the single-spindle wheel was
readily operable by the elderly and the children."

During my travels to Qipanshan, I was oblivious to this

complicated history, which had shaped the attitudes of every farmer in every village I showed up in to lecture about changing their ancestral practices. In my mind, Chinese farmers were still at the early stage of a process that would culminate in a European-style agricultural transformation. I thought I understood how farmers everywhere thought. My grandpa was a farmer, and I had spent the summers of my childhood guiding cows, feeding hens, pilfering raspberries from his garden and foraging for chanterelle mushrooms and wild blueberries in the fir forests of France's Ardeche plateau, roughly a hundred miles north of Provence. I respected the hard work of farming and the Provencal farmers' character and common sense. I admired their courage, grit and ingenuity.

In Europe and the U.S., agriculture is often more than just a job. It is a tradition and a craft, proudly passed down through generations. It isn't always easy; in Western countries, farmers cultivate crops and sometimes make money, sometimes lose some, or a lot. But in most cases, they own their land. It provides a cushion against fluctuations. It increases in value; it can be leased; it can be developed to improve next year's crop. It is the farmer's to care for, the farmer's to invest in or to dispose of as he chooses. But I was wrong to think I could relate to Chinese farmers just because I had spent time in the French countryside, where villagers raise animals and grow produce so tightly connected to the region's soils that the term "terroir" — or the region of origin — appears on labels.

Wanting to understand more, I asked Zhao Rongguang, a professor at Zhejiang University of Commerce and director of China's Research Institute of Dietary Culture, how he thought China's history affected the way farmers worked. I described the challenges I faced in Qipanshan and other places, hoping he could shed further light on the resistance to change.

"Things were different before the civil war," he said, referring to the conflict between the Nationalist government and Mao's Communists that stretched on and off through most of the 1930s and 1940s. "The environment was a mess, but Chinese still ate," he said "Farmers commonly referred to the land as a *laopo* (a wife). And they treated it as such—with care. The first separation came when the land got collectivized."

Soon after wrenching power from the Nationalist forces in 1949, Mao's Communists consolidated agricultural land into large, supposedly more effective communal farms. Now forced to move to the collectives, peasants suddenly weren't even farming the plots they had known and understood for years. They also weren't allowed to sell their crops or their labor at market prices, which could have provided much needed additional income. In order to preserve social peace in the cities, authorities kept a tight lid on inflation by forcing farmers to sell only to government-owned entities at a fixed price. This perpetuated Huang's involutionary process; without motivation to avail themselves of labor-saving and land-preserving agricultural innovations, the farmers' entrenched mindset—get as much as I can out of what little I've got—only deepened.

The government's favoring of urban stability over rural development translated into a strictly enforced household registration system that prevented villagers from freely moving to seek employment in larger towns where they could get a better value for their time. In contrast to the Arcadian image of the farmer that we have in the West, Chinese peasants weren't on the land they worked by choice. They were stuck.

Zhao explained that in addition to furnishing labor, every family on the collective from the 1950s through to the early 1980s when the system was revised, had to provide a quota of food to the single state buyer, which was a heavy strain on the average peasant household.

"In Anhui where I spent many years," he told me, "every family had to provide a pig weighing a minimum of 160 pounds. To get around the expense of raising an animal that large, people would deliberately underfeed their pigs. Instead of the 250-pound animals they traditionally groomed for the Spring festival, they aimed for a 160-pound limit, saved on feed and stuffed their pigs with water to artificially increase weight. On the day of the give-away, the queue to weigh the animals could last hours and those at the back were at risk. If your pig relieved itself while you waited, it could mean months of privation for your family. So, people forced a cork into their animals' buttocks. And they bribed officials to get to the head of the queue."

Having to come up with tactics like these didn't do anything to create a bond between farmers and their crops or livestock. On top of that, Zhao said, the farmers were further distanced from the land because the communal farms grouped everyone in work brigades and assigned them to various tasks on the farm as a whole; they were no longer tied to the family plot. Men's labor earned ten points, women's eight points and children's four points. The commune output was then divided by the total number of points and reallocated to each family. Whether they farmed well or not didn't matter. During winters — when villagers historically rested and planned for the next season — men could be mobilized to work on the construction of a large dam or a new road far away from home.

In the end, the "people's communes" didn't do well precisely because their overseers lacked the peasants' knowledge and intimacy with China's wide range of climates and soils. A grandma in Jiangsu province told me how central planners had directed her village to plant rice, a crop that villagers had little experience growing and that didn't fare well in the local climate.

"The varieties they gave us weren't any good either," she added, shaking her head in remembrance of those times.

For the thirty years the communal experience lasted, villagers tried to get by, covertly cultivating their own illegal private plots on the side as insurance for when things didn't pan out as planned. In the late seventies, some farmers in Anhui went one step further; they made a secret pact to each cultivate their own piece of land independently while officially operating as a brigade under the commune. Soon the first group of conspirators were followed by more—and production started to increase. Finally, recognizing that things had to change, in the early 1980s China's leader Deng Xiaoping allowed the reallocation of the land from the old communal farms back to individual households.

I thought I now had a complete answer, that it was the communal farms that had broken the bond between the farmers and their land. But Zhao disagreed with that simplistic view. He did agree that communal farms were the first severing of the ancestral trinity between farmers, their land, and the community of buyers they sold to. But centralization in his view wasn't all negative; he argued that though it stifled the free market, it also reduced corruption. For Zhao, the second and more intractable reason for the problems I faced in places like Qipanshan stemmed from the reforms initiated by Deng Xiaoping.

"After that," he said, "suddenly there was no limit to people's greed."

Free from commune rules, farmers from the 1980s were in theory increasingly able to choose what to plant and where to sell it. But nothing had prepared them for that kind of choice. Even before the commune, they had planted the same crops for the local merchants without much consideration for what the market wanted. Now, the reforms made it possible for buyers they didn't know—companies like mine among them—to come and buy their crop.

Many of these clients were unscrupulous. Zhao said, "Businessmen who knew what crop the market wanted bribed officials to direct villagers to plant it and bought it for cheap." The more farmers planted the same crop, the better it was for the traders as they played one farmer against the others. When prices were down, buyers withdrew and left peasants stranded—or invented concerns about crop quality that allowed them to back out of buying. That made villagers even more wary of outsiders.

Pressured to sell cheap, farmers reverted to the old involutionary mindset, extracting as much as they could from the land they tended without regard for the consequences to the environment or the quality of the food they were growing. With the development of road infrastructure, crops got shipped to ever-more distant and anonymous consumers, making it hard to feel shame over selling them tainted or sub-par products. At the same time, small unregulated chemical manufacturers sprang up around the country and sold their pesticides to villagers who saw them as an easy way to increase returns.

For a while, using cheap pesticides and other such dubious tactics worked. Statistics reviewed by Philip Huang confirm that chemical use boomed in the 1980s, initially causing yields to increase rapidly. But returns plateaued after a few years as soils got increasingly polluted. In addition, not all of the chemicals were what their labels advertised. Unscrupulous middlemen often mixed them with other substances to reduce costs. In China's first national soil survey in 2005, the government was so shocked by the data that it tried to label it a "state secret". Under public pressure, it finally disclosed that a fifth of the country's soils were contaminated with heavy metals, a substance harmful to humans.

In the age of reform, governing land-use rights also

complicated daily life for the overwhelmed farmers. Yes, they now operated their own farms again. But the little bit of land they got back under the reforms was broken down into small, often non-contiguous plots to achieve a balance across the village. The grandma I talked to in Jiangsu province explained that two of her plots were separated by a canal. At the age of seventy, she had to walk with her tools for half a mile, cross a stone bridge and walk back on the other side.

And, because both the collectivization and land reform happened in turbulent times, farmers' rights to a plot often lacked documentation. On paper, the plots were still owned by the state but they were theirs to farm. Yet, oversight of ownership and property remained in the village government's hands, leaving space for further corruption and manipulation. One piece of land might be abruptly allocated to a family that had bribed a local official; another plot might be sold to developers at well below market prices, with the official pocketing the difference. Local officials in league with corrupt middlemen and shrewd wholesalers also promoted the sales of toxic chemicals and fake seeds, to the very farmers they were charged with protecting. Once again, villagers were often locked into selling to just one buyer—whoever had the strongest ties to village officials—which further cut them off from the mass of city-dwellers who would have paid top price for foods they considered fresh and safe.

With supply and distribution chains that looked more like a racket than a legitimate market, it seemed natural that farmers would use every trick possible to increase productivity at the expense of sustainability and safety. In 2000, few talked about this unmooring of farmers from a social and moral framework, but this environment would later create the space for an increasing number of food safety scandals—all implicitly connected to this breakdown at the village level.

In their attempt to grow my lettuce according to my Western rules, Yang, Leo and Jimmy were up against a cultural wall of resistance shaped by this history of oppression and neglect. The villagers believed that continuing to do what they knew would protect them. Nobody wanted to try new methods for fear of losing the little bit they had. Yang slowly came to the realization that local farmers were happy about the higher return we promised them, but there just wasn't much space for risk-taking; anything out-of-the-ordinary could jeopardize a family's livelihood.

4
WAKE UP CALLS

IN THE STUFFY month of August 2000, I traded my suit and black leather shoes for a pair of work boots and jeans. I was still besotted with my internet project. But a potential investor had called asking to visit one of Creative Food's farms; I thought it would be good idea to check how things looked first myself, believing such visits had to be somewhat staged. I picked Jinyuan Town, near Shanghai, home to the nearest farm to my office. With Leo and Jimmy covering the bases in Qipanshan, Yang had started preparations in Jinyuan for the broccoli growing season, which was scheduled to start in November.

The operating pattern was similar to what I had in Inner Mongolia. I called it a "Creative Food farm," but someone outside the company ran it. Lu Qizhong was our supplier in charge of organizing the locals while Yang supervised the farming practices. Lu, a gentle character in his fifties came from a nearby village and had already been growing lettuce there for a few months.

As we neared the village, I heard my driver vociferate in Shanghainese dialect into his phone. By now, I knew this didn't mean much; it sounded as if he was just trying to find the best spot to meet. The car finally stopped somewhere on the roadside. Lu was there, walking briskly in my direction with a bright smile, his arms straight in front of him as he moved closer, finally closing in on my hand to shake it in the way Chinese welcome dignitaries. But there wasn't any broccoli in sight. What I saw were mostly thin rice seedlings emerging out of recently flooded paddies. Rice was the crop people here had been planting twice a year, year in and year out, for centuries, with a break during winter to grow wheat.

Lu and I walked through a maze of dirt paths between plots until I spotted the brownish, barren-looking fields he had rented from the village, behind a sea of paddies covered in lush green. As he spoke, I could guess through his heavy accent that he was concerned about a refrigerated truck, something Yang had asked him to buy. But I didn't need to be an expert to realize that no truck could drive through this labyrinth of tiny, winding paths. Farmers would have to hand-carry the harvest to the village, which meant certain damage along the way.

I noticed other potential problems on that first messy walk. Like lettuce, broccoli is first grown under greenhouses and then transplanted onto dirt beds after a few weeks. But the stocky lettuce seedling contrasts with the lanky broccoli one, which is perched on a narrow stem so fragile it looks like it could be wiped out by the first wind. After transplanting, the feeble plant needs all the nutrients it can take while adjusting to the new soil. That's when it requires fertilizer. The problem was that villagers not only used as little as possible to save money but they applied the organic type — without always giving it the time to compost. Everywhere, this place smelled of manure — human or animal, I wasn't sure. I knew we didn't allow it on the crops we purchased, but when all neighbors used it, there was no way to be sure whose crops were releasing the odor. That meant new risks of bacterial infections. Every empty spot along the path was planted with isolated cotton plants, which would bring a few cents more at the time of harvest. But they also carried bugs that would easily fly onto my broccoli. I didn't have the words in Mandarin to share this with Lu. And my own knowledge felt so new and anecdotal that it seemed inappropriate to express my concerns too forcefully; I had experts to deal with that.

Once we got to the broccoli field, I spotted Yang and Michael Tani, who were standing in one of the patches of earth. Tani, a California grower I had recruited six months before, was coaching Yang and his agriculture team on how to get Creative Food's suppliers closer to California standards.

A second generation Japanese-American from Santa Clara valley, Tani was cylindrically-shaped and sumo-like, with a bulldog face. But he spoke in a quiet, deliberate voice, as if mindful of softening his intimidating physical appearance. Tani's family farm had pioneered the export of fresh broccoli to Japan in the early nineties, but more recent competition from China had caused his business to shrivel. He was eager to prove that he could regain his edge in Japan by growing a better quality crop than everyone else in China. Today, though, he looked exhausted.

When he saw me, Yang waved his hand. Tani turned around and immediately came forward. As he strode over the beds, he lifted his rubber boots with strain, sweating and puffing with each step. Yang followed, watching the slow and painful gait of the man who supposedly would teach him how things should be done in his country. Tani finally got to the side of the field and shook my hand.

"How are you, Michael?" I asked.

"Oooh well, Xaaavier, you know, it's NOT easy," he answered still panting.

This year was meant to be our big break. I didn't want to hear bad news and it looked as if that's what he had in store for me. I had hired him to get it done. I wasn't interested in knowing how hard it was nor what it would take to get there. Of course it wasn't easy, I said to myself. Otherwise why would I bring someone all the way from California and pay him handsomely? I felt a burst of irritation at my American colleague; Chinese like Yang never complained about how hard it was.

"So, tell me how things are going here," I said to Tani, once we were standing along a neat row of broccoli seedlings. My arrival had interrupted a conversation between Lu, Tani and Yang. Once we were all standing along the neat row of broccoli seedlings, it resumed.

"Okay, I'll explain again," he said, sighing and turning to Lu, our supplier, who was expected to teach farmers how to implement California methods on Chinese soil. He looked at Yang, who was translating. "Try to translate clearly."

Tani looked at Lu, sweat dripping from his forehead. "When it comes time to harvest, you absolutely need to check the head-size before you allow people to pick," he said. Lu puckered his lips, staring at the circular steel piece Yang and Tani had designed to measure the circumference of the broccoli heads. They wanted to make sure Lu only harvested heads whose size met the exacting standards Japanese customers were accustomed to.

Tani went down on one knee to show how to place the disc-shaped gauge, which was pierced with a hole, roughly 30 inches above the seedling where a broccoli flower would soon sprout. "Here," he said. "When the broccoli head fits snugly inside the circle, that's when you want to harvest it."

The circular gauge seemed like a good practical idea to me. But Lu had a different view.

"*Hen kexi*—It's such a pity," he said in a plaintive voice, smiling as if trying to soften the blow for the American. Lu bought his produce from a group of farmers in a village where he had political backers in case things didn't go as planned. We had selected him because, unlike the majority of villagers, he seemed genuinely interested in trying new things. He bought the refrigerated truck and even invested in a cold room to pack and store the broccoli the way we wanted. Like lettuce, broccoli could bring multiple times the income that the farmers were accustomed to. But even Lu had a limited view of what Chinese farmers were capable of changing and what they would flat-out refuse to do.

"Broccoli is sold by weight in China, so heads are wider than in Japan," Lu said, half shouting, half smiling as villagers do. "It's completely unnatural for the *farmers* to harvest a crop earlier, before it matures completely and reaches the maximum weight."

Now it all makes sense, I thought. I had always wondered why vegetables sold in street markets looked so big compared to the ones in France.

Tani shook his head slowly in despair. He had already dealt with this type of feedback too many times. Larger size made vegetables taste worse; it was a proven fact. "It's not going to be easy," he said, looking at Yang and me. "People here don't understand that you can get a higher price for higher quality."

Yang nodded. "I understand," he said. "But Lu is right; farmers will try to cut corners. They're not bad people. That's just the way they are."

Tani kept looking at me, as if he expected me to fix the problem. Still irritated at his passivity, I jumped in and asked him more pointed questions.

"I smell manure here. How do you make sure people aren't using it on our crop?" I asked him.

"Well, we did deliver the fertilizer I had selected," he responded. "But they've taken it and sold it to pocket the cash."

Yang nodded. "Lu is on it and will try to get some compensation from the village," he said.

"How do we know they're not using dangerous substances on our crop, then?" I continued.

The two stayed silent.

"We can't really guarantee it," Yang said finally. "Next time, I will have our approved fertilizer and pesticide locked in this small shed and I will keep the keys," he continued, pointing at a small corrugated-iron barrack in a corner.

It all sounded so amateurish. Questions rushed through my mind: What prevents locals from breaking the locks? Will you need to be here each time to open the shed while you're supposed to supervise both Yunnan and Qipanshan at the same time? So why do we even employ Lu then?

But I said nothing. I liked my vision of containers stacked at Japanese ports so much I didn't want to know more. "Let Tani and Steve to figure this out," I thought. I nodded and said a silent prayer that Lu knew better ways of controlling the villagers.

As I walked back to the car, though, I couldn't help observing the stunted seedlings, some already under pest attacks. It didn't look at all as if we could ever meet the stringent Japanese standards I had promised during my last trip in Tokyo.

Why were we growing broccoli when lettuce was already complicated enough?

It was a matter of timing, mostly — and a dash of opportunism. Steve thought growing good quality lettuce in China could take a couple of years. Chinese farmers already grew broccoli for export to Japan, which meant that we could join and improve an existing operation. But because Chinese broccoli sold at steep discounts to the California crop, Steve felt we needed someone with a strong agriculture background to improve farming practices. With Tani, whom Steve had known for years, we not only got a good farmer but a man with deep experience selling in Japan, who could also teach farmers to grow better broccoli.

A few weeks before, Tani and I had travelled to Japan to meet his former clients. It was an impressive line-up; all of the attendees were key suppliers to McDonald's Japan or other large restaurant chains with thousands of outlets. It was exactly what I was hoping for. I had sat in meetings listening to Tani interact in Japanese and bowed to my unfailingly polite hosts without understanding a word of what was said. The trip went so well, the Japanese all promised to allocate some of their immense purchasing volume to Creative Food—provided we met their stringent quality standards, of course.

I wasn't completely oblivious to the challenge that it posed. In Tokyo's wholesale market, I had watched containers of broccoli arriving from California after two weeks spent on the ocean. The broccoli heads looked as if they had been generated by a 3D printer, all a uniform four inches in diameter and the same dark-green color. Nothing else passed muster in Japan. In the same hall a few steps away, Chinese broccoli looked completely different. The cheap-looking half-ripped plastic boxes displayed as many shades of green as you could imagine. Small yellow spots caused by sunburn made them look sickly. These "cat eyes"—as insiders called them—were caused by pearls of morning dew acting as a lens, burning the broccoli crown in various spots. Importers applied steep penalties for even the smallest defects. Light- or yellowish-green, or the purple discoloration caused by cool weather, weren't acceptable.

In Tani, I believed I had found the man to help us overcome this issue. And waiting for two more years until our lettuce operation was ready wasn't an option. I needed to show some quick progress so I could attract more investors. Broccoli seemed to be the perfect interim crop. Creative Food would be in Japan right away, trading and developing market networks until we could ship the much more valuable cut lettuce to foodservice chains.

Two years, I thought. It was only two years before we would hit the jackpot with our made-in-China bagged lettuce.

Tani worked like an evangelist, preaching his message about why California delivered the best broccoli in the world. But from the beginning, his sermons failed in the face of some stark facts. In the fertile valleys of Santa Clara or Salinas, pesticides and fertilizers were applied with precision by sprayers attached behind GPS-guided tractors. As a result, the entire crop came ready for harvest at the same time with identical quality. Long metallic wings pulled by a tractor and equipped with conveyor belts would then move methodically into broccoli patches as large as several football fields. Trailing them, a dozen hired laborers bent to pick the broccoli heads and methodically placed them in boxes set on top of the conveyers. Others at the end of one wing loaded the boxes into cold trucks, which then headed for pre-cooling at a nearby hub. Like a watch mechanism, every step a laborer made equaled one head of broccoli in a box.

In contrast, Chinese broccoli—planted across hundreds of small patches of land spread across the countryside—came to maturity at different times, preventing Lu and the other villagers from harvesting an entire field at once. Mature heads were harvested first, one by one, and thrown into a wheelbarrow that someone pushed along the dirt trails between the fields; it was then piled on the side of a road until a flatbed truck could pick it up. The broccoli might wait there for hours, sweating under the sun or rotting in the rain. Only a fraction made it fresh and intact to the cold storage facility, where it was sorted and packed. The same happened every day with the lettuce we were buying for KFC. Packing the produce in the fields, with mechanistic precision as in California, just wasn't possible.

So, Tani's effort to create new habits hit resistance wherever he went. He assumed that because he acted in good faith, people would trust him. But as in Qipanshan, leery farmers didn't trust anyone.

Despite my growing awareness of these issues, I mostly left Yang and Tani on their own and made only a couple of farm visits. I preferred to focus on I-Veg.com, absorbing myself in web search optimization and page-view numbers. Gone was my careful attention to cash flows, production costs and being thrifty at all. I spent more time dreamily reading *Fast Company* and *Wired* than worrying about how we might overcome the obstacles to getting good quality crops that I had now witnessed first-hand.

The goal for i-Veg.com was to provide information about the vegetable-trading sector and create a group of loyal followers who relied on the service to make decisions. The idea was to later connect subscribers directly with buyers and by-pass intermediaries as a way to increase profit for villagers like Yang's parents. Because this was before the widespread use of mobile phones, I envisioned a network of desktop computers placed strategically in a communal house in each village, where farmers would come to participate in online trades facilitated by i-Veg. com for a fee.

My early investors also continued to be infatuated with this part of the business. When I shared some concerns about early losses, one venture capitalist told me, "Xavier, do not worry about the money. Spend. Grow the business. We will take care of the rest." So, I did. I placed a young technology-savvy executive from Asiafoods in charge of iVeg.com. Since he lived in Beijing, we started a new office there, more than seven hundred miles away from the main team in Shanghai.

The old Asiafoods team had now dissolved. I had wanted

to hire Fang, my loyal accountant, from the finance team there, but she resigned as I was about to ask. Had she been on board at Creative Food in those early days, with her bluntness and business sense, things could have played out more favorably for us. Losing her was entirely my fault. A few weeks before, I had foolishly bragged about her accomplishments to a headhunter acquaintance I met over dinner. Subsequently, a fast-growing retail chain—that headhunter's client—made her an offer she couldn't turn down.

Steve did his part, supervising the construction of a new plant in Beijing and the transformation of our Shanghai and Shenzhen facilities into modern vegetable processing plants. I did tell KFC we were building the plant as a sign of our commitment to them. But the real goal was to use it as our model plant to impress Japanese customers.

In this summer of 2000, Creative Food had existed only a few months, but with one half-empty plant in Shanghai and two plants under construction in Beijing and Shenzhen, cash was flowing out very fast. The first financial results made it clear the "break-even business" I had touted to investors was losing a lot of money.

Creative Food after six months looked a lot like Asiafoods in its heyday. Foreigners held all the key positions at the company. Steve and Tani had hired a group of talented young Chinese managers who spoke fluent English, but apart from Yang and his team, very few knew what it meant to deal with the farmers. I certainly didn't. I was spending a lot of money on new plants and new equipment that didn't bring immediate savings or sales, and my internet venture was sucking precious cash and energy away. I found myself unconsciously using the empty phrases I had heard at Asiafoods, leading pep rallies that sounded a lot like the "Let's go team!" of the Johnson & Johnson pre-Family

Day meeting. As the fairy tale of my imagination failed to play out, I fell back on the same patterns I had judged so harshly when I arrived in China.

Back in Qipanshan as springtime turned into summer, Yang was increasingly frustrated. Unlike his parents and other rice farmers in the South, who harvested two to three crops a year, villagers in the north usually managed one annual harvest and were accustomed to long periods of inactivity. Yang was asking a whole lot more from them, but all he could see was dawdling and resistance—which could have serious consequences for the lettuce crop.

The potential for pests was one issue. Mornings were chilly, but by noon, the temperature was already above 100 degrees. Pests develop very fast when it's hot, Yang knew, which would mean the need for more costly pesticide.

And he had bigger problems: by mid-July, there wasn't any water left for irrigation thanks to faulty weather projections plus an unusually dry winter. If he didn't resolve the shortage fast, there wouldn't be a farm to supervise. It was decided that China Green Concept, the company that was supplying the lettuce to us, would buy water from village wells and channel it to our farm through a maze of ditches. Then during one of his trips north, Yang called me in Shanghai.

"We need to work at night from now on," he said bluntly.

"Why would you work at night?" I asked, sitting next to Steve and Tani, staring at the speaker phone in the Shanghai office.

Yang's voice stayed calm as he answered: "Because villagers are stealing our water."

We paid good rent money for the land villagers usually planted with scrawny potatoes and corn. On top of that, we paid those same farmers a daily fee to work for us. And now the village was getting more cash in exchange for the well water. We had been a boon for the community. "And you're saying they're stealing it?" I said, trying — and failing — to control my anger.

As usual, Yang was accommodating. "You have to look at it from their point of view," he said, pausing to make sure I was listening. "The water comes through ditches across their fields, so they feel it's theirs."

Before I had the time to ram another set of questions into him — I suspected farmers hadn't seen any of the money Leo had paid to the village — he added, "Don't even think of fighting them. The people digging holes in our ditches at night are the same ones who work for us during the day. We need them. You can't alienate the whole village."

Yang said China Green Concept planned to drill their own well on the farmland that we leased from them. They figured that they would find water after drilling for thirty feet. That day, I considered walking away from the project entirely. But I reasoned that, because someone else was paying for the drilling, it was worth waiting it out. Weeks passed; the drilling went deeper, down to two hundred thirty feet, and water never came. Yang's phone calls to me turned more agitated; China Green Concepts was running out of cash.

But even that was the least of our problems with Qipanshan. The quality of the first lettuce coming from our leased farms there was disastrous, and harvest volumes were far below projections. The heads of the lettuce were so small they looked like tennis balls instead of the large California-style basketball heads that Tani had promised. In my mind, I lumped together untrustworthy villagers and my California experts. I had done everything Tani had asked for, and I hadn't seen anything for my money. In the end, angry at everyone and frustrated at our many setbacks, I threw the issue back at Steve. I told him to figure it out and retreated back to my focus on the internet business.

Blocking out the bad news helped me concentrate on what was going well. The way I saw it, I had a lot to be pleased about. Three broccoli farms were in place for the autumn, Tani's customers had shown some interest during my exciting trip to Tokyo and I had even found an agent ready to represent Creative Food in Japan for the coming broccoli season. Our website for I-Veg.com was up and running. True, I also feared we were spreading ourselves too thin: new farms in Yunnan and Inner Mongolia, new plants in three cities, and the Internet, and Japan. But I didn't fear strongly enough to stop anything. The truth was, I still didn't really want to spend too much time thinking about farming.

One afternoon, six months after the official founding of Creative Food and right in the middle of the summer season in Inner Mongolia, I was working in our Beijing office, which dealt with the internet venture, when my cell phone rang. Warren Liu, vice president of Yum China, owner of KFC and Pizza Hut China, had somehow gotten hold of my number.

I knew Warren. Tall and imperious, he suffered no debate. Anyone speaking to him had to be well-prepared and articulate, or he would lose patience. I had spent a fair amount of time explaining to him that the separation of Creative Food from Asiafoods was a good thing for KFC. "Creative Food will be completely focused on growing and processing vegetables for KFC," I heard myself say, "while Asiafoods was a restaurant company that viewed vegetable processing as a distraction from its main business." I didn't believe a word of it. Japan and the internet were always my true dreams. But I still said it.

His voice on the phone today was portentous and slow, as if he were speaking to a child who had gotten into trouble. "Xavier, this is Warren Liu at Yum China," he said. "I am very concerned by what I am hearing, and I wonder whether you can help me make sense of it all."

Warren's team, he told me, had received a letter from Chennong, our biggest lettuce supplier in Yunnan—and the ringleader in the local cartel—claiming that Creative Food had not paid its bills for several months. I had been buying more than usual from Yunnan to offset delays at Qipanshan. As a consequence, he warned Warren, he would stop supplying lettuce to us, and we would be unable to process enough shredded lettuce to satisfy KFC's daily needs.

I was mortified. Warren didn't usually call me directly. Creative Food represented less than two percent of the total volume of supplies his company bought every year. But if I failed to deliver lettuce, KFC couldn't add it to its chicken burgers. And that part was worth his time.

It may sound strange that a senior executive in charge of hundreds of employees would concern himself with a shortfall in the supply of lettuce, a common and humble vegetable in the West. But iceberg lettuce is simply not grown in China. To the Chinese palate, which savors an immense variety of green vegetables, lettuce looks and tastes a lot like cabbage—that is, bland and boring. Fast food chains, however, love lettuce; its high water content and the white rib of its leaves make for a fresh and crispy contrast with the warm softness of buns and burgers.

In the late eighties when they arrived in China, KFC and McDonald's taught a few companies like Chennong how to grow iceberg lettuce, supplying them with seeds from the U.S. and then buying the vegetables back. *They* were the market—period. So, if even a single supplier stopped selling to KFC or to Creative Food, it was serious, simply because there was no other place to go. Creative Food processed more than seven metric tons of lettuce per day—close to one lettuce head every second. All the lettuce traders in the Shanghai vegetable wholesale market, the largest in a region of three hundred million people, stored barely half a metric ton on any day—and most of that was bad quality.

Given our tight financial situation, our accountants had indeed delayed payment to Chennong and other suppliers. This was in part a bargaining position: I wanted Chennong to believe that I could replace their lettuce with my own, hoping that they could lower their prices as a result. At the same time, I hadn't carefully reviewed our cash flows, leaving our accountants to decide who needed to be paid and in what order. Without clear direction, they simply delayed payments to everyone equally, exposing our flanks to a ruthless supplier who was hoping to cut us out of the equation and win business with KFC directly. I had neglected the dull, unsavory details that are essential to running a business, and now I was paying for it. Warren's call alarmed me, but not because I truly wanted to do a better job at serving him. My company couldn't afford to lose KFC: It would scare future investors away.

I flew back to Shanghai the day of the phone call to deal with this emergency. The next morning, I went to Yum China's headquarters in a gleaming Shanghai office tower to present to their executive committee. This was going straight into the sharks' tank. As I walked into the conference room, a dozen executives, all at least ten years older than I, sat around a large horse-shoe conference table, waiting to hear the many excuses I would give them about why we weren't paying our suppliers.

I pulled out my slides and then, as I often did with investors, I focused on what we were doing to develop the business: "Our exports to Japan will set the standards very high for our operations, and Yum China will benefit."

And then I-Veg.com: "We will be at the center of the produce community in China, able to identify quickly the best suppliers."

Finally, the clincher: "I am in advanced discussions with reputable investors such as ABN Amro, the largest Dutch bank, and FMO, the Development Bank of the Netherlands. They are committed to invest in Creative Food, but they need to follow their procedures."

The room was silent. Warren, in front of me, looked at his watch. On my left, a couple of people murmured something in Chinese to each other. At that moment, I realized I was the only foreigner in the room. I looked intently at Yum's vegetable buyer, hoping he would back me up, but he just stared, saying nothing.

I tried one more time, referring to another slide about the use of funds: "We've been investing a lot for you already.....the new plants.....the California experts..."

Then a man sitting along the right side of the table whom I hadn't noticed before started to speak. He was at least six feet tall—much taller than your typical Chinese executive—and he had a long, gloomy face, as if his role in life were solely to deliver bad news. I didn't know it yet, but this was Sam Su, the chief executive of Yum China, the man who had taken the company from five money-losing restaurants in the late 1980s to the more than six thousand it operates today.

"That's all very nice," he said in a booming voice, in perfect English, "but Yum China is paying you on time every month. You're using that money to fund your losses instead of paying your suppliers. By doing so, you jeopardize our business. You can't simply tell us to wait."

The room remained silent. The Yum executives sat in their chairs, all looking anywhere but at me. I felt like a fifth-grader being dressed down by his teacher for having forgotten to do his homework.

Sam Su wasn't done with me: "Cut expenses and reduce the amount you are losing every month, or we will find another supplier."

I looked back at him to show I took this seriously.

"In the meantime," he continued, "we request that you provide your accounts payable to our Chief Financial Officer every week."

He indicated a stern-looking lady near him and then turned back to me. "And our legal counsel will contact you to find ways to protect Yum China's business if you can't pay your bills."

He then asked with a tone that did not really require an answer: "Is that well understood?"

I nodded, not daring to say a word. Su and the others filed out of the room without waiting for me. I was stunned. It was the first time I had endured such a public dressing-down in the business world, ever. I knew what his words meant. Those middle-aged ladies in the cavernous canteens, cutting up lettuce for chicken burgers...It might be humble. It might be mundane. It might be bringing in only $300,000 a year. But that was the only money-making operation I had, and I had better make it work.

I wasn't ready to admit it, but Sam Su was right about a few things. By the time of my dressing-down, the money I had raised was quickly drying up. Worse, some of the investors had overcommitted. When the internet bubble burst in the spring of 2000, stock markets crashed and with it, all their hopes of listing companies with vague internet business plans in New York or Hong Kong. The very investors who had told me to go ahead and spend didn't return my calls. Several started to run low on cash, with many of their investee companies competing for what was left. They sent me the funds they had committed months before, but bit by bit only, when their cash flow allowed. I was in negotiation for a much larger round of funding, as I had told the Yum executives, but that money would take many months to materialize. My daily concern now was how to figure out creative ways of making payroll at the end of each month. If my employees were not paid, my dream of being an entrepreneur would soon become a nightmare.

I turned practical. Just a few months into the start of our Internet office in Beijing, I closed it down, an abrupt and unceremonious end to the enterprise that had distracted me from reality from the beginning. I put Tani's equipment purchases for the iced broccoli project on hold and did the same for the portable pre-cooling equipment Steve wanted for our range of farms. He was not happy about it, but he knew I had no choice. I delayed payments to travel agencies, packaging suppliers and equipment makers, none of whom could put us out of business. And I stopped paying myself. One angry supplier warned me that he knew where I lived. In the office, there was gossip about goons who had been hired to take care of me at night. For once, my inability to deal directly in Mandarin helped. I didn't sense the urgency as much as our buyers did when people yelled and threatened them on the phone. But because of this, and also to avoid more backchannel complaints to Yum China, I made sure that our vegetable vendors were paid at least some of what we owed them. That bought me some time.

I was not alone, though. Everyone had a hard time at Creative Food. "Why on earth are you staying on this sinking ship?" said a KFC junior buyer to Ms. Xu, our young customer service lady, when she called to collect orders for the day.

The negative gossip that my employees were subjected to was relentless. "This company is doomed; everyone knows it. They're going bust before the end of the year," said the Compass employees in the shuttle bus that drove them to the office in the morning. Ms Xu sometimes came to me for reassurance, and I would give her my pep talk, which only left me bitter when she left. In my mind, I was sounding more and more like Mike DeNoma, whose airy upbeat chatter had colored my earliest days in Shanghai.

By summer's end, though, we were shipping some test containers of broccoli and lettuce to Japan, and the Dutch banks had received preliminary approval from their head office in the Netherlands to invest in Creative Food. I was still struggling to scrape together enough cash to make payroll every month. But I looked forward to having enough resources to resume planning ahead.

One afternoon late in August during that summer of 2000, I was on my way back to Shanghai after a few days spent checking on our new plant in Beijing. As I lined up for check-in at Beijing's newly-built airport, I received a phone call from ABN Amro's Roger Marshall. I knew he was in the Netherlands for a final meeting to approve the investment in Creative Food. Documents were ready to sign.

He didn't waste any time with civilities. "I am sorry, Xavier," he said. "We got turned down."

At first, I thought this was a temporary setback, one that we could recover from with more negotiating. But Roger continued, "The newly-appointed bank chairman attended this committee, and he alone decided against it. Creative Food's business did not matter at all."

Then he went on, quoting the chairman: "'We don't want to be everything to everyone,' he said. "We do not invest in agriculture; that's all."

I was stupefied. ABN Amro had asked for exclusivity in negotiating a stake in my company during the past two months, and I had nothing to fall back on. In the far distance, a colleague of mine was calling me, telling to pass through the security gate, but I barely heard him. My head was buzzing. How was I supposed to explain this to Sam Su, to my employees, to my American experts, to other potential investors?

Later that day in Shanghai, I tried to cobble together a plan. The fund-raising community in China and Hong Kong revolves around a small group of people. Everyone knew that ABN Amro had been looking at investing in Creative Food. I had been very transparent about it. The exclusivity of the negotiation had sent a strong signal to the investor community. It showed ABN was confident it could quickly complete the investment, and it made Creative Food look desirable. Now, I feared that our company's name was tainted, that no one would ever want to touch us for fear that something bad had triggered ABN Amro's decision to walk away.

Roger Marshall, it turned out, felt guilty about how things had developed. He called again just hours later. "Xavier, I feel personally responsible for what happened," he said. "If I recommend an investment to my bank and it decides not to follow my advice, I should at least have the courage to invest myself. It may not be much, but I will gather friends' and family's money to provide you with some funds to help get you through this tough patch."

Along with Roger, the Dutch development bank called FMO stayed the course, but with one condition: I needed to find another institutional investor to co-invest alongside them.

Within a month, FMO verbally agreed to a package of equity and loans to support Creative Food, and the German Development Bank, DEG, agreed in principle to participate in the round. But I knew it might take much longer to receive funds. I kept on delaying investments and recruitment; I wanted to see our summer through and then dive into our Japanese broccoli exports in the autumn. It was the core of my plan, and shutting it down now was a sure way of losing the investors I had lined up. Money kept trickling in from existing shareholders, who believed I could pull it off. I feared I would run out of cash, and I feared even more I would lose good, competent people like Yang. If that happened, cash would not matter.

After months of what now seemed like merely playing around with being an entrepreneur, I finally knew, deep in my gut, what that meant. A sense of being alone at the helm, a knot in my stomach, the realization that no one but myself could save me. It stayed like that for years.

I wasn't the only one with cash-flow problems. Around the same time that I was struggling to find investors and scrape together funds to pay employees, Leo woke up at five as usual for another day at the Qipanshan farm. He dressed and headed for the kitchen to grab his rice porridge. The cooking lady Yang had hired to help prepare meals nodded at the window in the living room, indicating in her taciturn way that he should have a look outside.

"Villagers are not big communicators here," Leo thought as he pulled the curtain for a peek. Around fifteen farmers had gathered at the metal gate in front of the building, some crouching on the ground smoking cigarettes, all chatting away. They were his farmers, the people he hired, coddled and scolded every day. Some of them were carrying shovels in their hands. "Did they really walk the thirty kilometers from the farm," Leo wondered, "in the dark of the night?"

He quickly descended the stairs, walked around the building and opened the heavy metal door. There was a commotion outside. The farmers seized their shovels and turned toward him, one man shouting louder than the others, "Go back inside, go back inside!" Leo immediately knew why this was happening. When he came back into the apartment, Jimmy was standing at the door. "What's happening?" Jimmy asked,

"We can't leave the apartment," answered Leo. "We can't leave the apartment until we pay the farmers what we owe them." Then he picked up his phone to call Yang in Shanghai. "Please help," he said.

Leo and Jimmy had used up all their company's money drilling in vain for water. That's why they hadn't paid the villagers anything at all for several weeks. I had been paying for some of the bad lettuce they sent me despite my own cash flow problems. But they had gambled the money away — around $10,000 — on the drilling operation. Meanwhile, the fax machine in our customer service department regularly churned out complaints from angry KFC restaurant managers who saw their bags of Qipanshan-grown shredded lettuce go brown after a day or two instead of the five days we guaranteed. In these cases, I was forced to buy replacement lettuce from Chennong and the Yunnan cartel for triple the regular price and ship it by emergency airfreight to Shanghai, Beijing and Shenzhen. And I had to pay those companies first, or Sam and Warren were sure to come roaring at me.

The whole company was hemorrhaging cash. In my new daily ritual of dispensing our trickle of money, Leo and Jimmy in faraway Inner Mongolia came far down the list; I wasn't ready to pay for their drilling debts. At least, that's how I viewed the situation, until Yang rushed in to tell me that he feared for their safety. I had been wrong to assume this was their problem — because now I had to choose between forking out what their company owed or risk losing the season's lettuce crop, and maybe more.

Yang knew how villagers behaved. They hadn't been violent yet. But he thought it could quickly get out of control if we didn't do something.

"You won't gain anything by waiting it out," he said. "The police and the town government will always take their side."

In their eyes, we were a rich multinational. I mulled it over for a few seconds. In the end, I told him to try negotiations anyway. As long as the team up there was safe, I wasn't ready to cave in to the farmers' demands.

As dramatic as it was for me, such disturbances in the Chinese countryside weren't rare. As part of the economic reform policies in the early 1980s, farmers once again were allowed to till their own plot of land. But new rules overlapped with old ones, creating confusion and leaving much room for abuse. The old communal farm organization wasn't completely dismantled either. The production brigade or the production team simply shifted to the district, the town, or the village. The names of the entities might have changed, but the hierarchies stayed in place. Communes disappeared, but Communist Party secretaries in towns or villages stayed on as representatives of the state, with the authority to raise taxes, administer land and mediate conflicts.

This bureaucratic structure had advantages. When I needed to establish a new farm, I signed contracts with local village governments rather than with hundreds of individual farmers. Party secretaries were usually more educated than the local villagers; they knew that their performance depended on job creation, so a transaction with Creative Food could mean a promotion. Once the deal was done, they went out to convince villagers to lease out their contiguous plots to form one large farm or to agree to a supply arrangement. They spoke the same dialect as the villagers and understood their priorities in ways I never would.

But century-old family lineages, plus the bonds that had formed from years of working in the same production teams, created another tight network beneath the official hierarchy. In villages, it wasn't rare to hear a person talk about someone next door not as his neighbor but as a member of the same *shengchandui*, or production brigade. With such deep-rooted connections, people organized rapidly into large groups—and, when they didn't like new arrangements that were imposed from above, or might bring about unfair consequences, they were quite capable of mobilizing against authorities. During the roaring 1990s, the number of rural protests nationwide increased tenfold to around 40,000. Then that figure doubled again by 2005. Most of these acts of resistance were on a small scale and concluded peacefully, but some ended with injuries and even deaths, often caused by stone-throwing by protesters or police beatings.

As interesting as the number of protests were the reasons people rebelled in the first place. By the year 2000, annual per-capita income in the cities had soared to around $1,000, more than triple the rural figure. But people didn't protest because they were worried about lofty goals like income equality. They were motivated by practical reasons, such as when their land got misappropriated or a tax increase jeopardized their already meager livelihoods. As cities expanded, shrewd real estate developers came in and made deals with local cadres, using the same method that I had for my supply arrangements. However, farmers often received only a small fraction of the money that was raised from these deals. That caused anger and frustration, especially when reluctant villagers were expelled from their land by force, for what they felt was too little compensation.

If corruption among cadres and developers was one factor,

another was the sheer speed of economic transformation in the countryside. Farmers' land use rights were only partially documented, no land register had been set up, and laws administering the conversion of rural into urban land had not caught up to ballooning real-estate prices. In two-thirds of all rural protests, scholars have found abusive land grabs were the reason why farmers rebelled. Other causes included excessive or unfair taxation, and environmental degradation so severe that it caused serious health issues among villagers.

These protests could be dramatic, but what is remarkable is how slow, in reality, villagers were in resorting to shovels and shouting to make their needs known. In 1993, a decade after Deng Xiaoping launched economic reforms that began to allow a private sector to develop under the socialist state, the Chinese Academy of Social Sciences recorded around ten-thousand rural protests; that's less than two incidents for hundred villages. Faced with abuses, villagers preferred to petition the authorities in the nearby town or district, elevating the issue through the bureaucracy in a dispute resolution system already in place during imperial times. Residents might resort next to legal action, but suits against local authorities were not likely to end in their favor. When villagers finally marched to protest unfair practices, it happened mostly against egregious excesses, which explains why central authorities often backed them up.

While often neglected, China's sheer number of farmers represents a force that every ruling dynasty in the country's long history has watched carefully. The Three Kingdoms epic novel tells how the Yellow Turbans rebelled against the emperor in 184 AD. Most famously, in the mid-nineteenth-century, the Taiping Rebellion drove two million farmers angered by natural disasters, famines, abusive taxes and anti-Manchu sentiment, to take over Nanjing, the former capital under the Ming Dynasty.

And China's Communists understand better than anyone how peasant unrest can undermine a regime. The 1949 Communist revolution co-opted villagers to fight, and eventually defeat, the Nationalist government.

As the number of rural protests rose, the government in Beijing has seized on the chance to show support for the "Old Hundred Names." It essentially leveraged the farmers' anger to increase its own scrutiny over local cadres. In 2006, Beijing cancelled all local taxes affecting farmers and experimented for a while with elections at the village committee level.

When Yang insisted that I wouldn't get very far by pushing back against the Weichang protesters, he knew the context better than I did even though he didn't articulate it. Land grabs and local corruption were serious issues for any government official — but a company that was behind on paying salaries and a foreign one at that? I was fair game for anyone; the central government had nothing to do with it, local officials didn't want to get involved, and the media would probably take the poor farmers' side against the rich capitalist from abroad. Once again, I was alone.

For a few days, farmers continued to camp at the metal gate, day and night. The cooking lady was allowed to go out to shop, but Leo and Jimmy couldn't set foot outside. Leo tried a few times to bargain with the farmers about how much he would pay them, but nothing worked. The villagers were completely inflexible. Left with no choice, I asked Yang to fly to Weichang with $30,000 worth of cash in a gym bag. Leo and Jimmy were set free. The farmers returned home. We took the rest of the lettuce that we had already paid for but soon stopped farming in Qipanshan.

In stepping up for two men who did not even work for my company, I spent precious cash, which I never recovered from

Leo and Jimmy. I had to beg Chennong to let me buy more lettuce at a predatory price. Chennong, in turn, made sure KFC learned all about my management debacles and how its generosity had saved us.

Six months into its start, Creative Food was on its knees, bereft of funding, with bleeding finances, and distrustful clients.

In Qipanshan, the villagers went back to planting sweet potatoes and corn.

5

Partners

When Creative Food was six months old, I hired a man I believed could change the company's destiny. I was right about that, but not in the way I expected when Kevin Lam's resume first crossed my desk.

Kevin had worked as a vice president for sales and marketing at Kraft Foods, Colgate and Henkel, all respected multinationals in China. A Hong Kong native and recently naturalized Canadian, he was 46 years old, 15 years my senior, but looked much younger, tanned and athletic, with heavy-framed glasses that only accentuated his good looks. He often stroked his thick mane of hair as he spoke, tilting his head backward. He spoke fast, in what you might call approximate English — but who was I to judge him? The fact was that his words hit right where I felt we lacked substance at Creative Food. When he said, "decisive", "aggressive" and "in tune with the ways of China," I thought uncomfortably about my detached group of foreign experts, who were so often ignorant of the way things were done in this country. And it was flattering that for the entire interview, Kevin seemed so excited at the idea of working for a start-up like Creative Food. He would bring cultural and professional experience to our disparate group. His voice occasionally turned shrill when he got excited about something, but it was a minor annoyance. I liked him. As I signed his contract to become our executive vice president in charge of sales, I was filled with pride at having attracted such a talent to the company.

I was nervous about making such a pricy hire; cash was tight even before I got that fateful call from Roger Marshall while I was in the Beijing airport. But I needed a man to lead my sales operations. Tani and Steve were experienced in agricultural operations, but they weren't salesmen. Kevin told me he wanted a chance to be an entrepreneur; he wanted more freedom than he could get at a large corporation. I negotiated with him to reduce the cash part of his pay package and offset it with shares in Creative Food. That would give him a real taste of entrepreneurship, I thought.

A few days after he started, Kevin took me aside before a client meeting and asked if he could call himself a partner at Creative Food when he introduced himself to clients. He explained that the term, used for someone of his experience and caliber, would bring immediate weight to the company in the eyes of customers. I thought it was a bit early—Steve, who was closer to me, had never asked for that—but I felt that Kevin probably needed face now that he did not have the big title and company name behind him. In China's highly hierarchical society, I knew such symbols of status and prestige helped rank people. I had learned people could earn, lose or regain face, and even if the concept remained blurry to me, I was already keenly aware that the Chinese valued it highly. I also thought it would help soften his landing into the often-bleak world of the start-up. So, I started to call both Steve and Kevin partners inside and outside the company.

At board meetings, I made sure both men were invited to present their respective parts of the business. Their decades of experience brought gravitas to my fledgling venture. Bringing talented people into the company, I felt, reflected well on me.

A major reason I hired Kevin had nothing to do with his resume or his self-confidence: it was the simple fact that he could conduct meetings in the language that almost everyone at Creative Food best understood. Each time I led a meeting with my team of upper managers, most of them young Chinese men and women, I sensed I wasn't getting through to them. I tried to use colorful sayings in my presentations, things like "We are not selling lettuce; we are selling convenience," a tactic I knew worked with Western investors. But at these meetings in our Shanghai office, I often looked up from my PowerPoint presentations and saw no reaction at all. I assumed that they understood me—they had a reasonable level of English—but they were clearly disengaged. I searched their faces for signs of approval or even disapproval. What I got was nothing.

I had no idea what I and my other American managers were doing wrong. At Steve's staff meetings, people spoke more, but only to answer specific questions. The atmosphere was still restrained. Many of the foreigners I knew working at other companies faced the same issue. Most of them assumed that their Chinese employees were just shy and passive; they blamed decades of Communist rule and a rote education system. But to me, that sounded simplistic and judgmental. I had sat in on meetings at KFC. While I couldn't grasp what people were saying, the debates were lively and the managers engaged. Voices rose, faces showed frustration, heads nodded in agreement or shook in opposition, people talked over each other and some even exhaled with huffy irritation. Clearly, the Chinese were no more timid than Americans or Europeans.

When Kevin came on board and began to lead meetings, I noticed a shift. One of our first gatherings with the staffers took place just after I returned from a trip to Japan.

"This is Xavier, our CEO," he told the group of six with an air of grandiosity that I found slightly embarrassing.

"I've just come back from Japan," I said in English, "Our clients are really interested in what we're building out here."

I expected a smile or two; maybe a few pairs of eyes would widen with interest. But the meeting room table was completely silent. Most of the six staffers were staring at their hands crossed over the table, making me wonder whether they didn't care or simply didn't dare to speak up.

Kevin jumped in and took over. He spoke for a while in a long flow of Chinese words I didn't understand. One of the managers replied with a question.

Kevin praised him and then turned to me. "Mr Yu, our logistics manager, is asking about the recent concern with chemical residues found on vegetables from China in Japan and whether it's affecting our business," he translated for me.

Relieved that someone was interested at last, I gave him my usual pitch about how we controlled our growers and instructed them how to use chemicals. "That wouldn't happen to us," I said.

What I got back from Yu was another polite stare.

It didn't seem like I was getting my message through.

Kevin again came to my aid and translated in Chinese until I sensed the energy coming back into the room. I politely excused myself from the rest of the meeting. I didn't want to disturb the positive mood he seemed to have created.

The fact that I was shunted aside made me a little nervous, but I liked Kevin's lively meetings. My Chinese team did too, and it seemed good that they were airing their opinions. I didn't need to know what those opinions were, I decided. I didn't know enough about the language or the culture to judge, and I didn't have the time or energy right now to educate myself in those areas. After a while, I stopped attending Kevin's meetings altogether. I was often out of the office on fundraising trips anyway.

Soon after he arrived, I put Kevin in charge of a project I thought was ideal given his background managing brands in supermarkets around China. I had noticed that most of the farmers who grew lettuce and broccoli for us sold their vegetables to small traders, bringing their crop to corrugated-iron sheds on a tricycle mounted with flat wooden beds. The sheds were often located in the villages, which might be ten miles from the fields where the vegetables were harvested. The produce then followed a long chain of middlemen until it landed at large wholesale markets in Shanghai, Guangzhou or Beijing. Prices easily quadrupled between the farm and the large city markets. Worse, only about half of the original harvested volume made it there. Leaves withered under the sun for hours until farmers could haul them inside; other items were damaged or destroyed by successive loading and unloading into flatbed trucks without refrigeration.

I wanted to eliminate the middlemen and improve quality at the same time. So, I proposed using our network of growers in the countryside to package vegetables and then ship them directly to our plants in Shanghai or Beijing. I envisioned Creative Food building a direct link between our farmers and fast-emerging supermarket chains in those cities, while also moving beyond lettuce and broccoli to grow and trade a large range of produce.

Four months into it, by the end of 2000, the project was a fiasco. The two supermarket chains we had chosen, Homegain, a Shanghai-based company with hundreds of neighborhood supermarkets, and fast-expanding Carrefour, the second largest retailer in the world after Wal-Mart, promised us the exclusive right to supply them vegetables in Shanghai. But the project quickly proved too much for our network of growers, who were mainly accustomed to growing Western vegetables like lettuce or broccoli. To bring in the Chinese varieties that local consumers were accustomed to—bok choy, choy sum, and gailan for example—we had to resort, yet again, to buying from multiple traders. There was no way to find one a single vendor who was able to supply the fifty or so varieties of vegetables that we wanted every day.

Quality control was impossible. I had created a purchasing system that required layers of approvals in an effort to avoid corruption; my buyers couldn't buy anything without a signed order from their boss, and they could only purchase vegetables that met the quality standards that I had set. To check whether the price was fair, my manager usually consulted a government-run website; our quality people inspected the crop when it was delivered to the gates of our cold rooms.

But this system I had devised was too slow for China's fast-paced markets. Our people arrived at the office at 8.00am and left work at 6 pm. In contrast, traders worked 24 hours a day, frequently jabbering away on three cell phones at the same time. In the middle of each night, well before I scrutinized the figures entered into an Excel sheet by a junior government employee and waited for the vegetables to arrive, wholesalers were calling other merchants at the nearby markets to triangulate prices; then they would call villagers in two or three provinces thousands of miles away to understand harvest conditions: How much was coming to market? Of what quality? They knew, for example, that a late rain just before harvest could damage leaves, causing mold by the time the vegetable got to Shanghai, and they had time to take all of these variables into account well before they saw the vegetables arrive by truck.

The young and inexperienced recent college graduates we had

hired were no match for these ruthless merchants, entrenched in the wholesale markets for years, often working with cousins and family members, never counting work hours. No website could make up for this wide range of contacts and experience. Rejecting the poor-quality produce at the gate of our plants happened too late for us to replace them; by the early morning when our teams started work, the wholesale market was already empty. It was easy to dismiss these merchants, who could often be found dozing on wooden benches in the market during the day, their filthy white tank shirts rolled up just over their navels. But through the night, these ruthlessly competent men sniffed out and snatched up the best vegetables while our employees were sleeping at home.

We quickly decided that we needed a team working the night shift; I even resorted to paying overtime. But price and quality weren't our only problem. Both our clients and suppliers constantly changed their orders, a constant practice in the ruthless produce industry. The network of growers we assembled either harvested more than we needed or not enough, and they were dispersed all over the country. We had to constantly go back to the Shanghai wholesale market—the very place we were supposed to by-pass—to buy more or sell the excess that we had committed to buy on contract. And on top of all of this, our supermarket buyers were unorganized. Last-minute changes to their daily orders were common, forcing us to make expensive purchase runs to the market.

Waste accumulated. In the rush to get products out as fast as possible, our warehouse workers grabbed only the boxes stacked closest to the door of our cold storage facility. In the back, entire boxes of vegetables were left to decay or to freeze, as workers piled them too high and too close under the air conditioning units. We lost money every day on every product we sold. In what was perhaps the biggest embarrassment, we discovered that our supposed growers were actually buying products on the cheap from the same traders that we bought from, and then selling the goods back to us. In the market, Creative Food was like a wounded beast with a horde of bloodthirsty mosquitoes sucking away at it, weakening it further.

Kevin was in charge of the sales side of this operation, with Steve as liaison to the growers. I often crossed the office to collect a document or talk to someone and would see that Kevin had gathered a large group of employees in the glass-walled conference room. These meetings sometimes went on for hours.

One evening early in 2001, six months into his job, Kevin came to my office to rehash the day. We often did this after the rest of the staff had left for the evening. But that day he made a particular request.

"You're not really using the company car and its driver," he said.

I nodded. I was single and spent all my days in the office or traveling out of town. The driver was left idle most of the day, other than occasionally making trips to and from the airport.

"Do you mind if he picks me up in the morning and runs some errands for my wife during the day?" Kevin asked.

Kevin lived a five-minute drive from the plant in a compound where he had bought a townhouse. His request sounded strange to me. But I wanted him happy, so I agreed.

"You know, I need to take full control of the supermarkets project," he continued, as his voice rose to that shrill pitch I had noticed on the day I interviewed him. "Steve can't understand how fast things work in China."

He knew I would agree with him on that aspect.

"I need to hire someone to lead this project," Kevin said, "and

99

I have the perfect person." He opened his eyes wide as if he was about to reveal a wonderful surprise. "Her name is Kathy and she worked with me in sales at Colgate."

"One more recruit?" I wondered, thinking of the already dire state of our finances.

There was a contradiction between Kevin's wanting to run the project himself while also asking me to hire someone to do it. When I asked for more details, I found out that bringing Kathy on board would not be cheap. I had recently stopped paying myself and had also deferred part of Steve's and Kevin's salaries to save cash; they were partners after all, I told them. But Kevin insisted that hiring Kathy would make a difference, and he had caught me at a weak moment. I had just been dealing with my employee Sun being held hostage in Hebei province, and I was obsessively focused on getting new money for the company. I desperately wanted things to work. So, I agreed.

Deep down, I was not impressed by Kevin's performance so far. He talked too much; he seemed to run everything from behind his desk; he held endless meetings. But challenging him would have meant that I had to run things myself, to deal with dirty vegetable crates and the junior staff who froze in place each time I spoke to them.

"Kevin knows what he's doing," I told myself.

After six months of endless negotiations, the Dutch and German development banks had not yet signed any documents agreeing to invest. Busy with other deals, embroiled in their own politics, they didn't care about my problems and dragged out our negotiations by raising issues I had neither the time nor the energy to contemplate. I had to explain at one point how I would guarantee gender equality. Gender equality? I was all in favor of it, but it wouldn't matter if I couldn't pay workers' salaries.

Meanwhile, irate suppliers kept calling me, asking when I was going to pay them. I vowed that the money would arrive soon, but I often went back on my promises. I still had to provide proof to KFC every week that I had paid my lettuce suppliers, but I was doing that at the expense of many others.

In long fruitless conference calls with the banks and other potential investors, I repressed the urge to roar in frustration, and I spent long stretches of time in Europe, leaving Steve and Kevin in charge while I pursued the banks. In meetings, I remained outwardly composed despite the wrenching anxiety I felt. I believed that any alarmist talk from me would spook clients and employees alike. I didn't hide anything, but I focused on positives.

Not everyone bought into my show of calm. Among the realists was Stella Song, my new assistant. The sharp-eyed young woman with dark hair cut into a bob was as outspoken with me as others were shy. A graduate of Shanghai International Studies University, she spoke perfect English and expressed her views with a refreshing frankness. She sat in my office and overheard most of my conversations, so there was no hiding from her judgment.

"What's wrong with you?" she asked me one day, after witnessing yet another one of my upbeat performances.

I looked at her, both amused and surprised.

"How can you be so cheerful when things are so bad?" she continued.

I answered in my usual way. "It is normal to lose money when you're building up a company," I said. "And we've got great backers and an amazing opportunity ahead of us."

She didn't buy it; instead, she just rolled her eyes and got back to work. I did believe everything that I had just said. But I seemed to be the only one.

Finally, in the summer of 2001, we received $3 million from FMO, the Dutch Development Bank, and DEG, the German development bank. Blissful employees and shareholders celebrated what they thought was a huge payday. They were unaware that once the company paid its outstanding bills, we would be left with only a few hundred thousand dollars in the bank. And we were still burning cash at a rate of $2 million annually.

Despite that, I had bought us some time and was eager to build a role for myself beyond the thankless job of fund-raising. We had signed on new growers on Inner Mongolia's plateau, and the Beijing plant had just opened to process Steve's lettuce for Japan and serve KFC's northern cities. Because we had numerous quality problems there, I decided to base myself at the plant to keep an eye on operations.

Stella disagreed with my strategy. With her usual bluntness, she warned me that I should stay at headquarters in Shanghai and lead. "If you spend most of your time in Beijing," she said, "everyone will think you're leaving the keys to Kevin."

It made me sad that she would think I was so easily manipulated. But I didn't plan to change anything. I decided that Stella was bright but inexperienced, and slightly paranoid. I was a modern leader who trusted his managers, and I had enough self-confidence not to care about silly things like face. After all, I had raised enough cash to save the company from near-certain death. What more could you ask from a leader?

In an email to Kevin that summer, Steve's tone was controlled, but I knew he was upset: "If I write to you only, I do not appreciate that you answer by copying many more people as a way to make your point. This is politics. I don't play politics."

From my perch in Beijing, I followed such exchanges with

increasing worry. Feuding between Kevin and Steve derailed my efforts to have everyone work as a team. My exhortations to focus on the Japan market went unheeded. Kevin argued that we needed to focus all of our resources on the domestic supermarket business and viewed everything else as a distraction.

I called the Shanghai office each day, trying to micromanage every detail from a distance. Kevin seemed to enjoy our long and rambling conversations, reporting every night on the issues of the day and always careful to point out how Steve and Tani failed to understand the level of urgency at the company. He saw Tani as ineffectual, and he talked about Steve with the condescending respect accorded to old professors, slipping in barbs about his lack of experience in China.

In contrast, Steve was sounding more and more distant from me. When I asked for detailed reports of his progress, he would give me the same vague answer: he had a plan, he had a vision and one day everything would fall in place. None of that talk put me at ease. Our financial situation was disastrous and the atmosphere inside the company was getting more tense by the day.

Unlike Kevin, Steve never complained. But I could feel his irritation when I challenged him on issues Kevin had raised with me. He had apparently decided to ignore Kevin's griping and my haphazard leadership and just get on with the task at hand. "Just let me plod along," he kept repeating each time I asked for a status report.

My long phone calls with Kevin did not reassure me; I sensed that he had few tangible results to show, for all his talk. Yet, shortly after my arrival in Beijing, I made all our plant managers report to him, thinking that he would be more communicative than Steve and more accommodating of my requests. Steve didn't say a word. But when I negotiated his new contract, he asked for compensation if I ever terminated him before his term was up.

I told him he was overreacting.

I flew back to Shanghai every ten days. I would gather my managers in the same room and repeat the company's vision and strategy, urging everyone to stay focused. But it never occurred to me to have a meeting to address specific issues like the passive aggressive email exchanges, which might have forced Kevin to express his dissatisfaction with Steve in person and to give Steve a chance to respond and clear the air. Instead, problems kept simmering, unresolved. Steve and Kevin stopped e-mailing each other and started complaining to me instead.

In what seemed like a never-ending sequence of bad calls, I did make one good decision. But on the day I met the woman who would become my wife, we almost both got killed on Beijing's busy Fourth Ring Road.

"Are you sure you know what you're doing?" I shouted to Jane as she turned her race bike up a ramp leading to the freeway. She looked self-assured, so I rode along, only to realize too late we were caught in high-speed traffic. Cars zoomed dangerously near us, shaking our thin bike frames. The roar, the angry honks and the screeching sounds were deafening. Over her right shoulder, Jane looked at me slightly embarrassed, never mind that her bike was veering precariously toward what looked like certain death.

All my angst about Steve and Kevin went away. I shouted first—then I laughed. I already loved her style. While I labored under constant doubt, Jane displayed none of it.

A common friend had suggested we train together. Jane competed in Ironman triathlons and was always looking for training partners. When I didn't take our friend's hint the first time, he called again, interrupting the signing of Creative Food's final investment documents with the German Development Bank.

He had told me that Jane Lanhee Lee was American, but grew up in Korea. In my Euro-centric view of the world, North and South Korea were indistinguishable, just dictatorships along the lines of the old Eastern European bloc. I formed a vague picture in my mind of a broad-shouldered East German swimmer, towering over me while murmuring sweet words in a deep masculine voice. I thought I had good reasons not to call her.

In reality, Jane was the opposite of what I had pictured and the partner I had always dreamed of. Five feet two inches tall but tough as steel, she was born in Ohio but moved to South Korea at the age of seven when her father got a job there. That experience made her look at China with more nuance than I did. To her, the vagaries we experienced—like the hiccups in hot water supply during Beijing's freezing winters, the pushing and shoving at the ticket booths—were just a normal stage of development. She recalled how Korean news broadcasts when she was a child had shown helicopters dragging away the trash that had been left at tourist sites by "uncivilized" local residents. After a few years of shaming, people started to clean up after themselves. She remembered with nostalgia the smell of rotten cabbage when she crossed the fields on her way to school, the odd black-and-white television serials that looked so backward compared to America's, and the elementary teachers hitting her fingers with a ruler when she didn't understand their instructions in Korean. To her, nothing in China looked odd; she knew it was already changing for the better.

Sturdy and resilient on her bike, she left me in the dust on hilly slopes, relentlessly spinning ahead without ever standing on the pedals, biting away at the mountain while I puffed behind. After that first harrowing training session, we continued to court each other during 4 a.m. rides, curled up over handle bars on the slopes of Beijing's Fragrant Hills, then rushing back down so I could be on time for my 8:30 am staff meeting at the factory. Jane was studying Chinese on a fellowship at Tsinghua University, after a few years spent in South Korea as a foreign correspondent for the Reuters news service and the Asian Wall Street Journal. She was as confident and serene as I was doubtful and tortured. Training at dawn was a way of life for her. She was always preparing for the next race.

In the summer of 2001, I decided to move back to Shanghai. My first decision was to terminate Steve and Tani. Our trial shipments to Japan had been a failure, the lettuce and broccoli from our farms never met the quality standards of our prospective Japanese customers, and I could not afford to wait for a better hypothetical harvest in the fall. Time and money were running short again. Before he left, Steve warned me, one last time, about Kevin's duplicity. But it all sounded to me like bitterness. I still believed that Kevin had been transparent with me, and I shared many of his frustrations.

With Tani and Steve gone, I found myself even more isolated. I was now running all the company's departments but finance. I was the only foreigner in the business. I started to notice a change in the Shanghai office's atmosphere. Kevin continued to gather large meetings that went on for hours, but he no longer invited me. And he did not talk to me as much as he had before. I busied myself with what I knew best: making sure cash went to the right place and planning ahead for further financing needs. But it now felt as if the company was operating under a glass dome, and I was outside it.

As I walked through our office, I might sometimes pop into

an operations meeting to clarify a point or two. Kevin would look up with impatience, unable to conceal his irritation at my interruption. He had never shown impatience with me before. Now, he would nod at whatever I said, insert a couple of "yes, yes, yeses" and then eagerly see me to the door.

He also started to challenge the policy of working directly with farmers that Steve had implemented, saying that we had to stop relying on growers who effectively had no control over the quality of their crops. "We pay a high price, but we don't get the quality we pay for," he argued. I agreed with him on this, but disagreed with his solution, which was to revert to using only traders. I knew that relying solely on traders meant even less control over quality. We could end up buying vegetables contaminated with manure, pesticide residues, and pathogens like e-coli or toxic chemicals that could jeopardize the health of thousands of people. Even so, I did not oppose him on it or propose an alternative. So Kevin started to introduce more and more traders into our network, offering cheaper prices, trying to put pressure on the growers who worked with us to lower their prices.

In the fall of 2001, Kevin attempted, without consulting me, to move the Beijing plant manager I had just recruited to our Shenzhen plant in the south. Instead of agreeing to it, I called him into my office and steeled myself for a confrontation at last. "You need to consult with me on organization changes," I told him.

A long silence. "I like you a lot Xavier," Kevin said slowly. "You're a good person, you're a good financier, and you've raised the funds for the company. But you can't run a business."

The soft protective tone of the regent deferring to the ruler was gone. Instead, there was defiance in his voice. "The company needs a strong leader with experience," he said. "I can be that person. You can't. I'd be happy to have you as my finance director if you wish to stay, but you can't be the CEO."

I sat where I was, mute. I became suddenly aware of the bustle of Huqingping Road outside, a distant hum.

He stood up to leave, then turned around to deliver the death blow.

"Do not try to fight me on this. Everyone agrees with me; everyone is loyal to me. They will all leave if I leave. This company is dead without me." And as he closed my office door, gently, he said, "Don't take it personally. I do this for the company. I care for the company."

For several moments, I remained at my desk, staring at the road outside. I felt as if I had been hit by a tidal wave on a sunny day. I called Jane, who immediately took my side, outraged that Kevin had dared betray my trust. I tried answering a couple of emails, but Kevin's words kept ringing in my ears: "Everyone is loyal to me. They will all leave if I do."

Even more troubling, though, was that one part of me felt relieved. The almost two years of scraping by had taken a toll. For months, I had known that everyone was relying on me to find the funds to survive. But once that money was raised, I had struggled to find a role for myself. Moving to Beijing hadn't worked. And my Chinese was still too poor to dive into operational details or establish a relationship with the local managers. For the past two years, I had essentially stopped studying the language, rationalizing to myself that I should focus on more urgent concerns.

For several days after Kevin confronted me, I considered just going along with his coup. Showing up at the office became an ordeal. Every morning, I woke up nauseous and ran to the bathroom. Jane, who had moved for her job from Beijing to Shanghai, wasn't her usual blunt self either. She didn't push for a fast resolution even if her inner Korean warrior longed to flay every square inch of Kevin's skin. Instead, she knew instinctively that I needed to come to terms with the situation on my own. But I was despondent. I dreaded the hours spent alone at my desk. I knew that no one would come to ask a question or sign a document. I started to notice that people avoided looking at me, turning their eyes toward the floor instead of smiling at me as I passed them in corridors. Kevin and I still talked matter-of-factly, but we did not address what had passed between us. I was torn between anger at his behavior and guilt at having failed everyone over the past eighteen months.

If I fought Kevin and put down his mutiny, I would be on my own. That seemed more frightening than being pushed out of the company I had built. I had no idea what I would do to straighten the ship with its unruly cast of characters: hundreds of Chinese employees, including workers in the plants, sales staff and accountants, ruthless vegetable vendors, sensitive local officials, angry KFC executives, bleeding finances. I feared dealing with the minutiae of sales and operations in a language and a culture foreign to me. And I realized I didn't really know in depth any of the managers under Kevin.

This could well have gone on indefinitely. But one afternoon, our company lawyer, Frank Rocco, called. A portly man from Brooklyn, Frank's modest Italian origins translated into an insatiable curiosity for anything culinary. His shares-for-cash payments for service to us didn't amount to much for a man who had been Pepsico's in-house counsel in Asia, but Frank liked the thrill of entrepreneurship. Every morning he would call me on his way to work, and we had become friends. This time he gave it to me straight.

"You need to come to Hong Kong," he said. He added ominously with his characteristic accent: "Directors are *tawking*.

It's getting out of *controwl*; you need to come here and clarify what you plan to do."

Kevin had made one more move to assert his claim to leadership. He had written to the board directly.

"Xavier is running this company into the ground," he wrote in a long memorandum, listing all the management mistakes I had made since he joined the company.

"If you want to protect your investment, let me take over."

6

KEY MAN

THE DAY AFTER Frank's call, I made my way toward the exclusive Hong Kong Country Club. "We'll be sitting near the pool," Frank had written in the text message I received after landing in Shenzhen two hours before. With Creative Food once again in dire need of cash, I had taken to flying from Shanghai to Shenzhen in the far south of the country on a domestic flight, then taking the train into Hong Kong across the border. It cost much less than an international flight, which made it worth spending hours in interminable immigration checks or elbow-to-elbow on cramped trains, jostling with hundreds of Chinese travelers carrying plastic shopping bags full of electronics, clothes or pungent foods.

My taxi climbed a small hillside road lined with dense jungle vegetation and entered the gates. At dusk, the club felt like an oasis, nestled in a small bay on Hong Kong's south side and insulated from the tumultuous crowd that normally occupies the streets of the island. At the center of an immaculate lawn stood a group of low-rise white 1970s concrete buildings with large window bays overlooking the sea, housing several restaurants, a pool and a wine cellar. The ambiance, all understated power and wealth, represented a Mount Olympus to the earthbound Shenzhen commuter I had become. I cut through the grass, walking in the dark toward the pool. My suitcase felt heavier as the wheels dug into the soft ground.

The pool was lit from the bottom and cast a blue halo on the tall trees lingering over the white lounge chairs, all arranged with a freshly ironed towel rolled on top of the seat. I could see a couple of bugs zigzagging on the water. Frank was standing, facing two other directors sitting on pool chairs. Roger Marshall was chatting with Lewis Rutherfurd, an early investor in Asiafoods, the same man who had invited me to San Francisco to meet with Steve. They each held a glass of white wine; Lewis smoked a thick Cuban cigar.

The three businessmen weren't friends but they all had a personal stake in my project. Frank had been working for shares from the start, Lewis had the largest stake and Roger had a lot riding on me after convincing his sister and friends to invest in the aftermath of ABN Amro's abrupt withdrawal. Other directors on my board had been less engaged with me—they were either employees of the two large development banks or private equity investors.

"Hello Xavier, how are you doing?" said Lewis in a posh Bostonian accent.

Still out of breath, I launched into a long ramble, explaining about how I had made mistakes, and that I just wanted the best for the company.

"Maybe Kevin is right," I said at one point.

Distracted and anxious, I didn't pay attention to the faces of the men surrounding me. Unlike me, they seemed quiet, unfazed by the stream of disorganized thoughts and emotions that were spilling out of me.

"Maybe I should cast my ego aside and let him run the company," I ended lamely, half-hoping that one of the men would agree with me and give me a reason to walk away.

"Empires don't get built by nice fellas," Frank said in his New York accent, "they're built by egomaniacs."

Lewis blew a heavy cloud of smoke in the air before turning his steely blue eyes into mine. "My dear Xavier, it all sounds like you're browning your pants!" he said playfully. I noticed, with envy, that he was perfectly relaxed. This man had brought McDonald's and Ikea to Hong Kong. He had seen many wars in three decades of business in Asia.

Despite the friendly manner, it was clear that the three businessmen wanted to shock me out of my passivity before a meeting I had scheduled the next morning with them, plus the company's six other directors.

I needed to be clear on one point above all, they said.

"The larger question in every director's mind," said Lewis, pausing a little for effect, "is whether there is a general at the head of the army in China."

Frank and Roger nodded. I was still standing stiffly and in silence in front of them.

None of them saw Kevin as a credible replacement, they said.

"I don't know him; I don't want to know him," Roger added.

Lewis said that he had confronted the same situation many times. In each case, a high-profile recruit hired by a start-up company had turned against the founder and asked for the shareholders to support him. The rule was clear. You stuck with the entrepreneur—providing the man had the right mettle.

That's what everyone wanted to assess, they said to me.

Lewis—the same venture capitalist who once had gotten angry at me for presenting a break-even budget at Asiafoods—said, "In such circumstances, people are uncertain. They're bombarded with negative emails about the man in charge." Then with another puff: "Directors need to feel there is a George Patton leading the troops in China."

The three men encouraged me to take the evening to reflect. But by the next day, they said, I had to make a clear choice. I could not continue to wallow in the betrayal.

And so that night I made up my mind. I was still unsure how I would tackle the many challenges ahead. But I knew I would fire Kevin. The talk helped. For days I had blamed myself, thinking that I didn't deserve to run the company anymore. I didn't have Kevin's experience but investors had known me for years and that mattered more than anything else. Strong or weak, I was the man the board trusted, despite my many defeats, my failures, my procrastination. Leaving wasn't an option.

At the meeting the following day, I presented a set of practical measures to further reduce expenses and shut down the unprofitable trading business with supermarkets. Kevin's dismissal was barely discussed. It was one item in a long list of actions. A couple of directors tested my resolve by attacking some of my past decisions about Steve and Michael's termination. But I swiftly blocked the attacks, projecting confidence I didn't yet have. I even snapped with irritation, explaining I didn't need board approval to make management changes.

By the end of the meeting, they knew I was there to stay. I noticed a couple of satisfied smiles, pleased to see that their eleventh-hour intervention had succeeded. I'm sure not all of them trusted me completely, but I made them see that Kevin was not a viable alternative. I realized that day that he had never been.

In the wake of Kevin's mutiny, I wondered at both his behavior and my own naïve reaction to it. I also wondered why so few middle managers at Creative Food had expressed any resistance to Kevin's power grab. Steve and Michael had warned me about him, as did Stella, who knew me well enough to be candid. But I ignored them because I felt they were either out of tune with the ways of China or simply inexperienced. The majority of Creative Food's two hundred employees and workers stayed silent.

What had I missed? Was there anything I could have done to avoid what happened? It's always dangerous to make broad statements about a culture as ancient and complex as China, but as my intimacy with the country and its corporate culture grew, I discerned a few truths.

At the core, Chinese are more group-oriented than most of the people in societies in the West. Individualism exists but it's subordinated to the well-being of the community. The family is the foremost group, then the clan and village. In recent history, the Communists built cleverly on this by forming groups that replace traditional social blocks, such as work brigades on communal farms, and *Danweis* – or work units – in cities where a person's bosses and managers acted as village elders, passing judgment on all sorts of personal issues, such as housing and marriage.

These structures have been shaken by three decades of capitalist-influenced reforms and more assertive forms of individualism, but at heart the average Chinese person will always be reluctant to speak out, seeking instead a form of consensus within the safety of the group. That happens within companies too, whether they are local or managed by foreigners like me. Added to this are several sets of beliefs at play at any given time. First is Daoism, an ancient philosophy with deep roots, emphasizing how important it is to fit harmoniously in your environment. Trying to change this environment is viewed as an illusion. Often, in reaction to change and uncertainty – I think of my decisions to create new projects at Creative Food – people will revert to passivity as a default mode. Buddhism came later and introduced a notion of causality in people's relationships. To simplify, Buddhists believe that if you do good deeds, you'll have a better life next time. It assumes that people are good and that virtue can be passed on. But for this to work, you need to make sure that every participant shares the same values. That is not the case in today's society. Confucianism, the third current, emphasizes loyalty and obedience: son to father, wife to husband, citizen to emperor, employee to boss. Chinese employees tend to deal better than their Western counterparts with change imposed from the top or the idea that the boss calls the shots.

Dominant Judeo-Christian values in the West impart even young children with a strong sense of right and wrong. In America and Europe, an individual feels empowered to stand up to the society if he or she feels it has done something wrong. China can't be read with the same decoder. In fact, all three philosophical currents call for passivity and tolerance of one's circumstances rather than a direct challenge to them. Faced with tensions, Chinese people are more likely to put their heads down until they see where the group is heading.

Any organization in China with mostly Chinese staff will be infused with these philosophical currents. And each current's impact will vary depending on events, but they're always present to some degree.

As Chinese society has changed and modernized, it has gotten even more complicated. The younger generation tends to view some Western values — like the importance of cultivating cordial relations with one's boss — as a better fit than the stiff formalities of Confucianism. But that doesn't mean they can or want to abandon their own traditions. In contrast with their parents, who were indoctrinated by decades of communist teaching to deride traditional religions and philosophies, there is even a renewed interest in Daoism, Buddhism and Confucianism among young

Chinese even if it can seem superficial sometimes. In a fast-changing society, there is a gulf between them and their parents, between their aspirations and the brutal competitiveness of Chinese society. They don't know yet how to reconcile it all, but the first step is often to find a community of people that provides some sense of stability as their parents did in their village or "work unit". Today, classmates, alumni networks, work colleagues — each of these groups is a possible sanctuary. That's where the culture created in a company takes on a much larger significance in China than it might elsewhere.

My ignorance of this dynamic made the collective passivity of my employees in the face of Kevin's actions so surprising to me. Kevin, on the other hand, knew exactly what he was doing. "What Kevin Lam did to you sounds a lot like the classic 'clean the shelf — *jia kong* strategy,'" said Tony Zhu, a Chinese corporate culture consultant, when I told him about the attempted coup. It was Kevin using the power of the organization against me. "Mao used that strategy during the civil war in the 1940s. He isolated the cities by controlling the countryside. At the end, he wrested control of the cities from the powerful Kuomintang." And just so I got the point, he added, "You pull out the tiger's teeth by knocking off the powerful man's allies. Once this is done, it's easy to make him fall. The strategy is still very much in use in Chinese politics today."

It still didn't explain why nobody warned me, I replied. "If it's so obvious to you," I said, "then staffers must have seen that coming also."

Zhu smiled "You're right," he said. "But you also have to take into account the traditional respect for hierarchy that comes with Confucianism."

As Zhu spoke, I realized that I had made several mistakes during Creative Food's first months, the biggest being that I had failed to build a network of supporters around me. I had my reasons for that: I was distracted by fund raising, and my language skills made it difficult for me to form bonds with Chinese employees. Once he was hired, Kevin probably began working immediately at cutting away the tenuous affinities I had been forming prior to his arrival. My decisions to describe him as a partner and to let him use my car and driver were ill-advised. Leaving him in charge when I went off to Beijing was a terrible judgment call.

Unlike me, the staff cared a lot about the attributes of power. I had left a void that Kevin filled. Few of my employees believed he was genuine, but I was not an alternative in their mind. I was far away, nobody knew what to make of me and those people who might have supported me were intimidated by Kevin. Zhu explained, "In Chinese, we have a saying: 'The gun shoots the bird that comes out first (*qiang dachu touniao*)." Uncertain of where I stood in the hierarchy, the employees at Creative Food could not defend me. Nobody wanted to be the first bird.

Two weeks after the meeting with the board, on October 23, 2001, I once again flew from Shanghai to Shenzhen, crossed the border and made my way to Hong Kong's financial district. There, I entered the old Bank of China building and took the elevator to the fourteenth floor. The doors opened on the glamorous China Club. An affable host, smiling gently at me, approached to take my beat-up carry-on suitcase. The large round tables inside the restaurant were filled with diners in pinstripe suits, supping on delicate and aromatic broths. Bus boys in stylish white Mao-collared suits with red silk at the wrists swiftly moved from one table to another.

Tonight was my chance to meet our nine directors in a casual setting, to make sure that everyone was comfortable with my plan and that nobody would change his mind after reading one of the rambling emails Kevin was now sending them regularly. I had scheduled a board meeting for the next morning and I had invited Kevin as I normally did to present on his part of the business. but he was unaware of my real plan: to terminate him at the meeting. I was not sure this would proceed without complications. Since he had first confronted me, Kevin had been brazenly working to isolate me, prohibiting employees from reaching out to me and making sure I didn't attend company meetings. But lately, he had seemed more emotional and erratic. It was taking longer than he had planned to push me aside.

My cell phone vibrated inside the pocket of my jacket as I entered the China Club. It was Kevin. *I am your partner and you're not inviting me; I am disappointed,* read his text.

Other messages spooled out below that one, unread. *Why didn't you invite me? I know you're here and you're meeting with the board.*

"He sounds distressed and anxious," I thought, with a brief stab of pity that went away quickly. I remembered the endless days spent alone in my office, shifty looks as I walked the corridors at Creative Food, mornings when I woke up nauseated, dreading another day at work.

I am in my hotel room alone.

This company will die if you try anything against me.

I decided to call him because I didn't want him to delay things by flying back to China in a panic over my silence. I had decided to fire him in Hong Kong because I suspected that he would make a scene if I did it in the Shanghai office. I pictured him storming out and planting himself in the middle of the large common area, raising his arms, calling on employees to cast a vote of confidence in him and against me. "He is that sort of man," I thought.

He answered my call in a breathless voice. "I know you're meeting with the directors. You're trying to do something behind my back, right? How can you do that to me?"

I explained that the dinner was a casual meeting at the invitation of Frank, our counsel, who Kevin knew was a personal friend. I told Kevin that Frank wanted to introduce his new law firm's partners to potential clients. It was not about Creative. I hung up, leaving him somewhat calmer.

The part about Frank's new partners was true, but my being in that club was in fact all about solidifying my decision with the directors. In our financing documents, Kevin was listed—as I was—as a "key man," which would allow banks to foreclose on Creative's loans if he left. I had played up the value of my recruits so much during my fund-raising tours—Steve and Michael, already out, were also on the list—that their presence in the company was now enshrined even in legal wording. Within the last two months I had terminated most of the key men and was now on the verge of eliminating the last one, which I knew might create the perception that the company was in danger. I had made my case to each director already, but I was still worried about the Dutch and German development banks. I knew from experience that their investment officers could be supportive— they sensed the urgency of the situation because they talked to me regularly—but I also dreaded that someone else in Germany or the Netherlands could call on the clause in the agreements and push Creative Food into the abyss. I had stretched the company so thin that an event of default was sure to send it into bankruptcy.

Keeping an eye on my phone, I followed the host's black silk shirt through the tables into the Long March bar. There, my directors stood casually, each with a drink in hand, chatting with our lawyer's new partners.

The representative from the Dutch Development Bank quickly turned to me. "I've seen that story unfold many times in my career as a venture capitalist," he said. "The number two guy thinks he can do better than the number one guy."

"But," he added with a wry smile, "there is one rule in our business: you ride the horse you picked first; you don't swap horses in the middle of the race." He seemed confident he could convince any doubters within his bank and prevent a foreclosure.

I had similar polite conversations with all of the bankers and the lawyers that night. Like the Dutch banker, they seemed cool-headed and supportive. I left the club feeling I was on solid ground.

The next morning, I asked Kevin to come early to review his presentation to the board. We were scheduled to meet at the new Bank of China building, where Frank's firm leased an office. Kevin entered the conference room, looking cheerful. He didn't mention the frantic text messages from the night before.

As he put out his things on the conference table, I asked him to follow me into a small meeting room next door. There, Frank was waiting.

I sat down next to him, faced Kevin, and said, "I've decided to terminate your employment agreement. Here is a letter formalizing the termination."

Kevin took the letter from Frank. His jaw dropped.

His anxious messages the night before had revealed his suspicion that I was mobilizing directors in my favor. But he had not expected to be terminated.

"What? What does this mean?" he stuttered in a shrill voice.

I launched into the speech I had rehearsed all night long. He had repeatedly ignored my instructions. He might disagree with my views, but he had to respect the chain of command. Failing that, he had to go.

I can't be sure, but it looked like he had tears in his eyes.

"I just talked to my son in Shanghai," he said, starting to speak very quickly. "I've never been fired in my life. I made sacrifices to join Creative Food. What is my son going to say?"

Then he went on, "How can you do that to me?"

"I've always done my best for the *company*, I only care for the *company*," his plaintive voice continued, repeating the same things he had said since he first confronted me.

Did I feel bad for him? Sure, I wasn't completely immune to his distress. But I had realized at the Country Club that it wasn't about his brazen behavior or my past mistakes. There were hundreds of confused employees and concerned clients, and losses were piling up. And it was now clear that my shareholders had entrusted me, and no one else, with the millions of dollars that they had invested. The scope of what was at stake far outweighed personal feelings. There was a job to be done and for the first time, I was actually doing it.

Finally, Frank cut him off. "Please hand over your laptop. That's company property," he said without a sign of sympathy.

I was anxious about time. I wanted Kevin out; any scene he might make had to be over before our directors came for the board meeting in forty-five minutes' time.

He pleaded one more time as he gathered up his computer bag. "But my entire stock portfolio is on my laptop. I have a lot of personal data there!"

Frank was unmoved. "Don't forget the charger; that too, is company property."

At the board meeting that followed, I matter-of-factly informed the directors of Kevin's departure and proceeded with my presentation. By noon, I was ready to catch my flight back to Shanghai.

Frank pulled me aside as I was leaving.

"This is not over," he said. "Kevin was shocked this morning. He was weak and scared." He looked directly at me, tension all over his face. "But anger will follow, and then a thirst for revenge."

I knew all that. But as I headed for the elevator, I felt liberated. If more fight was coming, I was ready for it.

Back in Shanghai the same evening, I received a long e-mail from Kathy, the manager I had hired a year earlier on Kevin's recommendation. She said that the company's three senior regional managers were asking me to reconsider my decision. The letter was in English, so I figured Kevin was probably behind it. A similar letter went to each of the directors on the board. I learned later that all three plant managers had dinner with Kevin the same night. It wasn't a surprise—I had purposely asked all of them to come to Shanghai because I wanted everyone in one place when I returned from Hong Kong—but reading the e-mail made Frank's warning a reality more quickly than I had expected. I needed to move fast.

The next morning, I gathered the managers who had reported to Kevin and informed them of my decision. I sat at the small meeting table in my office and stared straight into their eyes.

"Now, I expect everyone to be focused on work. Do you understand me?"

Silence.

And since nobody responded, I added with a hint of threat, "It's now or never. Resign now or stay on to work on practical issues. No more politics."

More silence.

Eventually, Kathy repeated what she had said in the letter, adding that all the managers at the table agreed with her. I looked at them, but they all avoided eye contact, looking at their hands instead. No one resigned.

At noon, I came to the large open space filled with cubicles where all employees normally worked and found that everyone including the junior staffers had gone to lunch. The place was deserted. I reached Kathy on her phone. She claimed that she had an offsite meeting about our export program. I learned later from Stella that Kevin had turned up at the restaurant where they were and ranted at them, describing me as psychologically unstable.

"Xavier shed tears in front of me as he fired me," Kevin told his audience. "He's not a leader you can trust. He's feeling threatened by my experience."

The following day I agreed to meet the same three managers and Kevin at a driving range's coffee shop near the office so I could look him in the eye—without crying—and repeat in front of everyone the reasons for his dismissal. I prepared for the worst, imagining Kevin's screaming accusations. Instead, the conversation turned all syrupy. Kevin meekly begged to be reintegrated "in the interest of the company."

Someone made an analogy to a soccer team needing complementary players to perform at its best.

The regular *pok pok* of golfers hitting balls in the background filled the silence. There was nothing more for me to do but repeat the reasons why my decision was irrevocable. I then stood up and left the four of them behind.

The high sun outside blinded me at first, and the din of cars trying to get on the expressway near the practice range was deafening. Dust was everywhere, making me cough.

Suddenly I felt terribly lonely. I had left the entire company's senior management team behind me at that golf club. I looked right and left, but all the taxis were taken, and my driver was busy moving Kevin out of his office, sending cartons to his wife.

Still rehashing all the recent conversations in my mind, I found myself on the other side of the road, stuck on a small patch of grass, surrounded by traffic.

I was still looking for a way back to the office when my phone rang.

"Hello, this is Victor," said a voice on the line. Victor was the English name of Yu Haidong, our Shanghai logistics manager who worked under Kathy.

He continued in English, "Boss, I want to say I support you."

I was not sure I understood him. The noise around me was overwhelming.

He continued, "Me and my logistics team, we support you. We are with you, boss."

Then he added ominously, "But the job is not over yet."

He didn't say more, but he had said what I needed to hear. One by one, or in small groups, the workers at Creative Food called or visited me with words of support. They were essentially telling me in hesitating English that they were on my side. As I talked to more of them, it became clear that many employees had seen the plot unfold but had been afraid of taking sides until they saw I was re-asserting myself.

As I walked back to Creative Food after Yu's call, I did not even hear the traffic noise around me anymore. His support felt real.

That same day, I terminated Kathy. I found out that she was trying to gather signatures from all the staffers in Beijing and Shenzhen for a petition in favor of Kevin's reinstatement. I also learned that Kevin had indeed never been fired, but he had been pushed away from his two previous jobs for plotting against the general manager.

For a few more weeks, Kevin tried to woo employees at Creative, even calling them at night to cajole them into quitting.

But no one left. Instead, people complained to me about his harassment. It took only one call to end that: I threatened to stop paying the compensation he had been promised at his firing. He could sue me if he wanted, I warned him, but I would make it really hard on him. He called me vicious and ungrateful, but his calls to employees stopped.

In the wake of the attempted coup, I mulled obsessively over the details and the impressions I had ignored. One in particular had me puzzled: the blank stares at staff meetings. What did it mean? Did I simply lack charisma? Did my employees not have the foresight to fathom how great the future was? Was it simply a language problem?

When I asked him, Zhu, the consultant, put it simply: "Chinese people struggle with lofty concepts. It means too much change for them; it means insecurity. In China, the way you motivate people is to promise peaceful, sustainable development, not a great life or a great vision." He paused, then said again, "Not a great life, but a very stable one where you take care of them." Then he went on to tell me about Sun Yat-sen.

Sun was the first president of the Republic of China, founded after the last imperial dynasty collapsed in 1911. He stayed in power for only three months but remains revered by all Chinese as a revolutionary who overthrew the last Qing emperor. The slogan that defined his thinking was *Minzu, Minquan, Minsheng*. The three phrases repeated the sound *Min*, "the people", in Chinese — with potent effect in Sun's stump speeches around the country. The words literally mean "the people, the people's rights, the people's livelihood". The first two terms referred to the ideals of nationalism and democracy. But the third one was practical; it encompassed detailed plans to establish supplies of clothing, food, and housing for all Chinese people.

The three phrases weren't just Sun's slogan. Democracy and Nationalism meant a path out from under the imperial yoke. But Sun only gathered support for his revolution when he provided operational plans that translated these concepts into tangible improvements for ordinary people is supporters believed that if they supported nationalism and democracy, they would end up getting better food and clothing thanks to better infrastructure. The plan was so well thought through that a hundred years later, modern Chinese planners were still following it. Since Deng Xiaoping initiated a loosening of China's economy in the 1980s, China's leaders have followed a simple formula: Improve people's livelihoods in return for their political acquiescence. It's a formula that proved remarkably durable for almost four decades.

At Creative Food, I had thought I was providing a clear direction, one that inspired confidence in the future. I expected staffers to feel lifted and energized by it. But unlike Sun, I had failed to outline practical actions connecting reality and my vision, or to foster a sense that everyone was safe within the company. Instead, I assumed that everyone shared my thirst for constant change. So, the opposite of what I advocated happened. In reaction to a growing feeling of insecurity—fueled by gossip, client warnings and repeated strategic mistakes—employees decided to go with the flow, nodding without really believing me, but not daring to challenge me. Ancient Taoist tendencies resurfaced, reinforced by Confucian respect for hierarchy. It only looked like passivity. It took me years to really understand this.

For nearly three years, I had tried to prove that what worked elsewhere could be translated to China. Stubbornly, I had ignored warnings from my own Chinese staff, thinking instead that a few more millions in fundraising would resolve all my problems. I had driven the hundreds of employees who trusted me and the shareholders who had put their money behind me, to the verge of bankruptcy. Kevin wasn't wrong in his assessment—I had failed everyone.

That fall of 2001, I found myself with a chance to start over. I have since learned from Zhu, the management consultant, that once a group is formed, its impact inside and outside can be powerful, whether this group is made of classmates or colleagues inside the same organization. In such a way, Sun's revolutionaries overthrew the 300-year-old Qing dynasty, and Mao's Communist Party rallied millions of peasants. I believe in Zhu's words: "Once the Chinese feel secure, creativity erupts."

In the weeks that followed Kevin's termination, I knew instinctively that I had to regain my employees' trust and ignite that creativity. What I didn't know was how I would do it.

7

NUMBER ONE SOLDIER

AMID ALL this corporate turmoil, the business picture had darkened. By the end of 2001, our company's annual sales were only a little above two million dollars and monthly losses were draining the funds I had raised. To make things worse, KFC had found a new lettuce supplier, and was dividing its Shanghai orders between us, causing our sales in that city to drop by a third. In Japan, I had paused all lettuce shipments after terminating Tani and Steve, but I was still shipping broccoli. The business was sizeable, but it was still a money-losing venture. Despite my irritation with KFC, it was my only profit-making client.

In January 2002, three months after I had secured my position as the leader of Creative Food, I had a financial scare that almost sunk the company yet again. During a shareholders' meeting in The Hague, the Netherlands' capital, the Dutch bank threatened to pull out from a further commitment. It later reversed its position, but it was clear my investors had doubts about my business. In the end, we reached a deal for a shareholders' loan that could convert into shares at a rock-bottom price.

Mike DeNoma, the former Asiafoods CEO, was one of the attendees at the meeting. He had received some shares when I took over the small vegetable operations. When everything was said and done, he looked at me with his steely blue eyes:

"Operate as if this is your last money, Xavier. And hopefully it won't have to be."

For a second, memories of him blowing through millions crossed my mind. But I wasn't looking for an endorsement. What mattered was that the company was safe.

Once more, I had hustled my way to more investment money. In exchange for a million-dollar loan, I pledged to shrink the business to the bone: cut a third of the management and reduce our monthly losses to near zero. The only side project I kept going was the broccoli exports to Japan since it paved the road for selling cut lettuce there in the future. Essentially, I shrunk the business as Yum China's Sam Su had forcefully suggested I should do eighteen months before.

Having bought a little time, I returned to China. I had to get to know some of the managers. The executives who weighed most heavily on our expenses had left, but most middle-managers were still in place. I had been so detached from day-to-day operations that I didn't know any of them well enough to bounce ideas off them or trust the ideas they might bring to me. And I was nervous because many of them had been hired by Kevin.

One recruit I didn't want to lose was Mike Chen. We had hired Mike in October 2001 to manage our Beijing plant, but though I had interviewed him, I had little sense of his character. The week I terminated Kevin, Mike was spending a few days in Shanghai to get briefed on what I expected from the managers. He was scheduled to fly back to Beijing on the weekend.

I wondered where he stood. Did he plan to quit? I was already running the Shanghai region myself. If Mike resigned, I would have to run two regions at the same time. I hadn't been very good at managing one plant back in Beijing; managing it again from hundreds of miles away would be overwhelming at best and at worst a disaster. Mike was someone I had to keep—at least for a little while.

Jane sat on the sofa at home that Friday evening, listening while I rambled on yet again about work. She didn't need another update. She had already heard it all and had been a constant source of support since the day Kevin first confronted me. But I was still talking it out with her, hoping that she would notice something I had missed.

"Kevin and Kathy are out," I repeated to her, "while I've ordered Mike and the Shenzhen regional manager back to their posts. But I have this uneasy feeling that Mike will soon resign."

I had a hazy memory from Mike's interview of an organized and professional manager whom I had barely listened to, distracted as I was by my own qualms and my poor Chinese. "This guy obviously has many career choices," I continued to Jane. "He doesn't know me, so nothing ties him to the company now that Kevin is gone."

During the past few days, I had noticed that Mike had attended all meetings, careful not to take sides. But he hadn't expressed support for me either.

"Why don't you call him and ask to meet tomorrow before he takes his flight?" Jane said in her matter-of-fact way.

It was so obvious that I had not even considered it.

The call was short. One advantage of speaking poor Chinese is that you can do away with niceties.

"Mike, this is Xavier," I said. "Do you have time to meet tomorrow?"

"Sure, let's have lunch," he answered in a warm voice.

And he offered to pick a place to meet.

I had hired Mike under duress, during the period when I was locked in a power struggle with Kevin. Our biggest and newest plant in Beijing had been left without a manager because its former head had gone to Shenzhen more than a thousand miles south to run our plant there. Kevin had introduced Mike as a former employee of his who was immediately available. I was wary of hiring another one of Kevin's loyalists, but I didn't have much choice. The plant needed a manager, and Mike was available. I agreed to give the man a hearing.

The day of the interview, Mike entered my office together with Kevin. I quickly made it clear I didn't want Kevin to stay around and accompanied him to the door.

Mike put out his hand and feebly shook mine with a soft smile. "My name is *Maikeu*," he said in hesitant English.

"Please sit down and speak Chinese," I said to him.

Immediately, he appeared more comfortable. But that shifted the burden of understanding to me, and I couldn't keep up. As his words became unintelligible background noise, I concentrated on his appearance instead. He wore jeans, sneakers and a plain white T-shirt. His thick black hair, nerdy glasses and pimples made him look younger than he was. Yet he didn't display the nervousness that most Chinese applicants showed in their interviews with me. Every word he spoke came out well-formed, distinct. The overall message was: "This is who I am. Take it or leave it."

I deciphered from his Chinese-only resume that he was 35, three years older than I. He had run sales operations across eleven provinces for Henkel, a giant German manufacturer of household and personal-care products. Two-thirds of Persil-brand detergent sales in China wasn't small business; it meant he had had hundreds of salespeople under his lead.

"Why did you leave?" I asked.

A better question would have been why he even bothered to interview at my tiny failing start-up. I didn't understand his answer that day. But I learned later that Mike had been hospitalized a few months ago for a ruptured appendix. He had been traveling around China for months, courting distributors at boozy banquets, earning him the top ranking in a China-wide sales challenge. But it had cost him his health, and he had been recovering at home since. When Kevin called, he thought it might be a good time to get back to work.

He didn't mention a particular friendship with Kevin or an affinity with Creative Food's mission as a reason. In fact, he told me later, he saw it as a temporary job, a way to get back in the game. He never intended to stay.

As the interview went on, I asked probing questions. I missed most of the responses.

That day, a possible battle with Kevin about Mike's recruitment felt beyond my strength, and in any case, I couldn't find anything wrong with the guy. We did need someone in Beijing. So, I agreed to hire Mike and didn't give him much thought again until after Kevin's firing.

Mike's given name in Chinese — Yibing — means "Number One Soldier." It's not unusual for people born in the 1960s and 1970s to have such "revolutionary" names, especially when their parents, like Mike's, were dutiful civil servants. Graduating from college in accounting just as economic reforms began to pick up pace in the late 1980s, he initially worked in the government and in state-owned companies, distributing imported products. He belonged to the last generation of young Chinese to be assigned a job after university. After a fast rise in the Chinese administration, he made the jump to the private sector just as the Roaring Nineties shifted into high gear. He started as a low-ranking sales representative for Colgate, the American multinational, and within two and a half years, he was running the company's sales operations in seven provinces, nearly half of the country. He didn't have time to learn English well, but he became intimate with Western-style management systems and communication tools.

Colgate is where he met Kevin, who was instrumental in his rise. When Kevin moved to Henkel, he brought Mike with him to manage a vast and messy network of distributors the company had just acquired. Over the course of a year, Mike travelled across the country, sat with dozens of traders and negotiated arrangements for Henkel to be paid a lot of money that it was owed. He collected tens of millions of dollars, won the number-one ranking for salesmen inside the company and earned giant bonuses — until his health failed him.

All of this gave Mike an eye for the big picture. He understood the arcane world of Chinese state-owned companies and government bureaucrats, having been one of them at a senior level. But he also knew accounting and understood how professional multinationals operate. Perhaps even more important, he had a multi-faceted and sensitive understanding of people. After I got to know him better, he told me how he had learned this skill. His father, who was a Communist official, had been in charge of everything in his work unit from political education to practical work issues involving its employees. When colleagues and underlings came to the family apartment to seek assistance and advice, young Mike would pour tea as the older man passed judgment on marital issues, housing allocations and promotions. This experience gave Mike a revealing window into what people cared about, their fears and dreams.

For that lunch, Mike chose a restaurant named Shanghai Lulu that was nestled under an elevated expressway leading to the airport. When he saw me walk down the stairs into the small basement dining room, he got up and put out his hand with the same shy smile I had seen in the first interview. Above us, I could hear the noise of gears shifting as cars sped away from the traffic lights.

Things immediately felt right. Mike didn't make an effort to speak more slowly, but I somehow understood everything he said. His air of peaceful confidence quieted the tension and questioning in my head. It helped that his comments were insightful, based on actual conversations with growers, peasants, wholesalers, clients and our own employees. I was impressed, because what little I knew about the industry came from talking to Steve. I felt a pinch of guilt as I recognized that language was not the only reason I hadn't dug into our business. I just hadn't tried hard enough.

When I asked Mike for concrete suggestions on how to deal with our growers, he responded, "We need to work differently." Specifically, he continued, my initial idea of signing seasonal contracts so peasants didn't have to worry about price had failed.

"I agree," I said. "But I still feel there is no future in working only with spot traders as middlemen."

That had been a major point of tension between Kevin and me. Chinese traders would always be faster, cheaper and nimbler than we could be, I reasoned. They would run circles around us until one day, one of them would learn enough about our business to copy our plants and compete with us. I was adamant that we needed to get closer to the farms, even if Creative Food wasn't destined to be a farming company. That was the way to set us apart. That's why I signed supply contracts with farmers before the start of every season.

"No peasant will ever feel bound by a contract," Mike continued. "But it doesn't mean we can't work with them."

Farmers, he explained, viewed contracts as a framework that could always be renegotiated if conditions changed. They had been ripped off too many times across history to trust anyone, let alone a few words printed on a piece of paper. The guerilla actions I had witnessed with Sun and Leo had made me aware of this mindset, but Mike was articulating it in an original, more positive way, one that explained how everyday business was done.

"If you pay market price, you'll find them more willing to meet your quality standards," he said.

"Wouldn't the peasants want the safety of a stable contract price?" I asked, "Isn't that the only way to ensure good quality?"

"Not really," he answered, unflappable, picking up a piece of chicken in the plate between us with his chopsticks.

I thought about what Mike was saying. I could sign contracts, pay advances, and make guarantees until I was blue in the face, but if the other party didn't deliver the goods or the quality I wanted, I was the only one who suffered. The farmers and other middlemen I dealt with in the villages had meager assets; there was nothing to sue for when contracts were broken. Mike was saying that I needed to change the terms—to remake the binary choice that the farmers faced, so that they too would suffer if they didn't hold up their end of the bargain.

"So, you're saying I could pay suppliers only if they meet my quality standards?" I said.

I liked that Mike hadn't forced his point. But when he saw I was coming around, he dug in, talking as if it had been my idea all along.

"That's a great point," he replied. "Farmers don't depend on vegetables to survive. They have a bit of rice planted, a few hens and sometimes a pig. The lettuce they plant for us serves to raise some extra cash. They're willing to gamble a bit with it. They want the highest possible price."

I nodded. Coming from a world of predictability, I had

assumed peasants would want the same. But I hadn't realized that in fact they were comfortable with the risk of not being paid.

"And we can give them that price if we get the quality we want," he finally concluded with a smile.

Better-quality lettuce meant less waste in production. That was the shift nobody had considered before. Given the right incentives, paying a higher price could translate into lower costs for Creative Food overall.

The concept was clear. We would know where our lettuce was coming from, we would set quality standards in advance and we would support villagers with our teams of agronomists. But we wouldn't commit to any price until harvest time.

"That's risky," I said, thinking of all the ways we could be taken by surprise if a crop didn't yield the quality or the volume we wanted. "We still need lettuce every day."

"Yep," Mike replied, chewing on a meaty pork bone. "That's why we need those traders to help us until we form a stable group of growers. We can't do it alone."

That too made sense. We would work with local traders who helped supervise farmers and would pay these "aggregators" different prices for different levels of quality.

There were all sorts of details to sort out before Creative Food could be as savvy and nimble as the traders when working directly with farmers. First, we couldn't afford to pay cash-at-the-back-of-the-truck as traders did. We needed to pay thirty days after receiving the crop because that's when KFC paid us. Farmers would never give us credit and we couldn't finance the cash outlay ourselves. Second, I wanted my lettuce to have a minimum weight, no discoloration, no rot. My growers couldn't do that for me. What they wanted was to sell their entire crop for an average price. They were not set up to grade their production.

In contrast, traders bought from the same regions as we did

every day. They bought other crops than lettuce, but they had relationships there, and they had trucks coming back to Shanghai or Beijing. They had clients who would take the lower quality lettuce while I took the best grade.

Mike was probably the only manager at Creative Food roaming through wholesale markets at midnight to find out what lettuce or broccoli was selling for, but even that was not a solution because people often told him prices that bore no connection with reality. Prices weren't something you could easily check over the internet either, as I had experienced trying to monitor my buyers on wholesale markets. Reported data relied too much on what traders were willing to share. Their figures were mostly fudged to avoid scrutiny from tax authorities, and prices on the ground varied with crop quality. Moreover, once you thought you had it down, you had to take into account additional expenses like delivery to our plant. Bottom line: you had to be an actual buyer — as traders were — to know the actual price.

Mike explained that we could set up a reporting system, based on a number of farms and villages that we chose, to monitor crop conditions, accounting for daily changes in quality and volume. But traders would step in to make the purchase on our behalf. This would allow us to keep track of quality but leverage someone else's experience negotiating with farmers until we could do so ourselves. If we suddenly came short, the same traders could use their networks to get us lettuce without having to pay five times more as we had done with Yunnan's Chennong. Mike told me he had run the idea by some merchants and several were ready to give it a try.

There was another reason I needed someone between my company and the people growing the lettuce. Traders who already worked with hotels or restaurants understood better than any farmer what I would need, even if buying from thousands of peasants meant they couldn't guarantee the lettuce was always safe to eat. I needed stable pricing and volumes even more than I needed good quality lettuce. For the first time I understood that my desire to work with farmers didn't make sense unless I had a stable base of growers in place. Working with traders was a means to that end, and, for now, it was the most practical path.

Sitting at lunch with Mike, I considered the options. At our rate of loss, we had less than four months before we hit the wall again. The money I had raised in the Netherlands was clearly my last. I still wasn't completely at ease with the quality issue—even one compromised vegetable purchase could ruin our business—but I reasoned we could later try to convince the motivated peasants to expand their planted area or inspire willing traders to grow more of their own crops. If that worked, slowly, we would be able to start raising the bar on quality.

As we finished eating, I agreed to let Mike start selecting some reliable wholesalers upon his return to Beijing.

I came home that day excited. "He is so much smarter than Kevin," I said to Jane. She barely raised her eyes from the magazine she was reading.

"Then make sure you pay him as much as you did Kevin," she said.

Three weeks after I let Kevin go, I spent most of my time on the road between Beijing, Shanghai, Shenzhen and our suppliers' farms. I was not yet completely sure of how I would lead a 200-employee organization, but I instinctively felt that showing up in the places where they were was part of the answer.

I listened, asked questions, and tried to understand which issues concerned them most. After that first lunch, I found it easy to work with Mike. Like Kevin, he called me every day, but he didn't rant or ramble endlessly. He usually had prepared a list of points he thought could improve things and just called to get my go-ahead.

His first decision when he got the job in Beijing was typical. Shortly before his arrival, I had leased an apartment to use as an office for our sales people so they could be closer to downtown where our supermarket clients were. It wasn't the cheapest thing to do. I had approved it in a hurry, rushing through what sounded like small details at the time. The first thing Mike did was move himself into one of the apartment's bedrooms to live. In his view, he saved housing expenses for the company—and he kept an eye on the salespeople. It meant he was always the first and last one at the office. It was a shrewd move. Sales for the region picked up immediately.

A month after Kevin's departure, I visited Mike at the Beijing apartment. When I left, he came down the elevator with me, following me to the car until I opened the door, ready to step inside. I could feel tension building as we both stood there.

"Xavier, things are a bit complicated," he said.

I didn't answer, but I suddenly started to feel a bit queasy.

"I should resign," he said abruptly, looking down with embarrassment. "But I'll stay for a couple of months until you figure things out."

I had been preparing for this conversation, while also hoping it would never come. Despite our smooth relationship, I had felt that the fact he had been hired by Kevin would one day catch up with us. Also, I figured he was getting multiple headhunter calls every day offering much more attractive positions. The way I saw it, he was either over-qualified or loyal to someone else. As much as I liked him, I was careful not to take him for granted.

I sensed that the choice wasn't straightforward for him. My Chinese had improved enough that I could note a slight change in his tone—"I need to resign," he said, instead of "I want to resign."

Was it the choice of words or the awkwardness of the exchange? All I knew was that he wasn't completely certain. I also knew from experience that resignations I had received from Chinese managers before had been sent in writing, via email. By then, the manager's mind was made up, and he usually had a job lined up already. A resignation was a formal process to terminate a relationship. It wasn't the beginning of a discussion. The fact that Mike hadn't approached it that way made me feel I could change his mind. I was prepared to see him go but not without getting to the bottom of it.

I accepted his offer to stay on longer, sensing that the day wasn't right to inquire further or put pressure on him.

I came back a week later and sat down with him in a small Guizhou-style restaurant outside Tsinghua University campus where Jane had taken me a few times. Over a delicious fish wrapped and steamed with ginger and spices in a banana leaf, Mike finally shared with me that he felt pressure to show loyalty to his old boss. Kevin had been calling nearly every night for the past three weeks asking him to resign. Mike didn't like it, but he felt he couldn't ignore him either.

It all sounded so foreign to me; why not chase away the guy who bothers you at night? But as he shared his hesitation, I realized he wasn't being loyal to Kevin as a person—for his charisma, his leadership or his integrity—as a Westerner would expect. He knew what Kevin had done for his career when he propelled him up from ordinary sales executive to director level both at Colgate and at Henkel. Mike's Confucian beliefs told him it wasn't right to cut out a supportive former boss.

That didn't mean I couldn't do something about it myself.

I told Mike to let me handle Kevin and took care of it in the most Western way. Frank, our lawyer, sent Kevin a written injunction telling him to immediately cease his calls. For added proof of how serious I was, I made sure to delay Kevin's next severance payment. Kevin sent me the usual rambling email in reply. But he stopped calling Mike immediately.

As an additional incentive for Mike to stay, I offered to move him back to Shanghai, where his home was, to take over as head of China sales. I also hadn't forgotten Jane's advice about money. I promised to increase his salary five-fold over two years if he performed and if the company's financial situation allowed it.

"I'm not sure how I'll do that," I said, "but you have to trust me with it."

From then on, I boosted his salary every six months. Each time, I agonized about the new burden on our finances — and each time Mike delivered a deal that more than made up for it.

Mike's ability to keep a foot in both China and the West meant that he could be a hard-nosed and rational negotiator, methodically deconstructing any opponent's argument. He could also find himself entangled in a web of loyalties that seemed irrational to the foreign eye. As much as I liked to believe that he stayed on because of my efforts to intervene with Kevin, something else had tipped the scales in favor of Creative Food well before we shared that steamed fish. He told me about it only years later.

In the weeks following our lunch in Shanghai, Mike was back at the Beijing plant when the local accountant stepped into his office, she looked very concerned. "We only have three months of cash left for operating expenses," she said. Her fear was that I would have to close the plant, leaving her and other employees jobless.

Mike looked at her from behind his desk. He was uncertain himself whether he would stay. But he felt he needed to reassure her. Before he had time to take them back, the words were out of his mouth.

"Trust me," he said. "Things will get better. I give you my word."

As soon as he said it, he knew he had created a bond with Creative Food. He had made a promise, and he intended to keep it. That short conversation changed his life — and mine — for the next decade.

I liked Mike's money-saving move into the Beijing sales office so much that I upped the ante and banned air travel for all my managers. A few weeks before, I had started to travel by train myself. This was part of a package of austerity measures I had implemented following my trip to The Hague. I didn't really think that my decision could improve our finances on its own, but it sent a message to all employees. I did have a slight fear that people would resent it and leave the company, but it showed I understood the mess we were in — something I had taken eighteen months to acknowledge.

There weren't many left to complain about the flight ban, or anything else. If the remaining managers had been a platoon at war, ours would have been the one group forgotten behind enemy lines during a disastrous retreat. People who couldn't take the uncertainty had gone elsewhere. Some of those who had resigned in the past months were still sending emails and texts to their former colleagues, predicting our end. Everyone outside the company took it for granted that Creative Food would soon go bust. KFC was actively preparing for a replacement — the appointment of a second supplier in Shanghai was only a start.

But having nothing to lose was oddly liberating for those of us who remained: myself — a failed leader for two years — and a small team of non-English speaking managers, few of whom had any relevant experience in China's agriculture sector.

In this post-apocalyptic atmosphere, our train travels turned out to be a welcome adventure. One evening shortly before Chinese New Year in January 2002, I met Mike at the Shanghai railway station for a ten-hour train ride to Beijing. With Zhong Zhiyong, a KFC account manager, and Xu Shen, who had followed Michael Tani in his inspection trips around China, we boarded the night train on our way to a series of critical meetings. Xu was to negotiate the terms of our spring purchases, while Mike and Zhong planned to visit KFC in Beijing as part of their constant hustle for more business. I liked that we would not only save on plane tickets, but we would also save one hotel night by sleeping on the train. Small things mattered now.

The platform was crowded with factory workers already heading home a few weeks before the long spring festival holidays. Their fidgety eyes kept vigilance over large plastic-wrapped bundles or scattered relatives. Some were already carrying their unstable burdens into idling train cars, trying to keep their balance while also struggling to hold their place in the swarm at the doors.

"What do you think they carry?" I asked Mike.

"Oh, lots of presents and goodies mainly," he said. "It's all for relatives and kids they left back in the village. They only go back once a year so that's a big deal."

Returnees felt pressure to demonstrate that leaving the village had brought them wealth and prosperity, he explained. The presents were material proof that all the hardship their departure had imposed back home had not been in vain.

The jostling crowds, the noise and bustle: it still felt new to me. Before Creative Food, I had not travelled by train other than for tourism, and when I had, it had been in less crowded regions, far away from Shanghai. Yet none of my colleagues were fazed. Train travel was the mode of transportation by default since they had first been away from home as students. My symbolic ban wasn't a big deal for anyone except me.

We all gathered in a compartment with three bunk beds on each side. Two strangers settled in one middle and one top berth, pushed their bags inside and protectively lay down against them, turning their backs on us; we didn't hear from them until Beijing. Zhong, Xu and Mike insisted that I as "the boss" take a higher bunk while they settled on the lower ones to play cards. The bustle outside quieted a bit. When I left the compartment to see what was going on, I found that other passengers had crouched against the inside panels and were quietly munching on snacks, bobbing along with the rickety racket of the train. Near the end of the car, one man was carefully eating his way through a plastic bag filled with duck-blood jelly, moving carefully to avoid spilling. Another gnawed on rubbery chicken feet. Many around them were smoking. There was no sign of impatience with the constant rattle, the mixed smell of food and urine from the nearby bathroom, or the squeeze they would have to endure for the next hours or days. Many were traveling well beyond Beijing to regions in the far northeast, near the Russian border.

Back in our compartment, my travel companions' hands dipped in and out of a paper bag filled with watermelon seeds, then placed the bare hulls next to the cards on the table. Outside, the flat northern Jiangsu plains fell away, sometimes interrupted by the quick flashes of railway stations we passed without stopping. Everyone seemed content. I didn't know what to talk about, but I felt I needed to say something. I knew they would feel embarrassed if I engaged them about life, so I just talked shop.

"What's your forecast for lettuce prices in Beijing this week?" I asked Xu in Chinese, trying to assess whether he was ready for the negotiation to come.

Since we had started to buy from traders, we talked about market data every day. That too was new. Lettuce costs swallowed two-thirds of the revenues we collected, so keeping that cost in check was part of the job now. On any given day, I could now tell anyone who asked the price of lettuce across several regions in China.

"We're getting some greenhouse volume from Shanghai. That part is cheap, but it will end soon because it's getting too cold over there," Xu commented as he played a card. "The balance of what we need will come from Yunnan."

Mike had rolled his trouser leg up to his knee, a practice similar to the wholesalers at the night market, who not only rolled up their pants but also their shirts, usually to just over the belly button, when it was hot. Now, as he laid a couple of spades on the table, Mike stamped his foot in impatience. He already knew what Xu was telling me.

"I talked to Liu Baoping in Beijing, and he says we're still paying too much compared to local wholesalers," he said, mildly berating Xu while still watching his cards. Liu was one of the biggest wholesalers in North China; he knew everyone and every price on the market. We didn't buy much from him, but Mike talked to him regularly.

Xu didn't seem offended. He respected the insight: harvest volumes were falling in Shanghai, Beijing had been barren for the past two weeks, and Yunnan's harvest was delayed by a few days, causing prices to increase there.

I noted with satisfaction that while they bantered about the card game, the work chatter also never stopped. Xu, I realized, understood the planted volumes. But Mike had built a network among wholesalers, which gave him a better feel for the market. That night, by comparing their information, they concluded that suppliers in Yunnan probably had once again colluded before submitting bids to Creative Food. They decided to bring in an outsider from Guangzhou to keep the Yunnan suppliers in check.

I listened from my perch on the top bunk, interjecting here and there in Mandarin until the conversation faded away. On this train ride, unlike in meetings and phone calls at the company, there were no awkward silences. Everyone seemed engaged and content to be together in this compartment, now an ad-hoc meeting room. I was sure they still weren't seeing me as the charismatic and infallible leader I wanted to be. But I was there with them, and there wasn't anyone challenging the fact I was in charge. We were all learning as we went, learning from one another's insights and experiences. For me, survival was a pretty easy mission to explain, and though I couldn't be sure, we seemed to be making the right decisions for now.

The train's rhythm soothed me that night as it slowly progressed toward the capital. True, months after raising our last round of funds, the company was once again teetering on the brink of collapse. But that night I drifted off to sleep with a peaceful mind for the first time in a while.

Though I now understood more of the conversations like the one on the train, my Chinese language skills had largely been at a standstill for the past year. Politics and fund-raising hadn't allowed me to make any fresh effort in that area. Five years into my life in China, I still winced when the phone rang, as it did one day a few weeks after the train ride.

The caller ID flashed "Mike." The fourth ring was about to start, and I had not yet picked up. Sitting at my desk, I held the phone in front of me, watching the screen, mouth dry, hands trembling, thinking, "Here it goes again. He's going to speak Chinese and I won't understand."

I wanted to be a decisive leader in a time of uncertainty.

Instead, I still stuttered in broken Chinese. "Why," I berated myself, "am I not smarter, faster, and more dedicated at learning Mandarin?"

Fortunately, I seemed to be the only one annoyed by my language limitations. Everyone just adapted, glad they could at last reach me at all.

"Xavier?" said Mike with his tremulous English accent when I finally answered.

"What's up?" I said in Chinese, with the tone of someone who's been interrupted in the middle of something important. I didn't know the words to answer in a more polite and polished way.

Mike didn't seem to notice. As usual, he was all about the task at hand. "It's about the Wuhan market," he said. We had been trying to convince KFC to let us supply their Wuhan market from Shanghai. "I have an idea."

The call went on for a while in the same vein, and I realized I understood everything. Mike didn't speak more slowly, but it was obvious that he had made a conscious effort to think through what he would say before calling. He knew the words I normally used and chose his vocabulary accordingly. He also knew an email wouldn't cut it. I couldn't read Chinese, and translation caused delays that we couldn't afford. Like Mike, other managers soon learned to call me directly if they wanted things done. At first some tried in English, but they quickly realized that with a bit of preparation they could conduct the whole call in Chinese.

Though I didn't realize it at the time, my weeks of traveling and working with my Chinese colleagues were paying off. Sure, I occasionally had to ask my employees to repeat things, but I was learning more vocabulary, recognizing idioms, and grasping key sentence connectors. I could assess whether suggestions were well thought through. The fact that everyone had to speak clearly and logically, or I would be lost, meant that discussions were on-point. Managers and employees knew that if I didn't understand, they wouldn't get the decision they wanted. But if I felt that a caller was well prepared, I would decide immediately on equipment purchases, pricing and supplier selection without applications or pre-approvals.

In the same way that my mediocre Chinese forced people to speak clearly and logically, my inexperience forced everyone to take ownership of their jobs. I wasn't good at finding solutions to operational problems, so managers learned to outline options I could choose from rather than wait for my suggestions. The result was a strong sense that each manager could change the way things were done.

In my finance-centric world, I wanted formal reports for everything, including quality complaints. Su Hong, the newly-minted Beijing plant manager who Mike had identified to replace him, was a former quality manager in the plant. For months, she had dutifully filed such reports. But in her new role, she saw that this wasn't serving us well when she received deliveries of sub-standard lettuce from Yunnan's Chennong, the same trader who had once told on me to Sam Su. She realized that by the time a report found its way to me, her quality issue was already a few days old and aggregated with data from other regions. By that time, she had already received three other shipments from the same emboldened supplier, who had noticed he could unload onto Creative Food damaged produce he could not sell elsewhere.

Now empowered to reach out to me directly, Su didn't wait any longer for the report to be issued. She called to deal with problems as soon as they arose.

"Boss, this is about Chennong's lettuce," she started one such call, using Mike's direct approach to frame the context.

"The shipment looks horrible." Before I could suggest it, she added, "A formal complaint won't work. He needs to feel the pain. I suggest we knock some volume off the receiving record." That meant we were ready to push back by refusing part of the container.

I asked a couple of questions to verify this was all done in good order, that we had other sources of supply during the stand-off—and then I agreed. I hadn't known what "receiving record" meant in Chinese. It's the document that enumerates quantities received at the plant; it's critical because it is the base accountants use to calculate payments due. The supplier's driver usually signed it next to our quality controller.

In the minutes that followed Su's call to me, the quality manager inspecting the load called out the truck driver as he prepared to unload in front of the cold room. Unleashing a tide of frustration accumulated over the past months, she pointed her finger at the lettuce.

"I am wiping out a third of your shipment because it's wilted, it's partly rotten, and it doesn't meet our standards," she said. "Sign here, tell your boss what I did, and make sure it doesn't happen again."

Chennong lost a third of the payment it expected for that shipment, and the next shipment turned out much better. Chennong's boss whined a bit to Xu, but since we all called each other all the time, Xu had already spoken to both me and Su. For her part, Su felt she was getting things done for the first time in months.

This type of assertiveness had never happened before at Creative Food.

KFC quickly took notice of the changes. For the first time, their restaurant managers were able to obtain quick resolutions when a bag or two of lettuce from us turned out brownish, causing mayhem just when they were about to assemble thousands of burgers. We were able to solve the problem by shipping a few replacement bags immediately by taxi at our own cost.

"Something has changed at Creative Food," the junior buyer said to Mike approvingly.

When I visited KFC's headquarters with Zhong for the first time since Kevin's attempted coup, I braced myself for a scolding over my firing of the entire senior management team. But when I broke it to their purchasing director, he seemed surprisingly unperturbed.

"Is Susan Xu still working at Creative Food?" he asked after a pause.

I wasn't sure what to say. Xu was a junior employee in customer service, way down in the company hierarchy. Yet I had sensed the gregarious young woman was someone who cared about doing a good job. Every time I passed her cubicle, I heard her lively chatter and spontaneous laughs on the phone. Her job was to receive clients' complaints and quickly coordinate inside Creative Food to find practical solutions.

I stared back blankly at the tight-lipped KFC executive, seeking some indication of where this was going. The man did not often deal with Xu, but he clearly had heard about her.

"Yes, Ms. Xu is still with us," I finally replied.

Silence. Then he smiled. "So, we're fine," he said. "All those expats were useless anyway."

I continued to rely more and more on Mike, but in a more symbiotic way than I had leaned on Kevin. Mike and I carpooled together in the morning. As soon as he got in the car, our workday started. We rattled off a list of items that ranged from the latest news about lettuce prices to the evening calls we each had had with clients, employees or suppliers. We debated options and made decisions over the half-hour ride that allowed him to relay key messages immediately after we arrived at work.

As the weeks went on, I discovered that many staffers called him for advice before they called me. They felt that speaking to him was easier, and he was good at guiding them on how to structure their requests to me. There was a pattern Mike suggested they follow with me, and when I recognized it, I knew the manager or the employee in question had spoken to him beforehand. This had the added benefit of ensuring that Mike understood nearly everything that going on in the organization. He could quickly identify people who were frustrated, depressed or stuck waiting for a decision.

While KFC was happier and our employees were feeling nimbler and more empowered, we were still dealing with the unprofitable business of shipping broccoli to Japan. Our big idea of commanding higher prices because we used a special slush or better-quality control had failed. We were merely buying, packing with middlemen, and selling at the same price as other Chinese players. But we were shipping around 150 containers a year and—being my usual determined self—I still hoped we could capitalize on that. So, we made no plans to exit the business.

It was obvious Japan was not the answer to the survival question. But what was? Turns out it was our original thorny client, Yum Brands/KFC. The day in March 2002 that Mike called me to talk about the Wuhan market was the turning point.

"We've been trying to ship to KFC's Wuhan market for a year," he began after I answered the phone.

Wuhan is a city of six million roughly halfway between Beijing and Shanghai. KFC had its own small-food processing center there with stainless steel tables manned by a few older ladies in white, a set-up very similar to the old Asiafoods processing room.

Creative Food's operation didn't look at all like that anymore. I had bought crisp-looking stainless-steel processing lines for our three plants. Workers stood at a custom-made conveyor belt, trimming and coring the lettuce heads passing in front of them. The belt then moved up, pouring the vegetable into a formidable professional slicer that then spat the shredded lettuce into a torrent of chlorinated water. After a good rinse, the leaves were collected onto a vibrating table and drained before moving to centrifuges for drying and then packing. This was exactly what Yum had wanted when they gave Asiafoods their ultimatum.

But for Creative Food to replace KFC's existing set up Wuhan, we had to offer the same price they paid for their own humble operation. We had been head-butting with the KFC buyers for a year because the cost of processing the lettuce in our Shanghai plant and then trucking it to Wuhan made us too expensive.

Mike had an idea, but he was unsure whether it made any sense.

"I have analyzed the situation," he said. "We can either keep trying to reduce our price to meet KFC's demand or we can take advantage of our geographic position in Beijing and Shanghai."

Unlike many before him, he was not complaining about KFC's unrealistic expectations or the fairness of their attitude, complaints that were justified given we had invested millions for this customer, but ultimately unproductive.

I asked what he meant.

"Instead of trucking lettuce from the north to Shanghai in the summer, we could process it in our Beijing plant," he said. "The savings on transportation would bring costs down a lot. Both plants could alternate shipping to Wuhan when the season changes."

Then he showed me how he had already worked out the

details, including the transportation costs.

It was creative. Our Shanghai competitor couldn't come near us if we could put this together, I thought. Mike outlined other alternatives, concluding that he leaned in favor of the split production, but he wanted me to make the call.

He was very careful to make sure he got approval every time he had an idea, quite a contrast with what I had dealt with before. I told him to go ahead and test the idea with Yum. He hung up, then called back a few hours later to report KFC had agreed to restart negotiations.

In the end, we got the contract in Wuhan.

The goodwill that emerged during these tortuous months paid off. With the Wuhan win, everyone started to believe it might all work out. By end of 2002, sales doubled, and the company broke even for the first time.

8

TRADE-OFFS

CLIENTS ASSUMED that I tracked where my vegetables came from. And I did track them—but I had learned that there wouldn't be a company to run if I did everything squeaky-clean on the food-safety front. The turmoil of the first two years had tested my ideals. I had become a ruthless survivor.

I didn't lie. In fact, I did everything I could to know where my lettuce came from, and that's what I communicated to clients. But what I didn't say is that my select group of traders—the ones Mike and I agreed to work with—moved fast to tap their networks and get lettuce from other regions when the one I had originally ordered from was suddenly short. Each time this happened, and it happened frequently, I closed my eyes to the fact that such emergency shipments blended heads of lettuce grown by thousands of unknown villagers scattered around multiple regions.

In their many visits to Creative Food's processing plants, KFC auditors were thorough.

"Do you have control over your supply of vegetables?" said their questionnaire.

"Yes," was my answer by default.

But the fact that I had a system in place to identify where my supply came from didn't mean that it always came from one place. And for small quantities of vegetables other than lettuce, I bought most of the crop from traders simply because it was too risky to sow my own. If I did, I was sure to harvest either too much or too little. Using traders neutralized this risk, but it meant I had less control over my sources.

Why not buy from fewer and larger farms directly? Because there weren't any farms of such scale. I had tried to replicate California in China, and it had been a disaster. I wasn't ready to risk my company again. So now I was operating much more like a local entrepreneur. I kept growing the business and hoped I would be able to correct the safety situation later. While I was at it, I made some choices that would have appalled the moral and judgmental young man I was in my early Asiafoods days.

Once we had won KFC's Wuhan business, Mike adroitly fended off the relentless pressure to decrease prices. He added new clients and more cities and convinced customers that we could do much more than coleslaw and shredded lettuce. Business was going well. As Chinese New Year approached in January 2003 — one year after my first train ride with the team — we were now making elaborate salads, soups and pasta sauces for newcomers Starbucks and Pizza Hut and for hospitals in Hong Kong.

But our Japanese exports weren't doing as well. Our company had built a decent volume there, but we still hadn't reached profitability. Suddenly, the safety issue forced itself on us. A Japanese newspaper had published an article in December 2001 claiming that 47 percent of vegetables grown in China were contaminated with chemicals. Within weeks, Japan started to test every container of fresh vegetables coming from China for chemical contamination. By the spring of 2002, spinach from China was officially banned in Japan. In the aftermath of the decision, all produce exported from China suffered as many products failed the new tests.

In the autumn of 2002, it became clear that our third year in Japan would be our worst yet. At the meeting I called to assess the damage, Xu Shen, the supply manager who was now handling our export business, reported on broccoli sales.

"Market prices are coming down fast," he said with a grim face.

I was irritated. "More excuses," I thought. Japan was the project I had described as a sure win to everyone. Mike was doing a good job with sales on the domestic front, but I had put my own stamp on the Japanese business and I wanted it to work.

"What do you mean prices are down? What caused this?" I asked.

"After the article about Chinese vegetables, Japanese customs increased the sampling tests for spinach imported from China," he replied. "And they found chemical residues a hundred times higher than the acceptable threshold."

I didn't know or care much about the article or the ban. "When will it return to normal?" I asked Xu.

He gave no answer to that, probably thinking I would contradict anything he said that day. Mike was quiet too. He wasn't a fan of my Japan efforts. To him, things were hard enough at home, in a market we knew better.

I began to wonder if our own vegetables might be contaminated too, but instead of acknowledging that, I turned my frustration on Mike.

"We do some chemical residue testing on the vegetables we receive, right?" I asked.

"Yes," he said. "Our quality controllers in all plants apply a paper strip to samples of vegetables selected from each lot before they enter our cold rooms. It changes color if there is a residue."

"So, we're good then?" I pressed.

"Not really," he said. "When the color changes, it means a toxic level that will kill you." He paused. "But it could still be very dangerous below that level. There's just no way to know."

In other words, our tests only caught contamination of truly deadly proportions, but pesticide residues below that level could still exist undetected – and could still make people very sick.

It was easy for me to hide behind the fact that we did test, which was more than many other players in the market did. Deep down, though, beneath all my other worries about keeping the company afloat, paying farmers and dealing with KFC's whims and politics, I knew that those tests wouldn't save us from any scandal that might erupt should someone fall ill or die after eating our vegetables.

Of all the food-safety dangers looming over Creative Food, the kinds of chemical residues that sparked the Japanese ban were the most insidious. Such residues were leftover traces of pesticide that hadn't neutralized because they had been applied too close to harvest or toxic substances embedded in the soil that had been absorbed by the plant.

Unlike other contaminants, chemical residues affect the body only after a while; they aren't something you can immediately connect to the consumption of one food. But the long-term effect is frightening. Excess use of products like antibiotics in fish or meat can cause increased bacteria resistance or help create superbugs. Heavy metals and other toxic substances in leafy vegetables can have carcinogenic effects. Think cancer and still-born fetuses – not something you would want to bet the future of your company on or have on your conscience.

The vegetable scandal in Japan cast light on a problem that had its roots in the early 1980s: Chinese farmers used far too much pesticide and fertilizer. From the earliest days of agricultural reform, they were seen in the countryside as the magic wand that allowed productivity to rise even though farming methods hadn't evolved.

Authorities didn't really check whether these chemicals were applied safely. No government agency had asked me this question. Even Japan, for all its meticulous attention to detail, wasn't very thorough when it came to chemicals. It tested for far fewer substances than the number recommended by the Codex Alimentarius, a branch of the United Nations' Food and Agriculture Organization tasked with compiling which categories of chemical should be tested and how. China was worse. Codex recommended testing for more than 2,500 chemicals' Minimum Residue Levels (MRLs), but China only covered 485. And within the Chinese standard, only a fifth complied with UN recommendations.

Nevertheless, when the Japanese problem grew big enough to become a national issue, Beijing took drastic measures. The Administration for Quality, Supervision, Inspection and Quarantine — which regulated quality standards for all exported products — black-listed the insecticide found on the spinach in question. Inspection of each load heading for Japan became compulsory. All residue limits in China were adjusted to match Japan's newly-established standards. During the period of the ban, the government introduced a new certification process for all agricultural-products exporters, which reduced their numbers to only the handful of companies able to meet the new stringent regulations. To comply as an exporter, you now had to lease your own farmland — instead of buying produce from other suppliers — and buy gas chromatographers, equipment that identifies the exact quantity of residue in a sample. Out of 448,000 companies previously involved in exporting, only around 11,000 got certified. Spinach exporters were whittled down to a dozen companies. Traders moved to other categories.

These new rules killed my broccoli exports. I couldn't buy from the likes of Linhai's Wang any longer. And I couldn't afford to lease my own land. Soon after my impatience at the meeting with Mike and Xu, my three years of efforts in Japan petered out.

The new rules, however, applied to exporters only, so I didn't have to change much for my domestic clients. KFC climbed back to represent a disproportionate share of my sales. For them and for my other domestic clients, I kept buying from the 97.5 percent of companies whose produce wasn't clean enough to export but was cheap enough to allow me to squeeze out a profit.

Chemicals may have been the scariest source of contamination, but since residues weren't tested thoroughly inside China, what I feared most on a day-to-day basis was bacterial contamination. Bad bacteria, like E-coli, listeria and salmonella, cause food poisoning and sometimes death in the space of a few days. These nasty bugs can find their way into your stomach via even innocent-looking foods. Starting at the farm, they leach into crops from stables and animal manure. From there, anyone touching the vegetable during harvest, loading, storing or processing (and that includes a person chopping meat or vegetables in his own kitchen) can then be a potential carrier. In the United States, bags of salads sold at the supermarket must be free of pathogens like salmonella and e-coli. In China, no test was required for pathogens. Since nobody asked for such tests, I just skipped them.

It didn't take a lot of imagination to guess that Wang's workers in Linhai didn't wash their hands as they returned from the open-air trench serving as their latrine. These workers handpicked our precious broccoli, destined for fastidious Japanese consumers, and placed the florets in our super-high-tech sanitized ice slush —

and they probably did it with dirty hands.

Inside our plants, the situation wasn't much better. We had hygiene manuals and standard operating procedures based on a well-recognized American hazard monitoring system called Hazard Analysis and Critical Control Points. You had to wash hands, wear white coats and spray disinfectant on your palms each time you entered the production area. But I wasn't sure the workers did these things as regularly as they should have. My twenty-something quality controllers didn't always stop fifty-something female workers leaving the bathroom to inquire whether they had washed their hands before entering the production room. They lacked experience—the rules were new for them—they lacked confidence, and, above all, they lacked a strong mandate from me.

It's easy to blame China's lack of standards. But I realized only years later how my own lack of commitment to safety and quality affected Creative Food. At one point, I travelled to England to visit a food-processing plant as part of my effort to understand how the best companies in my sector operated. The plants were larger, cleaner, and more automated than mine. But what impressed me most was something else. One day as I walked through the chlorinated pools between the changing rooms and the production area, I heard a heavy voice bark from the locker area behind me.

"Hey, you!" said an imposing man with a red beard; he was only half dressed, suspenders at his sides, pants half down but green rubber boots on.

"Get your hairnet! You can't get in without your hairnet," he said, pointing at me menacingly.

The company's owner was ahead of me. He looked back when he heard the man and confirmed that I needed to go and put on a hairnet beneath my plastic white hat. It was embarrassing.

The red-bearded man could see I was with his boss, but that didn't matter to him. Everyone without exception followed the rules inside the factory. The boss's assent reinforced for all those present that it was acceptable for the man to speak to me like that. In China, I could have come into the factory stinking like a polecat and wearing manure-covered boots, and nobody would have uttered a word. I was the supreme leader; status mattered more than safety.

In the United States and Europe, bacterial contamination risks have been mostly dealt with via a complex system of operating standards, strict controls and transparent communication between government agencies and companies. There is also a shared understanding of basic biology concepts and contamination threats. Government or clients' inspectors raise mostly valid issues, and operators propose corrections. They don't always agree, but in the end, they will come up with reasonable compromises.

That wasn't true in China. Health inspectors lacked basic knowledge and were swayed by industry trends that were not always effective. For hours during regular inspections, they toured our plants, demanding the installation of a wind tunnel at the entrance to the production area, more masks for workers and — yes — hairnets. In my view, wind tunnels only moved hairs from one shoulder to another and therefore didn't solve anything. But they were the fashionable thing. Masks and hairnets were necessary but only to control basic cleanliness. The post-Japan-scandal gas chromatographers were trendy too. But did it make sense to invest in a device telling you the exact quantity of residue if 95 percent of what you bought wasn't tested?

Local inspectors didn't comment when watching my coleslaw production team come in and out of the raw material cooler with dirty cabbage to shred, while others in the same room were mixing clean cabbage with mayonnaise. My workers were exposing clean coleslaw to dirty unwashed cabbage that could contain harmful bacteria. I learned later that in the world's best plants, raw materials and finished products are processed in separate rooms and never cross paths. The clean rooms even have separate teams wearing colored uniforms and dedicated air filtration systems.

If workers in my foreign-invested HACCP-certified plants didn't wash hands and didn't respect the rules, imagine what could go on in a traditional wholesaler's warehouse managed by somebody's second cousin. Consumers were even more in the dark about what happened to food before it reached the supermarket shelves. Jane stopped buying local milk when she learned from an executive at a reputable foreign company, while reporting an article, that farmers urinated in the milk to increase nitrogen content, an indicator used by dairy processors to measure protein levels.

"Xavier, we have a problem," said Frank Rasche on my cell phone one day.

I didn't know Frank well, but I had followed the expansion of his company, Element Fresh, the restaurant chain he had set up with two partners on the model of the British chain Pret-a-Manger to serve sandwiches, salads, soups and juices to the emerging crowd of office ladies and other health-conscious Chinese in Shanghai and other cities. separately salads pre-washed in large bags.

"A customer found a plastic glove in his salad today," he said.

"Oh no!" I said in response, trying to sound as surprised as he was. But I wasn't surprised at all, and I was more annoyed than anything, for I knew someone at my plant had once more failed to follow the rules.

According to our manuals, quality controllers checked in and checked out all gloves before and after production. But I also knew they sometimes didn't. When they were in a rush to get the products out of the plant, production managers pressured lower-ranking quality controllers to cut corners on some inspections to save time; one of those cut corners was not checking all gloves back in after work to verify that none were missing. And in my plants, there wasn't any red-bearded man to stand up in protest. I had created a culture where the production manager — the man with control over the profit — far outranked the lowly quality controller. While I can't say I was comfortable with all the implications of this situation, I also wasn't ready to do anything to change it yet.

Still, I couldn't ignore my client. A greasy latex glove had found its way onto Frank's customer's plate of grilled salmon salad; I had to investigate.

After looking into it, we verified that the glove counts were constant in our records. So, no workers had lost any. We came up with two hypotheses. Either a disgruntled worker at Creative Food had hidden a glove inside a bag or someone in Frank's restaurant had been paid off by a competitor to cause trouble. We installed cameras inside our production room to catch such instances. But I felt that my actions were more symbolic than effective. If someone wanted to cause harm, there were many ways to do so. Accusing a competitor was a cop-out. I knew that we weren't faultless, that contamination of our products by unwelcome objects was a day-to-day food quality problem for us.

A bug in a bag can be spun as a sign of freshness. It gets harder to justify when it's a plastic glove. A month later, Frank's staff claimed they found a needle in one of our salad bags. Frank switched to another supplier that day. Nobody used needles in our factories, but it wasn't impossible that a disgruntled worker or a corrupt restaurant employee had placed one in there before or after the bag was opened. I felt helpless and exposed.

In December of 2002, Jane and I got married. It wasn't exactly the timing I had planned. I would have preferred to wait until the company was on more solid ground.

"What does marriage have to do with your business?" she had snapped when I told her I wanted to wait a bit. We had been together for 18 months.

I knew that I would marry Jane. I just wanted to be able to provide for a family first. She clearly disagreed. In her eyes, I was hesitating about an important matter. The change in her tone was perceptible: Jane didn't get mad, she just got cold.

"I am Korean," she said. "Koreans marry."

I countered rhetorically—and regretted it as soon as I did—that she was American too, and that couples in the West tended to live together for a while before they committed to each other. It took her a fraction of a second to dismiss that; I watched her lips pucker in disgust at my loose European morals.

"You marry me, or I am moving on with life," she said.

The resolution in her voice made it clear it wasn't a bluff. I had no intention of letting her go anyway. The showdown was so typical of Jane it made me smile. She was the steadiest and most radiant human being I knew. But when she picked a battle, you wouldn't want to stand in her way. We married late in 2002 and decided to use the New Year lull in 2003 to honeymoon in the mountains of Hokkaido in Japan.

Around the same time, in early 2003, KFC was busy putting the final touches on its launch of the *Lao Beijing Jiroujuan* (Old Beijing Chicken Wrap), a new product backed by heavy marketing during what is usually a peak in sales for the brand. The Peking

Duck-like burrito would be served in thousands of restaurants spread across several regions in China. Ingredients included chicken fingers, cucumber sticks and green onions topped with a plum sauce. We were in charge of shipping small bags of cucumber and green onion cut in sticks, so that restaurants could assemble the wraps quickly.

Everyone can cut a few vegetables in his kitchen for a dinner party. But it is much harder to guarantee that thousands of restaurants across China will get the identical shipments every day, come rain or shine, from January to December. You can't store fresh vegetables to make up for ups and downs. Size, taste and color changed all the time because none of the thousands of farmers who worked for us indirectly did things the same way. On top of that, plans for harvested volume went awry if a cold snap, a sudden drought or heavy rains hit during the growing season. And such events were common given China's continental climate.

For the green onions and cucumbers that KFC needed, I arranged planting in three different regions to cover a year of supply, settling on the coastal province of Shandong to kick off the program. KFC wanted a sweeter type of green onion than what the Chinese typically consume so we picked a variety that was grown specifically for Japan. But that meant I wouldn't be able to do a night run to the wholesale market if I was short. Any mistake would ripple directly to hundreds of angry restaurant managers scrambling to make up for the missing ingredients.

The wrap was an overnight success. Orders far exceeded what we had planned for. We didn't have enough people to process all the cucumbers and green onions required, and the volume we had stored in anticipation of the launch was quickly exhausted. Most of my regular workers had gone home for the lunar new year. Even small farmers in Shandong didn't bother to harvest during this most traditional of holidays.

My honeymoon in Japan didn't last long. The day after I arrived, Mike called.

"Xavier, we have a problem with the new wrap," he said.

Like everyone but a few supervisors at the factory, he had been on holiday with his family in his hometown of Nanjing, three hours by car from Shanghai. A day before his call to me, he was asked to sign off on a fax agreeing to the launch, and he had noticed a mistake in the way that volumes had been calculated. Nobody at Creative Food or at KFC had caught it. But anticipating problems, Mike drove back to Shanghai.

On the road, the factory called to tell him that incoming orders were four times higher than the forecast. There weren't enough workers. Worse, there wasn't enough space to trim, clean and sort the vegetables that didn't meet our quality standards before we could process them.

Mike brought me up to speed quickly about the ongoing whiplash. KFC had spent tens of millions of dollars in prime-time TV advertising across the country, and nobody there wanted to tell Sam Su that his new wrap couldn't be sold because of a lack of some cucumbers and green onions.

Complicating the matter further, the green onions that we received were much thicker than planned — and they tasted spicy, nothing like the intended sweetness. Zhu Jun, KFC's manager in charge of new products, was to blame. In his insistence on selecting an uncommon variety of green onions, he had picked one that was sweet when it was young — but neither the growers nor Creative Food's agronomists had alerted him that the flavor would change as the vegetable grew.

Tables inside KFC Shanghai restaurants were littered with white spicy stalks of green onions that customers had pulled out of their wraps. In Beijing, it was better. Green onions are eaten there as snacks. But we had designed a product for all Chinese palates, not just northern ones, and we now had to peel away 80 percent of the green onions we had grown to mitigate the pungent flavor and fit into the wrap's specifications. The problem was that our pre-launch calculations had assumed we would lose only 10% in production. Our purchasing and planting plans were based on this estimate.

When he received the fax to sign off for the launch, Mike had noticed that the onions described on paper didn't look at all like what he saw in our coolers before he left for the holiday. That's when he decided to drive back to the plant. When he arrived, managers were in a state of panic, production had slowed to a trickle due to lack of people and materials, and the supervisors were at a loss about what to do. Meanwhile, with a 90 percent waste in production, we were losing a fortune on every bag we processed.

As we spoke on the phone, Mike was amid what sounded like a war. In contrast, I was standing in a forest in northern Hokkaido amidst pristine powder snow with snowshoes on. A hundred yards away there was our cabin, kept warm by a wood-fire stove. We had just returned from a long hike, and Jane was waiting for me with curry rice. For a good hour, as I stood in the cold, Mike brought me up to speed. He had called back a large part of the team to help manage the crisis in Shanghai, Beijing and Shenzhen. Everyone was now on deck in three cities. Managers were knocking at nearby semi-conductor factories' doors — most hosted their workers on site in company-built dormitories — offering triple the normal hourly wage if they came and cut vegetables for a couple of hours.

Mike had convinced Zhu to let us shred the onions into flakes, so we could throw the coarse material into our powerful industrial cutters and reduce the spiciness. But that only partially helped. Cucumbers were even slower to process. You needed to wash away dirt, then wait endless minutes while they were dipped in chlorinated water to kill bacteria. Once you took them out of the large garbage-bin-like gray plastic crates, you still had to peel them, slice them in two and remove the core seeds before you could cut them into sticks. There weren't any machines to do this. And in any case, no equipment was able to distinguish the straight cucumbers we needed from the twisted and curvy ones filling our boxes in the cold room.

Already, several KFC restaurants outside the big cities had stopped selling the heavily advertised wrap. Having green onions didn't help if cucumbers were missing. Mike had called Zhu to explain.

"I get everything you say," Zhu said. "But you have to figure out a way, and you had better not drop the ball." As Mike repeated the exchange to me, I understood there was no way Zhu was going to take the blame for the mess.

Still standing in the snow, I kept weighing the pros and cons of cutting my honeymoon short. I had been married all of 30 days. I could vividly picture Jane's reaction if I announced I was needed back in Shanghai. I prayed that Mike had a plan I would judge acceptable.

"You remember Yue Caihua in Beijing," he said.

Yue was the accountant who had come to him worried about the state of the company. She had since then taken a job in government as vice mayor of a small town near the airport.

"Sure," I said, wondering where he was going.

"She wants us to move our Beijing plant to her town."

It was true our Beijing plant was getting too small for us. I had started to look into new locations for a much bigger plant.

"I told her we could look at it if she helped with this crisis,"

Mike said.

"Cucumber, new plant, ex-accountant turned vice mayor." I was having a hard time connecting the dots.

But Mike hadn't lost his practical touch. His plan was to ask Yue to mobilize school canteens in her town to do all the basic preparation of the cucumber and green onions. Unlike the big cities where our plants were located, workers there were all local villagers, so it was easy for Yue as vice mayor to summon them back to work. The trimmed vegetables — sorted, cleaned, and peeled — would then be further sanitized and processed into sticks inside our Beijing plant an hour away. Mike wanted my approval for similar schemes in kitchens run by small lunchbox providers he had identified in Shanghai and in Guangzhou.

I knew too well from my Asiafoods days that these local operations were nowhere as safety-conscious as our plants. Picture a metal roof over concrete sinks and countertops set with filthy, rusty kitchen tools, greasy black woks, and wooden chopping boards harboring invisible colonies of bacteria. And forget about hand washing. Mike knew that, too, so before I asked, he promised to get our quality team to train and control the makeshift kitchens.

I approved the move, figuring that we would catch contamination problems — if any — in the large chlorinated baths inside our plants. One thing bothered me, though. Mike insisted we not inform KFC because it would put Zhu in a tough spot. The kitchens clearly didn't pass muster. So Zhu would have to make a harsh trade-off: stop us from doing this and admit that his onion mistake had cost his company millions of dollars, or agree to our plan and appear to be complicit. "Don't drop the ball," Zhu had said. For Mike, the message was clear. We had to do whatever we could to make sure KFC could still supply its new wrap to millions of consumers or Zhu would find a way to punish us later.

I called the head buyer at Yum to reassure him we would have his back and guarantee delivery for every order coming our way. I left out how I would do that, but he sounded relieved and grateful; he hadn't slept for three nights. Restaurant managers were calling him from everywhere to complain that people had come to buy the Old Beijing chicken wrap and couldn't get it.

When I finally hung up and walked back through the snow to Jane and my cold curry, I wasn't sure I had made the right call, but it was too late to turn back. Over the next days, I spent guilty hours on the phone with Mike, hoping that Jane wouldn't feel I was completely ignoring her while trying to stay as involved as possible with the people in Shanghai. But Jane wasn't the type to rant about my business crashing her honeymoon. Instead, she spent two days holed up in a dimly-lit café, editing the business plan I had prepared for new investors, while other couples skied.

Back in China, all our staff scrambled to make sure our risky gamble on the small kitchens worked. Each night, Mike and other colleagues collapsed in sleeping bags on the floor of the Shanghai meeting room after a day spent dispatching tons of cucumbers and green onions from the traders' coolers to the lunchbox kitchens, then to Creative Food's plants, and finally to KFC's distribution centers, all along negotiating small delays so we could allocate enough to each region. Often, he sent trucks directly to the restaurants to make up for shortages. If the production manager called for help, he and other managers dropped everything and rushed to the plant to help workers on the conveyor belt.

On the third day, I picked up Mike's call early in the morning to hear he was on his way to the Shanghai kitchen we operated under the radar. Someone had blown the whistle to KFC. That morning at 7 am, a group of seven managers from KFC had shown up at the gate of the small stealth unit. Zhu was one of them. When he got there, Mike explained the steps we had taken to keep food safety risks at bay. Zhu made a gesture with his arm, pointing inside the small building.

"Shut this down," he ordered. "This is unacceptable."

Fortunately, the holiday period was coming to an end. Workers were slowly returning, the peak of orders had passed, and our stealth kitchens were no longer needed.

Mike suspected that someone inside Creative Food had betrayed the team and called KFC. He was dejected but still practical. He guessed the whistle had probably been blown a few days earlier, but Zhu, worried he wouldn't get supply, had sat on it before acting. It was an all-around win for him. He appeared to have stopped our bad behavior but without jeopardizing supply for the company in the middle of the holidays.

Later that day, Mike called to say I had been summoned in front of KFC's head buyer the following Monday. Over the weekend, he negotiated with the junior buyer what the penalty for Creative Food should be. Everyone knew we couldn't be too severely sanctioned, the junior explained. But an example had to be made.

When I showed up to meet his boss, I played along uneasily with the choreography Mike had staged. The man scolded me for not disclosing the matter.

"We would have worked that out together," he said. But we both knew nobody would have had the courage to pick up the phone to tell Sam Su that his marketing millions were about to be thrown out the window. In the end, KFC took away a third of our Shanghai business for three months and gave it to another supplier.

I appeared as contrite as possible. But in my view, we had won, just as Zhu had with his own high-wire act. The hit was easy to digest. Accounting for the penalty, my sales were still triple what they had been the year before, and we had made no enemies inside Yum.

Within a couple of weeks, the head of our quality department left Creative Food to join Yum's ranks and Zhu's team. Mike looked at me pointedly: "I told you someone from inside had betrayed us. Now comes his reward."

The arguments against my actions during the green-onion-and-cucumber crisis still echo in my head: "You should have been upfront with your client." "This could have turned out very badly for everyone." I'm not proud of what I did, but I also believe it was a necessary trade-off. It was a choice between setting up three stealth processing plants with dubious quality control or causing a huge crisis in the middle of Chinese New Year for our budgets client, one that I was sure to be blamed for.

Nothing in my history of dealings with Yum encouraged me to be transparent. For the previous three years, my treasured client had watched in silence and actively looked for other suppliers as I struggled with my own financial crises. The pressure to cut costs was relentless. They had introduced an annual tender system that forced prices down every year, ignoring periods of inflation or seasonal changes. And now they had poached a manager without even giving me a heads-up.

The endless maneuvering at Yum had turned Creative Food's honest managers and workers into a fiercely protective and secretive group. Together with Mike, I had indeed built a tight team. But in protecting my own narrow interests, I had made compromises on the larger issue of food quality. We had done things I would have thought unthinkable three years before.

I wondered if someday I—and the company—would pay for that.

9

SAND-TEA NOODLES AND TAINTED SHRIMP

THE LACK OF concern around food safety in the factories of China belies China's tremendous passion for anything culinary. Over the years, I've heard many people affirm that Chinese cuisine is unmatched around the world. Only French cuisine, Chinese people tell me, shows comparable sophistication—and they probably only say that to me out of politeness. The Chinese love food. Rich or poor, intellectual or illiterate, city dweller or lettuce grower, everyone hungers for the right dish at the right moment.

It was a quest I shared, though with different intensity the longer I lived in China. Starting with the first recipes I saw at Asiafoods, Chinese dishes and ingredients sounded foreign and remote; in fact, I knew so little about them that I associated Chinese food with the Vietnamese food I had eaten in France. In those early years, I desperately hung onto my Western culinary heritage, looking for familiar flavors. I ordered noodles hoping to see fresh Italian-style pasta. What I got looked more like watery soup with a piece of bony meat in it. I usually ate the noodles and left the rest. The broth brought back too many memories of being force-fed soup as a child. Why couldn't I get a simple plate of spaghetti?

Over time, my tastes improved, somewhat thanks to Jane, who guided me through her own Asian favorites. But I didn't make much effort to learn about ingredients or cooking styles. I carefully avoided the seasoning section when shopping at supermarkets. It wasn't just taste; the unknown bean pastes, vinegars, and oils on the shelves called me out for my ignorance about anything culinary in a country where I was supposed to be selling foods to the natives. And a few years after my arrival, the newfound comfort of finally knowing a few dishes that I liked further numbed what little curiosity I had had. When I got lost in a restaurant menu filled with enigmatic descriptions, I reasoned it was just part of being a foreigner.

The night I had dinner with my American friend Eric Rosenblum on Beijing's *Guijie* — "Ghost Street" — probably marks the moment when all my assumptions got shattered.

Eric had already played an outsize role in my life as the man who had repeatedly insisted that I meet Jane. Shortly after that introduction, one night in the summer of 2001, I traveled to Beijing, and he suggested we meet another friend for dinner. Tucked behind Dongzhimen gate, Ghost Street was a small stretch of road packed with dozens of food stalls. The name, dating back to the Qing Dynasty (1644-1911), supposedly came from the flickering of the lights emitted by the shop owners' oil lamps at night, giving the market a spectral atmosphere. Then surrounded by the rubble of Beijing's pre-Olympics transformation, Ghost Street at the turn of the 21st century was still a great place to go for a late-night meal. Patrons sat on plastic stools under light bulbs hanging from wires connected to generators. Gas-powered woks threw flames through the darkness as cooks working under tents or corrugated iron sheds, infusing the air with the heady smells of fried chilies, garlic, hot oil and diesel fuel.

As he sat next to me studying the menu, I watched Eric while holding up my end of the conversation. I knew he had studied Chinese at university, but I assumed this broad-shouldered, blue-eyed foreigner from Pittsburgh would do what I always did: ignore the menu and ask the waitress for one of the limited range of dishes I knew how to say.

The laminated menu covered in characters was as bewildering to me as an ancient parchment. I was ignorant of most characters, but four years of trying to decipher menus had taught me that even when I could read some, it didn't help me much. Names on a Chinese menu require a level of culture I didn't have. Someone more knowledgeable than I could guess if the name included key ingredients or flavors—a *Suanla* ("Hot and Sour") soup for example—but few menus will explain that the soup includes bamboo shoots, tofu skin and black wood-ear fungi.

It's harder when names refer to a cooking method. *Chashao* ("Fork-Burn") dishes don't mean anything to the uneducated eye. But Chinese diners immediately understand that it refers to roasted pork dishes with a caramelized sauce common in southern China. At other times, dish names sound grand but give no indication of what goes into them. Knowing how to read the characters for *xiaolong bao* ("Little Basket") dumplings won't tell you anything about the delicious pork soup captured inside a tiny wrapper and usually served on Shanghai streets in bamboo steamer baskets.

In some instances, Chinese cooks use proper nouns to create an emotional connection with their dishes. *Dongpo* pork is named after Su Dongpo (1037-1101), a respected Song Dynasty poet and statesman from Hangzhou. Su supposedly perfected the stewing of pork in a garlic, soy, ginger and sugar-based sauce until the pork fat becomes so soft it melts in the mouth.

"Oh, look at this!" Eric said with genuine excitement. "I think I'm going to order this amazing *mala* crayfish; it's one of the specialties here. Or maybe I should go for the *shuizhuyu*?"

I knew that the first dish was *mala*—numb-spicy—something-

or-other. And the other dish must have been the fish cooked in a huge vat of boiling red chili oil that I had seen people order in restaurants. But I had never ventured to sample these fiery dishes on my own.

He pointed at a group of Chinese characters printed in the middle of one page of the menu. I didn't want to reveal my ignorance so I nodded along, careful not to express an opinion for fear of saying something obvious or stupid in front of such an expert.

Our dinner companion was as excited as Eric. "Oh yes, I'd love this," he said. "It's been such a long time since I had *shuizhuyu*."

Shuizhyu literally translates as "water-boiled fish," a rather tame evocation for something so spicy that diners often need to wipe sweat from their forehead. The two of them went on to debate the pros and cons of stewed lamb spine, spicy crabs and other flavors of crayfish while sipping their chilled beer.

"*Mala* crayfish?" I repeated to myself. I could barely recognize the character for "rice," but Eric knew how to read "Sichuan-flavored numb and spicy crayfish."

I was far too insecure to ask how he had learned so much about Chinese food; it just so obviously demonstrated how little I knew about the place after four years living here. Eric later explained that when he was forced to close down his internet business following the 2001 dot-com crash, he had opted to take three months of his life to dive into Chinese street markets and learn how to cook the local way. Unlike me, he didn't settle into a boring but comfortable routine, choosing instead to immerse himself in subtleties like the art of differentiating between a young and an old chicken and how the old brought out the best flavors in broths.

I didn't say anything to my friends that night, but after that dinner, I resolved to embrace Chinese cuisine with much more daring that I had so far shown.

My first solo adventure with this new mindset took place on a trip soon after to Xiamen, a port city on the southeast coast opposite Taiwan. In my search for a place to eat one evening, I asked passers-by where I could find a good noodle shop. A woman with a toddler indicated I could find *shacha mian* – sand-tea noodles – down the road at a place called "Old Zhao." Each time I got to a street corner, I asked the same question of a different stranger. "Old Zhao" seemed to be the place to go.

When I got to the shop, it looked unimpressive. An older lady stood behind a huge pot bubbling with gray solids suspended in a whitish foam. It smelled of fish, but there was also a slight spicy fragrance in the air. There was no finishing room, just two laminated tables outside with orange plastic benches. Most patrons grabbed their noodles and walked away, slurping loudly. It wasn't the charming guesthouse filled with wooden stools that I had imagined, but it was too late to try something else. I asked for a bowl and, as usual, nodded along blandly at the two or three questions the gruff lady threw at me, acting as if I understood. Without a look, she grabbed noodles from a skimmer and put them in a paper bowl. Then she took a ladle of broth from the giant pot and poured it over the noodles.

The milky liquid covering my dish smelled surprisingly good even if it looked appalling. And when I took a mouthful, something clicked. I actually tasted the complex broth brimming with flavors. I sat on the orange bench, slurping through the bowl, wondering why it had taken me so long to dive in. I learned later that *shacha*, or sand-tea, was the transliteration for the satay sauce you usually find in Indonesia and Malaysia. Local merchants brought it to China a few centuries ago. In Indonesia, it's a mix of peanut butter, chili, shrimp paste and spices like galangal, the local ginger. But the Chinese, as they've always done, localized the recipe and replaced the peanut butter with a soy-bean paste and fish marinated in spices and fermented rice.

In the years that followed, my quest for a good meal became more like that of the Chinese themselves. On the road, I still struggled with the expensive but rubbery sea cucumbers, jellyfish and clams that people ordered at banquets to make me feel important. But more often, I delighted in the simple fare of villagers: baby bok-choy stir-fried in garlic, baked sweet potatoes and foraged mushrooms braised in a sweet rice wine sauce, and smoked ham or carp steamed with ginger, scallions and soy sauce. When I later turned to eating mostly food from plants as a way to control my sky-rocketing cholesterol levels, I found in Mike a partner-in-crime, as he himself needed to avoid meat for health reasons. With every meal as a non-meat eater, I became more comfortable with the wide variety of Chinese steamed, stir-fried and pickled greens. After a while, they became my first choice—fitting for a man who sold vegetables for a living.

When we all travelled abroad together, my Chinese colleagues were a lot like I had been—somewhat suspicious of new foods. On one occasion, Mike was chaperoning a group of Chinese officials on a tour of food companies in England, and I flew over to join them, bringing with me some Chinese snacks—duck blood jelly, chicken feet and instant noodles. This was Jane's idea. As an Asian, she knew better than I how much they would be missing the flavors of home.

The night of my arrival at a small country inn north of London, the officials were so happy to see the snacks that they stayed in their rooms for dinner, eating with delight what I had brought while playing cards on top of their beds with their pants rolled up. I still remember their relief and the grateful words as I unpacked my box of goodies. The week without their favorite foods had been tough—the Chinese restaurants Mike had found in England tasted off to them.

So, what makes food such a central part of China's identity?

Over the course of centuries, China's large population has regularly stretched the country's agricultural resources. China's percentage of arable land is small — less than a quarter of its land mass — so when floods, droughts, or diseases hit crops, famines have often followed, as part of the normal cycle of life. In addition, China's continental climate causes brutal temperature changes between seasons, shortening the time left between planting and harvesting of crops. In a land squeezed between mountains and deserts, Siberian winters and scorching summers, the fields must be worked to yield as large and varied a harvest as possible to support all of China's people.

As a foreigner in the country, I always found it striking how the Chinese shaped and bent their environment to feed everyone. They built dams, canals, and tunnels, flattened some hills and terraced others, destroyed forests and replanted them — all for the sake of producing more food crops. From centuries-old rice terraces cut into steep slopes to valleys flooded to make room for the Three Gorges Dam, the tamed wildlands serve as a resource. I never saw in China the mystique associated with the preservation of countryside that you see in the U.S.; people there just can't afford it. Across its history, Chinese society constantly labored to master nature so it could feed its people.

A relatively small amount of workable land, however, doesn't mean a smaller range of foods. In fact, the flora is incredibly diverse. China has 31,000 plant species, many more than the 20,000 catalogued in the U.S. and Canada together. Many species still growing in the wild in China today were eliminated in North America during the Ice Ages. Biologists around the world travel to China for a lot of their work. I learned this firsthand when I later advised New Zealand's largest kiwifruit exporter.

The country is well-known for the green-and-gold fruits it named after its eponymous furry bird, but the kiwifruit actually originated in China, where it's called "monkey peach." New Zealanders brought it to their island a hundred years ago and perfected its cultivation, yet all of its rootstocks are in China.

So, while the geographical and climatic limits on agriculture make food production a constant concern, the varied plant life gives cooks plenty of the raw materials to experiment with, feeding a curiosity for anything culinary that could only increase with a third factor: the arrival of foods from outside of China.

Chinese speak so highly of their food culture that you would think they invented it all, but a lot of their ingredients originated elsewhere. China's main contribution to the world of foods is actually the way its cooks cut, slice, grind, ferment, pickle and cook other cultures' plants and animals, in ways never seen before. As E.N. Anderson explained in his seminal work *The Food of China*, foreign travelers like the British botanist Robert Fortune couldn't help but note the variety of Chinese cooking skills: "The food of these people is of the simplest kind—namely rice, vegetables, and a small portion of animal food, such as fish or pork. But the poorest classes in China seem to understand the art of preparing their food better than the same class at home. A Chinese can dine in sumptuous manner upon his rice, fish, vegetables, and tea; and I fully believe that in no country in the world is there less real misery and want than in China.[1]"

Born in the Yellow River basin, Chinese agriculture goes back to 6,000 BC when millet was the primary grain consumed, but they weren't the world's first farmers—cultivating crops started many thousand years earlier in the Middle East. Continental trade routes from the Middle East to Central Asia brought these

---

1   E.N Anderson—"The Food of China" pp117

foods to China, where people tweaked and experimented until they came up with something they viewed as superior. Flour-milling technology came from Central Asia, but the Chinese perfected these techniques into noodles. Buddhist monks from Burma probably brought tea during the Tang dynasty; Chinese connoisseurs codified it and made it a quintessential part of their culture. Soybeans, too ,came through Central Asia, but their transformation into the bean pastes and bean curds that confused me in my early days, and delighted me later, happened in China.

For centuries, eras of abundance alternated with periods of scarcity like a pendulum that never ceased to oscillate, producing an ever-increasing range of edible choices. When there was plenty, cooks got creative. In times of starvation, every plant, insect and animal became a food. Over time, virtually every living organism has been studied and arranged by the Chinese into a dish, ranging from the simplest to the most hedonistic, ready to be summoned for either a feast or a particularly harsh time. Shark fin soups or sea cucumbers often come out when Chinese want to impress guests. But diets in times of starvation looked jarring. Jonathan Spence in "Chinese Roundabout" quotes what foreign travelers recorded: "Flour of ground leaves, sawdust, thistles, cotton seeds, peanut hulls, ground pumice."[2]

Food is also central to traditional Chinese medicine. In every culture, you'll find remedies associated with foods and plants, but what's different is how China combined centuries of folk and religious practices into a science. Chinese medicine classifies foods into those that possess a cooling quality, *yin*, or a heating quality, *yang*. Even in today's China, the first thing people do when faced with an ailment is to figure out whether the body is skewed towards *yin* or *yang* based on the foods they have been

---

2   Jonthan Spence – "Chinese Roundabouts" pp166

eating. A healthy person must balance the intake of cooling and heating foods; eating too much of either one leads to sickness. Thus, eating in Chinese culture is also a search for inner balance.

Whether it's about balancing food supplies or maintaining good health, the preoccupation with food has been uninterrupted throughout Chinese history. The search for the right food for the right moment has come to represent a point of balance in itself — continuity amid external turbulence.

A few weeks after my cucumber crisis, another panic hit the country. Shortly before Chinese New Year in 2003, newspapers had reported a strange type of flu affecting people in the southern province of Guangdong. The virus was highly contagious and sometimes lethal. But while the rest of the world started to read and worry about deaths and illness caused by what was now called Severe Acute Respiratory Syndrome, or SARS, the Chinese government and media simply denied the presence of the virus within China's borders. This was a hallmark example of how the Chinese bureaucracy tends to respond to crises: Pretend they don't exist in the hope that they will go away and not present a risk to social stability.

Local governments, in particular, preferred to suppress potential problems rather than risk being punished for allowing something bad to happen on their watch. As a result, there were few domestic SARS cases identified officially. According to local authorities, the virus, a pneumonia-like infection that causes coughing, high fevers and, in some cases, death, was a foreign problem; we were all in the safest place on the planet.

Around March 2003, Jane and I were biking in the hills north of Beijing when we hit a road block assembled by local villagers. When we asked why we couldn't get through on a path we had used many times before, one man acting like he was in charge replied in Beijing's guttural accent: "The road is blocked to prevent contamination from SARS."

Others around him nodded in agreement.

"But there are still people crossing, and you're letting them through," I said, pointing at other bikers going back and forth through the makeshift fence, despite the warning signs.

The villagers laughed first, probably wondering why I even asked the question. It was obvious. "Well, they're not foreigners," the man said. "Foreigners are infected, and they brought SARS to China. That's why you can't go."

The villagers weren't aggressive. They were, in a way, being logical. The Chinese media said China was safe while the rest of the world was infected. It made total sense to bar foreigners from coming in.

I tried to explain that "quarantine" meant that they should stop everyone, not just the one white man. They laughed as if they agreed with me. But they didn't budge. The virus, they believed, simply couldn't pass to a Chinese person. The man in charge continued: "The only way Chinese get infected is when foreign blood has been in contact with theirs."

Another villager jumped in: "Chinese eat a lot of garlic; they've become immune to the virus."

After half an hour of back-and-forth questions and answers, they said they would let Jane through. Chinese in the countryside tended to assume that she was one of them because she was Asian.

Jane looked at me with an ironic smile. She was in and I was out. I thought about launching into a tirade against profiling and racial bias, but I knew there was no way I could reason with the villagers. To them, their logic was ironclad. Laughing at my outrage, Jane decided to follow me as we took a path around the village after waving good-bye to the unwavering but still smiling gate-keepers.

When I talked to our staffers at Creative Food about my Beijing story, I found that they too believed the local media. Nobody had any idea how anyone could block this virus from crossing the borders, but if the government said so, then it had to be true. Even Mike said, "China is different."

For weeks, I read about international health authorities scrambling to make sense of the new threat. In China, though, health officials suggested there already were a number of drugs to fight SARS. Rumors abounded, and as the villagers had suggested, garlic prices shot up when someone wrote that garlic contained SARS-fighting chemicals. But nobody wanted to address the truth. The official number of SARS-infected patients in Beijing was twelve cases as of March 2003. At a press conference on April 3, the Minister of Health even called out a foreign journalist wearing a mask with a mocking tone. "You're safe here, whether you wear the gauze mask or not," he said, chuckling.

Finally, after weeks of reports in foreign media about the prevalence of cases in different Chinese cities and statements of concern from health authorities around the world, Beijing came clean. The government acknowledged the existence of hundreds of SARS cases within its borders. The new prime minister, Wen Jiabao, sacked the Beijing mayor as well as the health minister, blaming them for hiding the true scale of the disease in China. A prominent vice premier took responsibility for fighting SARS as a way to show the leadership's commitment. Reports became more transparent and regular. Beijing's official numbers jumped to sixty cases. Shanghai was strangely low, with only two cases. Guangzhou, with 1,511 cases and 58 deaths,[3] was the worst-affected in mainland China, while Hong Kong, where the first

---

3   NCBI-Zhonghua Yu Fang Yi Xue Za Zhi. 2003 Jul;37(4):227-32.

rash of cases had been identified, saw 1,755 cases and 298 deaths.

All this was bad news for me, coming as it did just as things were starting to improve for Creative Food. Our plant in Guangzhou, which shipped lettuce to Hong Kong and Guangdong province in the south, was too small to accommodate the new business we were winning. I had convinced KFC to stop its search for a second supplier there, promising that Creative Food would build a new plant near KFC's distribution center before the summer. But now that the central government had recognized the severity of the SARS crisis, all travelers to infected areas such as Beijing and Guangzhou were quarantined at home upon their return for ten days, the period needed for the virus to incubate.

That meant each time any of my employees went to Guangzhou — we needed engineers, quality experts and all sorts of managers down there during construction — the person was out of reach for two weeks.

I kept a complicated roster to make sure that my key managers were not all travelling to the south at the same time. I bought laptops and video cameras so they and others in quarantine could join our meetings. And we continued to talk daily on the phone.

But scrutiny increased. The hygiene bureau requested that we record every worker's temperature at the entrance of our premises. From a state of denial only a week before, health inspectors now roamed paranoid inside our facilities, grabbing random workers to check their temperature with a gun-like device they stuck in people's ears. If ever anyone got caught with a simple flu, I knew they would get dispatched to a special hospital together with SARS patients. In the worst-case scenario, my plant might even be shut down.

By the summer, SARS news slowly fell away from the front page. The lady at the vegetable stall down the street from my apartment, who had emerged as an enforcer of the neighborhood committee to control outsiders, took the red band off her arm, and a warm smile reappeared on her face. But while that crisis was over, it had made me very aware that the systems in place to control diseases and other forms of contamination — including pathogens on foods — were inadequate.

The earlier battle over tainted spinach exported to Japan had exposed huge gaps in the way China treated food safety. But there was always a suspicion that the Japanese had made it a bigger deal than it really was. After SARS, the government couldn't claim any longer that critics of its supervision and crisis-management systems had vindictive agendas or that China was immune to outside risks. Because China was an increasingly large exporter of foods to the rest of the world, its systemic flaws were starting to show up in the accumulation of tainted foods caught at borders. And it wasn't just in Japan.

A year before the SARS epidemic, in November 2001, several European nations stopped shipments of Chinese chicken, honey, and shrimp after the foods were found to contain banned substances such as chloramphenicol, a potent antibiotic capable of damaging bone marrow in humans banned in food processing in the EU since 1994. The investigations of the European Union's Food and Veterinary Office that followed these bans revealed more weaknesses across the Chinese system charged with ensuring food safety. There was a lack of coordination between regulatory agencies, no central registration of veterinary drugs, and many inconsistencies in the allowable thresholds of those drugs at the provincial level. Taken together, the reports showed a secretive culture among the very officials who were supposed to guarantee safe food production in China — the same attitudes I had seen at work myself.

European experts who came to China could only visit

places that the Chinese authorities had selected and vetted. I can imagine that they were shown what were perceived at the time as the best aquaculture farms, labs and veterinary centers. The fact that even these heavily-supervised visits managed to produce reports that uncovered problems tells a lot about the general level of ignorance among their minders.

The reports were damning. There was no clear set of civil or criminal sanctions for the companies caught using banned veterinary products or exceeding approved thresholds, one report said[4]. Even worse, food samples destined for lab tests were collected only when accidents happened rather than systematically throughout the year. Rules regarding which veterinary product could be used and what residue level was acceptable weren't applied or weren't consistent across the country. One circular issued by the Ministry of Agriculture referred to minimum residue levels for chloramphenicol ten times higher than another document issued by the same ministry. Chloramphenicol on-farm tests were required by the Ministry of Agriculture in six provinces but not in Shandong, home to ten of the fourteen poultry exporters approved by the EU. Meanwhile, as no livestock prescription system existed, antibiotics were available over the counter and could be procured in one province for use in another.

The honey and aquaculture farms Chinese authorities showed to the Europeans had all the trappings of modern farms; the problem was they weren't in operation yet. When experts asked to see the plants behind the tainted foods caught at their borders, they were told that the factories weren't producing during their visits.

---

4   EU-Food and Veterinary Office DG (SANCO) 3280/2001 Final: "Final report of a mission carried out in China from 8 to 22 November 2001 in order to evaluate the control of residues in live animals and animal products"

Another key issue that jumped out from these European reports was how little communication there was among government agencies in China. The system was described as a hodgepodge of bureaus and ministry branches, each operating in its own region, issuing different sets of rules and reacting haphazardly to food crises. I witnessed how disconnected the system was with my own broccoli exports after the Japanese spinach crisis: agents from the Administration of Quality Supervision, Inspection and Quarantine, the agency supervising exporters, tended to react fast and demanded strict monitoring of our farms. But the local branches of the Ministry of Agriculture, whose responsibility it was to actually monitor the farms, never showed up to check anything.

So, given the obvious gaps in the system, how did China respond to the reports' findings? By first denying that the problems even existed, as they had with SARS. When confronted with the presence of a banned antibiotic in frozen shrimp exported to Europe, the Chinese response was to dismiss it entirely. The justification was even more puzzling. "The chloramphenicol came from a cream that the factory workers used to treat wounds on their hands," a statement from the Ministry of Agriculture said.

I suspected that the Old Hundred Names working in the factories didn't use any cream on their hands—period. They barely took any medicine if they were sick; I was sure they viewed hand cream as a useless luxury.

After the EU investigations were completed, it became harder for the Chinese authorities to deny the existence of any problems. So, officials switched gears, saying the problems were isolated and that the tainted foods in question "were not representative of China's larger set of exporters."

This statement resembled declarations I had seen during both the spinach and the SARS crises. First, deny the issue. Then argue that the problem is limited to a few bad apples. Finally, when confronted with hard facts, blame the foreigners' ignorance about all things Chinese. "EU experts don't understand China's legal system," one of the official responses to the report went on.

As China emerged on the global scene with its much-celebrated joining of the World Trade Organization in 2001, these issues just looked too bad to be acknowledged officially. But the reality was that the regulatory system, the network of inspectors, and the laws and the practices hadn't kept up with the speed of growth in the food factories of China.

At my level, meanwhile, almost nothing changed. The only new rule I saw—the requirement to register farms—was just for the products I exported. It didn't affect the lettuce I cut for KFC. So even as my own uneasiness about food safety issues at Creative Food grew, transforming from a vague consciousness to a real worry, I remained able to shove it aside amid more immediate concerns—like the rapid growth of the company, growth I wasn't sure I would be able to keep up with.

After a drop in sales during SARS, business at Creative Food quickly recovered. Customers stayed away from restaurants for a while, worried about mixing in large crowds and possibly contracting illnesses. But as soon as media reports faded, sales picked up so fast that by end of 2003, I was exceeding all my targets.

There was a reason KFC had pushed so hard for Creative Food to invest in new machinery and plants. During the 1990s, the brand had built around 500 stores in China. By 2002, its store numbers exceeded 1,000. In two years, it had built more stores than it had in the preceding decade. More impressive, by 2003 KFC was on track to reach 2,000 stores in China—another doubling of its business. Its biggest push was in southern provinces, where

McDonald's historically had a strong foothold. That was why I was rushing to build that new plant in Guangzhou in the middle of the SARS crisis. KFC had named the military-like advance "Strike-Back" — an army pushing its fried chicken deep into hamburger-and-french-fries territory. It wasn't hard to guess who was on the dark side in their corporate metaphor.

In this battle for supremacy over the Golden Arches, Sam Su, true to his character, wasn't subtle. In large events for KFC's more than five hundred suppliers, he hammered out the same message: "We've built this amazing company, and you guys have been lucky to grow with us. But you need to prove yourselves."

Two years earlier, I would have been elated. But now, everyone at Creative Food was showing signs of exhaustion. Problems piled up unresolved, and the phones were so constantly ringing we couldn't have a meeting without being interrupted. KFC's mandate that we prove ourselves meant more investment and more expansion, while we also, somehow, had to bring our prices down.

To reach its goals, Yum created an annual tender process for all its food purchases. This meant there was no more negotiating on the prices they paid us, no consideration of how much I paid for my lettuce or for my workers. If the price I offered them was the lowest, then I got a larger chunk of their business. Every year, I spent weeks trying to calculate what the winning price would be, offsetting concessions here with increases there, as I calculated the right price for the tender.

But I had no control over what my competition would offer. In every region, new companies who had watched Creative Food's fast expansion with envy started to set up plants and knocked at KFC's door to get a piece of the vegetable-processing business. In Beijing, my own supplier — one of the rare professional growers I had developed — built a factory and turned into a competitor.

To its credit, KFC conducted a long technical review, and many would-be usurpers didn't pass muster. But by the time companies were approved, desperation after such a long wait led to very aggressive pricing.

When I lost one-third of my business in Shanghai to a new competitor and was offered the right to match the much lower price or lose even more volume, it felt so unfair that I called a meeting with the local KFC buyer to try and change his views. The man, a Shanghai native in his late forties with years spent in state-owned companies, greeted me with an openly bored expression on his face, barely squeezing my hand as if I wasn't worth his energy. He sat down, flanked by two junior buyers.

I made my case: My long experience supplying KFC should have given me an advantage in the bidding wars; I should not have to match the aggressive prices of all these newcomers.

"If others judge they can make money at that price, why wouldn't you?" he said, echoing what Sam Su had said to me in that fateful meeting two years before.

I argued that I had been around for more than five years, since the Asiafoods days. "Surely you value stability among your suppliers?" I said, trying to suggest that some of my new rivals might close shop as fast as they had opened. It didn't move him.

"Well, these are the rules, and you can't just come after the fact and try to change them," he said.

I insisted that as I was investing in other regions to help KFC, I needed to keep the volume I already had, but he turned visibly annoyed.

"*jiu shi zheyang!*" he said bluntly, which meant "It is what it is!" He continued: "There are plenty of candidates to replace you if you aren't happy with the system."

Before I could think of what to do next, he gave me a big smile. "How do I know a supplier has given me his best price?"

I waited in silence, trying to show respect rather than annoyance.

"When the supplier goes out of business," he said.

The two junior buyers laughed.

I had no choice. Once again, I had to figure ways of improving productivity while we were building new plants. Meanwhile, our employees were complaining that they hadn't had a pay raise in two years.

Reacting to the pressure from Yum, I pressed my own suppliers in turn. I didn't organize tenders, but I negotiated hard, demanding that they bring prices down in exchange for more volume, while requiring them to expand in new regions. It's a safe bet my suppliers squeezed farmers further as well to offset the lower costs they charged me. The squeeze culture went down the chain, forcing everyone to cut corners.

My story was really a global one. More people around the world wanted cheap goods from China. The market grew bigger while the supply stayed fragmented, giving buyers more ammunition to push costs down and leaving less money for suppliers like Creative Food to invest and modernize.

The more I expanded, the more villagers got involved in growing lettuce for me. But none of them got any better at it. Amid all the pressure, farmers threw unsafe chemicals into the water, sprayed them onto their crops or injected them into their animals. My suppliers dipped their vegetables into water buckets to increase weight or reduce temperature when they didn't want to use costly refrigerated trucks, causing waste, mold, and bacterial contamination, not to mention low-quality lettuce leaves. In other areas of agriculture, more dangerous practices took place daily. Some producers added toxic coloring agents to brighten red meat or diluted milk with plastics that showed up on tests as protein.

I felt increasingly uncomfortable showing investors Shanghai's glittering skyline as a way to convince them that my business had an amazing future amid China's exponential growth. Behind the curtain of China's modernization loomed this shadowy food chain that had no connection whatsoever with the modern-looking store fronts and factories I showed my visitors. I knew that thousands of my farmers pushed wheelbarrows full of lettuce off their fields and onto dirt roads, where it sat until flatbed trucks could come to pick it up hours later. These trucks then carried the wrinkled and molding vegetables away to other trucks in nearby towns in a grinding process of repeated loading and unloading that ended at my plants.

The national preoccupation with food remained as the Chinese people spent more of their hard-earned cash at new restaurants and on expensive items like meat, milk and seafood. But in the race for a piece of growing markets at home and abroad, a moral vacuum had been created. There was a strange absence of guilt among the people I worked with.

One KFC executive acknowledged as much. "After three years of price decreases thanks to the tenders we implemented, who will now have the guts to turn to Sam and say we need to increase prices if we want our suppliers to do a better job?" he said. "You're talking tens of millions of dollars."

Everyone knew that tackling food safety risks made production slower and more expensive, so we all looked ahead instead. I myself felt the pull. I didn't do sampling tests or control what I bought as I should have. Years later, I remembered those days as I watched cycling champion Lance Armstrong admit to doping. To defend his well-oiled drug procurement system, he said that it was impossible to compete cleanly because the use of drugs was so widespread among competitors. Cycling authorities couldn't keep up with the new techniques used to hide the performance enhancers, and some speculate they didn't want to. Armstrong was saying that he *had* to dope to compete.

I didn't want to be like Armstrong. But I still needed to find ways to stay competitive for all the people who had trusted me with their money, and all of Creative Food's devoted employees. In the end, the dilemma brought me back to the heart of the issue: the very countryside I had deliberately avoided for the past couple of years.

10

THE LETTUCE POLICE

MORE THAN two years had passed since the villager's riots in Qipanshan and the hostage crisis in Linhai. After those dramatic failures, I had stayed away from farming. But 2003 was going to be my comeback year. I knew I couldn't go on ignoring food safety threats.

The network of traders I had relied on since the turnaround had now morphed into a solid group. Confident that they now had a steady buyer for their vegetables, many had even started to grow some lettuce themselves instead of buying from an intermediary, partnering along the way with villages and even investing in their own farms. A dozen Creative Food suppliers indirectly employed close to five thousand farmers.

When I started Creative Food, I signed contracts for lettuce I never saw. During the turn-around years, I watched traders guard those crops in ways that were totally foreign to me. Near Shanghai, one of them had local policemen surround the fields so that villagers wouldn't plunder his crop and sell it to higher bidders. "Without your police to watch over my lettuce," this trader told the local party secretary, "I'll take my business to the next town." That would mean the loss of hundreds of local jobs, so every season, the party secretary sent a cordon of policemen to block access to the crop for the few days before the harvest.

Now, policemen were no longer necessary. Creative Food was here to stay, and farmers knew that selling their crop to me would guarantee them long-term business. In a rural economy where cash was king, I was even able to negotiate terms up to thirty days. I had finally created a community where everyone benefited. Life was becoming predictable, which turned out to be invaluable for everyone: The villagers made money, the traders had a steady stream of orders—and Creative Food had dependable volumes at stable prices, while I kept busy building new plants.

But that had resolved only the issue of consistent supply. Still baffling us was the problem of ensuring that our lettuce was free of harmful pesticides and germs. And there was so much we didn't know. I remembered that Michael Tani, whom I had hired to improve farming operations, had talked about temperature-resistant seeds and fertilizers adapted to certain soils. But none of my suppliers had the time, interest, knowledge or resources to try out those innovations.

In moral terms, my position was getting more ambiguous, too. I could explain away some unconventional choices when the company was new. But now that I was expanding and turning a profit, it was harder for me to ignore the fact that tens of thousands of people ate my lettuce every day. Reputable restaurant chains worked with Creative Food because I implied that no food scandals would erupt if they bought from us. They relied on us to keep their brands untainted.

Our options were limited. We could try running our own farms, but farming is risky. We could lose everything if the weather turned bad or if pests and diseases hit. And I badly needed all my cash to fund new factories and stay ahead of KFC's long line of suitors. Also, I had neglected my team of agronomists as I retreated from farming in order to save the company.

There was a lot I could offer to improve farming practices: new varieties of seeds, different types of fertilizers, better practices for pesticide application and some modest mechanization. But before they would even consider changing their ways, suppliers, like farmers, needed to see that the new practices would work. Lu's plaintive voice in the broccoli field two years before, when I had asked him to harvest his broccoli earlier than villagers normally did, continued to play in my mind. The only way to convince the farmers was to show good results myself.

I hit on the idea of building a small model farm, a place where I could try new ideas, new seeds, and new tools. If these experiments didn't work, the financial impact would be limited. But if they worked, employing a set of safer practices would set me apart from the crowd of competitors—and ease my conscience.

Once more, I had to find enough cash to fund the idea. My shareholder, the German Development Bank, had an aid department separate from its investment arm for funding poverty alleviation programs. I applied for it and was awarded a $160,000 grant to cover all operating costs for a model farm for one year, including the hiring of a technical advisor.

With the lettuce farms that supplied our company spread widely from the Vietnamese border in China's southwest to the Inner Mongolia plateau in the north, I had to choose the most relevant place to set up the two farms I had in mind—one for the summer season and one for spring and autumn. Two years earlier, our company's winning bid to supply KFC in Wuhan, in central China, had marked a new start for me there. I had been shipping to our Wuhan operations from Beijing in the summer and from Shanghai in the winter, but I knew KFC would look for someone else locally if I didn't quickly build a plant in Wuhan. I decided that one of the two model farms would be located near the new plant we had built there in 2003, in a town called Xinzhou. The other would be based in Inner Mongolia, the place where we could grow lettuce in the summer when the rest of the country was too hot and humid to grow anything.

Once again, I resolved to change one thousand years of farming behavior, but this time respectfully — by showing, not telling.

To begin, I needed an expert. I conducted a search by posting ads in agricultural trade magazines in the U.S., but not one application resulted. China probably sounded too scary or too foreign. I changed tactics and posted an ad on Monster.com: "An agriculture start-up in China is seeking an adventurous professional to train Chinese farmers." I was looking for someone with an attitude, rather than just a set of skills. When Doug Trett saw it, he immediately applied.

Doug was a certified expert on pesticide application — someone with the very skills we would need in China. But above all he was a farmer, a man who loved toiling in the earth. He had run his own cotton farm in the arid San Joaquin Valley, in Chowchilla, northwest of Fresno. At 770 acres, it wasn't a large farm by California standards, and his stepbrother's 4,500-acre spread nearby dwarfed it. But it was Doug's little piece of heaven, and a great place to farm raw crops like cotton. He leased most of the land that he farmed, except for 120 acres he had bought two years before.

"I put in all my savings to buy that piece of land and that was a mistake," he told me when we first met. "I had no more cash to get me though a bad season; that's what got me in the end."

In October 2000, his local bank decided to stop all small loans to farmers, and suddenly, Doug had to come up with hundreds of thousands of dollars or close shop. His wife of twenty years, a certified public accountant, refused Doug's suggestion to mortgage the house or use family savings to keep the farm afloat.

"I never liked the farm," she said when he pressed her.

"You never liked the farm," Doug answered, "and I never liked the marriage."

That was that. As much as he regretted those words when they came out of his mouth, he couldn't take them back. They had met when he was fifteen, married when he was nineteen and had a son together. The ensuing divorce was bitter. Running Creative Food's model farms became the adventure that helped him forget the pain of divorce and the loss of what had been his life's dream.

"I like farming," he said. "I like the change of seasons and being able to start afresh every year. I will bring my sleeping bag and stay wherever your farm is."

Doug's unkempt gray hair and blue eyes behind round glasses gave him a professorial look belied by his broad fingers and thick nails. His worn jeans and heavy boots indicated what mattered to him. He arrived in the autumn of 2002 and worked with Sun Guoqiang, my agronomist who had been held hostage in Linhai. He translated for Doug, and I also trusted him to balance out some of the American's less realistic suggestions. In our new company culture, I wanted foreigners to act as advisors, while Chinese led. Doug's mandate was to experiment with lettuce-growing practices, not to overhaul Chinese agriculture.

I enjoyed the comfort of sharing a common language with him, but I was careful to treat him like any other employee, avoiding falling into frequent one-on-one meetings and casual lunches. He was our company's only foreign employee at the time, so it probably wasn't easy for him. But I knew staffers instinctively lumped foreigners together, suspecting that all outsiders were united by a secret pact. I didn't want to break the fragile bond that I had finally forged with my ever-watchful

Chinese colleagues. While Doug was here to help everyone improve, I hovered over his project like a hawk—and I wouldn't have hesitated to send him back home if he refused to listen to people who knew less about farming but had been dealing with Chinese farmers for much longer than he had.

Doug's early comments were encouraging. For the first time, I was hearing practical suggestions to improve farming instead of complaints about the dire state of China's agriculture. He didn't grouse about China and the ways of its farmers. He didn't complain about how backward they were or claim that the only way forward was to replicate methods from California. He understood intuitively, for example, that the amount of capital needed to buy the equipment he used in the U.S. would never make economic sense given China's short growing seasons and cheap labor. Instead, he made an effort to blend his experience with reality. I also liked that many of his suggestions didn't cost anything at all.

"See, Xey-vieurrr," he said one afternoon at a farm near Shanghai during his assessment period. "Look here, how the roots of our seedlings are attacked by rot."

I nodded while looking at the tiny plant quivering between his fingers.

"That's because you're waiting too long before transplanting them," Doug said.

Creative Food's suppliers grew small seedlings inside greenhouses during the winter to protect them from the cold, and then transplanted them into the fields when temperatures turned milder. Why, I wondered, hadn't anyone mentioned that before? If transplanting earlier meant healthier plants, it meant larger lettuce heads too—all for the same cost.

After a few weeks of observation, Doug determined that he needed to buy certain pieces of equipment, but he would do the designs himself and have them custom-built in China. Michael Tani had always seemed lost in China, uprooted from the vast tracts of land and high productivity he had known back home. Doug in contrast rarely referred to California except to highlight how different things were. He would need lighter, transportable pieces of machinery that he could move through the patchwork of plots surrounding our land and from farm to farm every three months or so.

First, he needed a tractor to pull a ripper, a piece of equipment that helps loosen and aerate the soil, while cutting down weed roots. The giant jaw-like device plowed deeper and more consistently than the traditional tool of choice, a chisel pulled by a water buffalo. With those, local farmers plowed down only about eight inches into the soil. This upper layer, cultivated every season for decades or centuries, had lost all its nutrients. It did not provide the crop with the energy to grow.

"Xey-vieurrr, you put weaklings in poor ground, you'll only get tennis balls," Doug would tell me. By "tennis balls," Doug meant Chinese heads of lettuce that were roughly one third the size of lettuce heads grown in California. The quality of the leaves was inferior, too. Workers on the processing lines threw away nearly 70 percent of a lettuce head to meet KFC's specifications. In California, the loss was only half that.

In Qipanshan, Yang had already observed that shallowly plowed soils meant weaker lettuce. But Doug analyzed it for me better. "Here," he showed me, again with a small seedling in his hand. "The root pushes down vertically in the smooth upper layer."

He dangled the small root in the air as if it was drilling through invisible soil. "But then it hits the hard part and it starts growing horizontally," he went on, holding the small root with his other hand to form a perpendicular angle.

Years of built-up sedimentation had created a barrier impossible for small plants to push through. This prevented the roots from digging deep enough. Each time the weather heated up, the shallow upper soil dried out and the lettuce, unable to dig deeper to capture the water it needed, wilted and weakened.

"I just need a ripper to open up the soil," Doug concluded. Not only did it make perfect sense from an agronomic point of view, but with $10 million worth of lettuce purchased that year, I would save a lot if I fixed the issue and got even slightly bigger heads.

"I'll buy as many rippers as Doug wants if it saves me money," I thought.

The problem was that nobody wanted to build Doug's ripper. Many of the tools he had in mind were actually "made-in-China." But the factories that manufactured them did so based on specifications from foreign buyers—and in large quantities. They sent all their production toward export markets, simply because there wasn't a demand for it in China. When Doug asked, established Chinese manufacturers ignored him, mostly because they didn't want to be bothered customizing a piece or two while they rammed hundreds of standard machines into containers every week. Doug spent days roaming Shanghai's machinery shops, often lined up along the same road and selling the same basic spare parts.

But he did buy a tractor. It took him only a few days to locate a John Deere joint-venture in North China, but much longer to find how to make a purchase from the Kafkaesque state-owned maker. He and Sun spent hours begging for the right to buy one of their tractors while the salespeople argued that they couldn't sell to a foreign-owned company in China. In the end, they found a reasonable executive, who made an exception.

But locating a ripper proved impossible. He also needed a

chisel plow to break down pieces of mud and aerate the soil, then a share plow to form the beds on which lettuce would grow, and finally a sprayer to uniformly apply pesticides to the crop. A sprayer pulled by a tractor moving at a steady pace, as Doug wanted, would remedy the problem of inconsistent pesticide application Yang had noticed back in Qipanshan.

He would need to build all these things himself.

Since none of the big manufacturers wanted to help, Doug found a basic scrap-metal workshop in a village near our factory and, side by side with Sun and the shop's owner, worked until he got the design and the quality he wanted. It was a learning experience for a man who, despite his farming background, was no agricultural engineer.

Doug also wanted to find a plastic tank for the pesticide sprayer but never found the shape he wanted. So, he built one from scratch out of stainless steel and bought the necessary spray nozzles on one of his trips to Hong Kong to renew his visa. He had no idea about issues such as pump pressure, or insulation. But he and Sun searched the internet, then tried and failed until they got it right. That street workshop trained Doug for life in the countryside. There too, he would be on his own.

The site of our model farm near Xinzhou Town on the central China plain near Wuhan was anything but charming. The land was flat; stagnant fish ponds encircled the fields. The town had planted trees along the roads, but otherwise the landscape was bare. Garbage of all sorts littered the roadsides: seed sacks, fertilizer, empty plastic pesticide bags. The architectural style might be called Chinese Provincial Generic, its buildings faced in white ceramic tile with blue-tinted glass windows. Most houses were bare concrete frames without heating and sometimes without electricity. Many villagers' homes had dirt floors, as their occupants could not yet afford to lay concrete.

The fields surrounding Xinzhou mostly grew rice and cotton from spring to autumn. During the winter, farmers switched to wheat. As in most parts of the country, farming was done on a very small scale by village families who wasted nothing, using the wheat straw left over after harvest to make bricks, and planting cotton rows next to wheat rows to speed up the transition from one crop to another as seasons ended. Harvested cotton was left to fluff up on the roadside. As a former cotton grower, Doug wasn't impressed. "It's made of knotty balls of very poor quality, nothing like what we do in California," he observed on a drive through the area. And there were better places than Xinzhou to grow lettuce, like the slopes Doug saw in the mountains far west of Wuhan, where China would later open the world's largest power station—The *Three Gorges* Dam.

But he did like Xinzhou's Communist Party Secretary. Wu Meiying was a short heavyset woman getting close to retirement age. She spoke in an earthy local dialect that I didn't understand, smoked cigarettes non-stop and drank bottles of *baijiu*, the local sorghum-distilled alcohol. Her leathery face was worn by years of sun exposure, and her voice never got below the "loud" setting. When she spoke at me—rather than to me—I could imagine her haranguing crowds in villages around the county. Behind her smile lay thirty years of life in the countryside, the brutal tactics of decades of political campaigns and the hard life of pushing wheelbarrows and weeding fields.

"Chairman Li!" she bawled at a banquet for my visit, using my Chinese name. "Xinzhou government will iron out any difficulty for your investments here!" As I smiled back noncommittally, she grabbed my arm and pushed a glass of *baijiu* into my hand, shouting, "*Ganbei* (bottoms-up) to the great future of Creative Food in Xinzhou!"

Wu and Doug had the kind of straightforward relationship

that transcends language barriers. Doug could see that behind her theatrics and blunt demeanor, she genuinely cared for her community and forcefully pushed for change. Banquets were just a platform for her, not an end in themselves. After an initial visit by Mike and I, Wu had viewed our plan to set up a model farm as an opportunity for her underdeveloped county. She directed officials at a state-owned experimental farm to set aside seventeen acres of contiguous land for us. The plots were near a place known as Village Number 9, named after a communal production brigade formed during the 1950s collectivization campaign.

Doug immediately ran up against local resistance. He needed to access irrigation water, but the state farm officials delayed digging the promised well. He needed to hire locals to work for him, but villagers, knowing there was no competition, asked for salaries that were much more than the $10 day-rate they charged among themselves when helping with farm work. He needed to train and direct them, but they thought their ways were better than his. But each time he struggled with villagers or the National Farm officials, he asked his Chinese colleague Sun to reach out to Wu, and things usually fell in place.

Doug often said, "People lie, but Ms. Wu fixes the problem each time I call her. She gathers people for a meal, they drink three bottles of *baijiu*, smoke two cartons of cigarettes and she makes things happen."

Doug rarely complained, but his life in Xinzhou was bleak. For nearly a year, he lived in the village's guesthouse. The path to his hotel was a dark, narrow and slippery street, littered with plastic bottles and discarded rubbish. At dusk, the shadows of enormous rats flashed through the small lane. The hotel where he and Sun lived was built of concrete once painted white, but the layer of cheap primer had gotten moldy and black streaks were visible everywhere. There was no indoor heating, and Doug bought a small portable heater from Shanghai, but the uninsulated concrete let the wet cold seep through anyway, freezing him as soon as he moved away from the heater. Amenities outside weren't much better. Once while visiting, I walked around the town looking for snacks, but I couldn't find one single piece of chocolate—the local treat was jellified duck blood and dried gizzards, both wrapped in thick vacuumed plastic and covered in labels vouching for the safety of its origin. Whenever I visited Xinzhou, I hurried back to Shanghai as soon as I could. But Doug stayed there for months on end.

As the long winter of 2003 turned into spring, Doug was more and more impatient waiting to get his tractor into the field. He had sat through endless meetings with town and village officials and waited out continuous hard rain. He had a piece of land, the equipment he had worked hard to acquire and, in some cases, had built himself, was ready. He knew he needed to start working the field before April or the harvest would be delayed, and if summer came earlier than expected, his lettuce crop would be subjected to a deadly June heat wave that could wipe it out.

One day, seeing an opening after a couple of days without rain, he rushed his John Deere tractor into the field. But an oil-fluid leak in the steering wheel caused it to drive into a ditch. Doug had to get fifteen people to help fill it and extract his beloved machine. From day one, something had broken each time he had tried it. The day he tested the ripper, the jaws bogged down in the wet soil and it fell sideways with a thud. The first intense pull had torn off one of the blades they had carefully welded onto the frame in the Shanghai workshop.

Increasingly when he talked to me, Doug's voice sounded shaky as he described whatever had caused a new delay—the incessant rain, uncooperative villagers, or another equipment breakdown. I too started to get anxious, so I kept calling, adding to his distress without providing any practical advice. Deep down, I believed he wasn't making enough of an effort and I began to worry that he was another of "those" expats after all, doing nothing but complaining about China. Dismissive of what he had to deal with every day despite my experience in Qipanshan and elsewhere, I unconsciously bullied him. Doug told me later he feared that he would be fired.

By the time he pulled into the field on a day in late March when the endless rain had finally stopped, he was no longer the confident hand I had met in Shanghai. That day, he finally attached the ripper to the tractor's trailer, drove the tractor to the edge of the field, and maneuvered between the trees that the government-run farm had planted to beautify the site. He was ready to do the work of plowing deeper than this land had been plowed in decades.

Suddenly, a group of local farmers stepped onto the field, halting his progress.

"What's going on here?" Doug asked with some irritation.

The farmers told him that the land belonged to them.

Doug didn't think twice, answering like any American would: "I have a contract. This is *my* land."

He then engaged the gears of the tractor, and drove on, very slowly, expecting the farmers to move out of his way. He was relieved to see that the tractor seemed to be working in the deep mud. But, as he later recounted, "There was this woman in front of me who stayed there, like the guy in front of the tank in Tiananmen."

He turned the machine away from the group of around twenty farmers toward the opposite corner of the field, but the woman followed him and once again threw herself in front of the tractor.

"It can't be all her land," thought Doug, who knew the parcel had been put together from the former holdings of several villagers.

Then the woman tripped on a mud clod and fell on her back, and the tractor's wheel ran over her right foot. Doug stopped, horrified. The women lay in the mud, seemingly unconscious. An ominous silence fell on the field. Doug was in shock.

"Wrong, wrong, wrong," Doug thought in desperation. "I hurt that woman, I'm going to jail, and I will never see home and family again."

Sure enough, people started to scream and wail. Some scrambled around the woman, some grabbed shovels and moved angrily on Doug. That's when Sun told him to run as fast as he could to his hotel. Doug obeyed. And once behind the locked door, he picked up his phone and called me.

I was visiting our Beijing plant, where the cellular signal was patchy at best and my bald head froze as I stepped out of the office into the factory yard with the phone still ringing. When he spoke, Doug didn't waste time with niceties.

"Xey-vieurrr," he shrieked, "you gotta come and get me out of here! It's World War III here!"

His voice rose to an even more frantic pitch. "I am locked in my hotel room. They want to get me! They want to kill me!"

Images of angry farmers with shovels and pickaxes kicking down his door floated before my eyes. Then the line went dead.

In the seconds that followed his panicked call to me, I took a deep breath and stood alone at the gate of our factory, waiting for my phone to buzz again as darkness set in over the hills behind the Beijing plant. But no call came. His phone was unreachable.

I called Mike and then a manager named Xu Shen. Xu had handled our broccoli shipments to Japan, and was now my head of procurement. He supervised all our suppliers' farms, including the model farm. He ranked above Sun since Yang had departed, and we agreed he would fly immediately to Wuhan and find out what had happened. After a few calls on his way to the airport that night, Xu reported that Secretary Wu was already on the case. She had ordered the farmers to go home, but nobody had told Doug. Sun was busy trying to calm down the villagers. Doug was so frightened that he hid out in his hotel room.

"I feared they'd come and lynch me," he told me later.

The next day, Secretary Wu called a meeting with my employees also present. Xu discovered that the funds we had paid for the land to the experimental farm had only partially been distributed to the farmers. Had someone been shuffling money on the side? Was there an agreement for the farm to retain some of the proceeds to fund village expenses? I didn't know because my contract was with the state-owned farm, which acted as the villagers' representative. But the good news was that the woman protestor whom Doug thought he had seriously harmed had not been hurt. The soil had been softened by the rain, and her foot only got bruised. The villagers even said the woman was known to be a little unstable. The farm agreed to increase payments to the farmers, and everything got settled with Secretary Wu presiding around a few more glasses of *baijiu* and a couple more packs of cigarettes.

Doug was no quitter. The day after Wu intervened, he resumed his simple daily routine that started with coffee and noodles prepared by his hotel's owner, then continued with a twenty-minute taxi ride to one of his greenhouses full of seedlings. The plan was to transplant the lettuce seedlings to the fields as soon as the rain stopped. His seedlings grew inside the greenhouses in small square boxes tucked in black plastic trays, rooted in fertilized peat and protected by plastic tunnels from the cold outside. Doug entered these warm, clammy tunnels and knelt on the floor surrounded by curious farmers, examining the precious plants for signs of disease or overgrowth, both of which could affect their survival chances once in the field.

Part of the arrangement with the German Development Bank was that we would train hundreds of farmers in our new techniques. With Sun acting as translator, Doug spent time in the greenhouses with groups as large as twenty at a time.

"See here, how I do this," he said, looking at the villagers. "I try to remove seedlings delicately with the peat square formed around the roots. I don't pull harshly or it will tear the roots. The peat provides the plant protection from the shock of acclimatizing to a new soil environment. It increases the chance of survival and therefore reduces costs."

As Doug spoke, the villagers made loud comments in a local dialect so thick that Sun could not comprehend it. But he knew exactly what they were saying: "Mostly they were criticizing the new way," he told me later.

The villagers in Xinzhou, like the ones in Inner Mongolia more than a thousand miles away, didn't believe they needed special seeds that would thrive in low temperatures, or expensive peat or additional fertilizer. Rooted in their habits, they couldn't grasp why a buyer would pay a higher price for nicer-looking vegetables of a uniform size.

Doug was frustrated, but he also understood their point of view. "What I am telling them is so counterintuitive. I am telling them to spend up-front, put more fertilizer to kickstart the crop. That's all money!"

Our farm was adjacent to the main dirt road heading into the village, so Doug could drive his tractor straight into the field. But everywhere around it, people continued to farm as they had for hundreds of years. The first day he had used his chisel plow with the powerful John Deere tractor, Doug had Sun take a picture of him driving, which also featured a villager wearing a blue Mao suit and straw hat on top of a square plywood-chisel pulled by a water buffalo, oblivious of the giant machinery next to him.

It took some more massaging of relationships—what the Chinese call *guanxi*—before Doug finally got the farmers to at least listen to him. Secretary Wu could make sure he got irrigation water and that the farmers were paid what they were owed for our use of the land, but when it came to managing the way they did their work, she had little leverage. As much as Doug enjoyed noisy banquets with Wu, he understood where the real power lay in this little village. The one person the farmers respected was Xia Lihua, the Village Number 9 committee leader.

"Things really only got better when I won Mr. Xia's trust," Doug said.

Xia, was probably in his mid-thirties, but looked many years older from having toiled under the sun.

"People respected him naturally," said Doug. "Before he spoke, he made long pauses to make sure he was heard."

In countless lunches and dinners with Xia's family while playing with the village leader's primary school-age son, Doug observed life as it was for the villagers. During these meals, chickens roamed free in the house, pecking at the bones and gristle spat out or thrown on the floor by the diners. Doug loved to observe the animals' dance below the table, watching how they jumped and skipped as they tried to grab a morsel of food without being kicked by one of the guests. After the meal, women swept the floor up to the front door, where the less-fortunate chickens fought over what was left.

"The indoor birds, I swear, do not shit in the house," Doug told me. "I often wondered why, and the only reason I can find is they'd become tomorrow's dinner if they did!"

There were also nesting boxes in various corners of the house, where the chickens would lay eggs. "Best eggs I had in China were on that farm," recalled Doug. "Best flavor, best color—a nice dark yellow yolk. It was delicious. If only I could have gotten them over-easy with bacon and hash-brown potatoes."

When villagers employed on the farm saw the relationship between Xia and Doug developing, they finally started to pay attention to his instructions. It may sound strange that workers who were being paid by Doug would ignore him, but that was the mindset. Throughout the decades, those who had survived were the ones who looked with circumspection at every shift in policy. With every good idea Doug brought, farmers took a step back and assumed that both he and the idea would soon disappear. How, they wondered, would all of this impact what they still saw as their own fields?

Under such circumstances, the hardest aspect of village life for Doug was distinguishing between the farmers' valid objections and their automatic resistance to any kind of change—a hard task for anyone blind to the language and the cultural nuances. Xia became the link that was missing, allowing Doug to implement some, if not all, of his ideas. When things got deadlocked, Doug called on Xia to organize a formal meeting with the workers and resolve the issue. Xia was more than just a power broker. He was an elder, a wise man, who helped Doug navigate the intricate mesh of personal and family allegiances that formed a countercurrent often invisible to the outsider.

In one particular case, Xia's help was essential. As he had explained to me in Shanghai, Doug believed that by using his equipment to break soil that had never been plowed deep, the roots of his plants would grow deeper, strengthening the plants in times of drought. His workers disagreed, and even Xia raised objections. "The village was founded on land reclaimed from former swamps," Sun explained to me later. "The deep soil was made of wet clay, so locals knew that the soil Doug was about to turn up would be sopping wet and poor in nutrients."

Doug dismissed this as another obstacle he had to overcome on his way to basketball-sized lettuce. "A bit more fertilizer will compensate for it," he assured his audience.

And maybe because of the respect they shared for each other, Xia chose to back him against his own instincts.

Once the weather got dryer, Doug reploughed his field entirely in just a few days. And while the farmers might have doubted his methods, they were impressed with what he could accomplish with his machinery. Until Doug arrived, farmers had flooded their fields each time they irrigated. When the water encountered an obstacle, they dug a ditch so it could flow away. There was no overarching field slope, only a collection of ditches and a maze of irrigation canals constructed manually over the years. When Doug came in with his tractor, he wiped all of that out.

"We ripped it, broke down all the lumps of dirt, and remade the beds for planting," Doug related to me. "At the same time, I shaped a slope to help water flow away. They all thought I was crazy. I was destroying the beds that they had carefully preserved from one year to another. It had taken them one week of work with hand shovels to make those beds. It was backbreaking work."

In half a day, Doug had cleared out seventeen acres of fields and rebuilt the plant beds with the help of a lister, an attachment to the tractor that smoothed down the mud clods. Ordinarily, this work would have taken twenty hardworking men a full week.

"I could see the relief in their eyes when I finished the beds," Doug told me. "They would not have to redo it manually when we failed and moved away!"

Xinzhou Town and Village Number 9 benefited from Doug's

presence in other ways. As Doug walked along the little irrigation canals that fed into the aquaculture ponds, he often saw plastic containers of pesticide thrown in the water. He also noticed the farmers' unsafe practices when applying pesticides. Over time and the course of many training sessions, Doug explained to hundreds of farmers the risks associated with the use of such chemicals. He showed how contamination worked and how dangerous it could be to everyone's health.

"Xia got it," he said. With the village leader's help, Doug relentlessly reminded people to protect their environment. And day after day, Doug noticed that there were fewer discarded pesticide containers in the water.

As Doug worked through these problems, getting to know the land and its people, he gradually gained a good reputation. Pride in farming as a profession is unusual in China. Over the past twenty years, the Old Hundred Names like Sun's parents have sent their brightest children away to study and work in the big cities. The last thing the sons and daughters of farmers in China want to do is farm themselves. Even if they've chosen to study agriculture or agronomy, their parents would see that as a failure. Yet here was Doug, an educated American with a university degree, clearly in love with the dirty work of fields and seeds and fertilizer. He often joked that our Chinese agronomists walked around in blue suits and leather shoes, checking the fields from the outside, looking at them with apprehension. In contrast, he wore rubber boots and went down on one knee in the middle of the field, grabbing fistfuls of earth to feel its density and its quality, showing it to the local farmer standing next to him, communicating, using hand choreography and a ballet of nods that only other farmers could understand.

As the months went on, workers saw that Doug was here to stay, and that salaries got paid despite delays, mechanical breakdowns and poor harvest results. The beds got formed in just one day, many times faster and easier than with traditional methods. Mostly, Doug's passion for the land came through in his daily interactions, and people started to listen to him even when Xia wasn't involved.

Nobody complained that Doug could not speak Chinese. When he was on the farm, he spoke the same language as the local farmers. By the time the model farm project ended, he had gained their respect. *Dugelasi* (Doo-ge-la-seu), a transliteration of Douglas in English, was his Chinese name, and it seemed everyone in Xinzhou knew who he was.

Unfortunately, Doug had been right to be anxious during the long rainy winter. The summer heat came early, and by June, the lettuce we planned to harvest bolted to flower stage without forming a ball.

I had hoped that Doug's new way of preparing the field would compensate for that risk, allowing the plants to dig deeper in search of water and nutrients, giving the plants enough strength to form a ball despite the heat. But in this case, the villagers were right: the layer of clay, once brought up to the surface, proved to be very poor soil. It sucked in all the fertilizer that Doug threw at it and tripled the cost of growing without much to show for it.

Next, Doug found out that roughly half of the field was showing even poorer results than the rest. He asked around and discovered that this part of the land had been used to grow wheat and sprayed with a herbicide containing sulfonated urea. He looked it up and found that such chemicals remain for five years, though the Chinese label claimed it was only six months.

Doug moved to our summer farm in Inner Mongolia in July 2003, leaving a young agronomist in Xinzhou to plant some watermelons during the hot months as a rotating crop. By the autumn, when Xinzhou's seedlings were ready for transplanting,

Doug was still busy at the Inner Mongolia farm, so he managed the Xinzhou farm from afar. Our agronomist did all right, but not enough to convince people to change their old methods and plant lettuce for us the next season. By then, Doug's one-year contract had ended. I was once more pressed for cash, and I decided to send him back to the US. He offered to stay on for less, but I couldn't afford the team around him without a substantial grant from the German bank. The day I informed him, he looked visibly crushed. "I feel shorted," he said.

The Xinzhou model-farm land returned to its previous rights-holders, the farmers reverted to farming as they always had, and Creative Food continued to move lettuce bought from our network of suppliers in refrigerated trucks from Shanghai to Wuhan.

But the model farm project wasn't a total failure. At the Inner Mongolia location, farmers had already been growing lettuce for one of our suppliers for three years, and Creative Food's farm was able to capitalize on their experience. The farmers had learned to grow seedlings in trays to protect them from diseases. They were still using pesticides, but they had learned to spray more consistently. Doug ran a competition daily with our supplier's managers on whose methods would yield the best results. In the end, local farmers learned a lot and continued to farm lettuce for years after Doug's departure, allowing us to supply a wide range of our businesses from central to southern China instead of relying on unreliable produce from other regions.

Creative Food's story was not unlike those of thousands of companies in China. Unable to really change how our products were produced, we re-focused on meeting booming demand. The problem of ensuring clean supplies, though it never came back to bite Creative Food, also never really went away. Periodically, food-safety scandals would erupt in our industry, all traceable back to the unresolved tension between the demands of 21st-century consumers and the medieval-era agriculture methods still practiced in China.

Doug Trett is now back in California working on pest-control programs with fruit growers there. He often reminisces about his adventures in China and wishes he could go back. Even though the model farms didn't work as he envisioned, he succeeded in other ways. The people he met and the experiences he had in China transformed his life for the better, he says. "I am not a successful man, that's for sure," he said to me. "But the only time I can see admiration in people's eyes is when I talk about my China adventures."

On his final trip before he returned to the U.S., Doug exchanged gifts with the local friends he had made. The taxi driver who had regularly shuttled him between Xinzhou Town and Village Number 9 offered him a special gift: a bottle of his favorite brand of homemade *baijiu*. *Baijiu* (literally "white alcohol") is the 120-proof spirit that Doug drank on many occasions with Secretary Wu during their banquets. But this one was different. It came from a four-gallon bottle that the driver kept at home. That bottle was filled with herbs and spices—and infused with the juices from three snakes, whose pickled bodies gave the liquid a dark brown tint. The man decanted a liter for Doug in a separate bottle and forced him to pack it in his luggage, telling Doug that it had medicinal benefits.

At the Wuhan airport, Doug was pulled aside by a security guard and questioned with suspicion about what was in that bottle. The officer uncorked it, smelled it, then looked at Doug with a wide smile before waving him into the departure lounge. Doug still swears this *baijiu* can cure the common cold.

11

MODERN PEASANT

APPEARING ON a high-profile Chinese television talk show about business personalities had never been part of my plan, but there I was. I paced the empty concrete yard between the several brick warehouses which are Shanghai TV's studios, rehearsing my lines for an interview set to start in just a few minutes. But pacing didn't help. It's daunting enough to appear on prime-time TV anywhere, but I had the added fear that millions of viewers would mock my awful Chinese—or, worse, not understand me at all.

It was August 2004. Producers of the famous "Fortune Time" talk show, which focused on telling the personal stories of business leaders, had found me and Creative Food—I'm not sure why or how—and told my marketing manager that there was a last-minute opening for a guest. "Are you interested in stepping in?" the manager asked me.

I wasn't sure about the offer—I didn't watch local TV—but Mike was uncharacteristically enthusiastic.

"It's a really good program," he said. "It could really improve our standing with customers. And by the way, Ye Rong is my favorite talk-show host. She has this mix of elegance and professionalism."

Mike was never buoyant about anything, so his reaction

alone got my attention. And when the news that I was going to be interviewed by Ye Rong made its way through the company's ranks, everyone at Creative Food suddenly turned giddy. In the canteen, staffers recalled how Ye Rong had made a guest's wife cry by gently leading her to recount long evenings spent alone at home while her businessman husband was traveling.

After I accepted the offer, it dawned on me that my performance might not turn out at all as expected, that I could let everyone down and make myself a national laughingstock. But it was too late to turn back, so while technicians barked orders and moved cameras, I sat myself down on a brightly-lit soundstage beside Ye Rong—elegant and professional, just as Mike had promised—in the seat previously occupied by Chinese executives including Li Kaifu, the China CEO of Microsoft and later Google.

A few weeks later, the show aired on a Saturday evening at 8 pm—the most prime of prime times, when roughly 220 million Chinese viewers were sitting in front of their TV sets. It started with a series of pictures I had given the program's producers, photos of me as a child in my mom's arms and a later one featuring me touring one of our plants, as a male Chinese voice provided a slightly pompous narration of my history over a soundtrack of syrupy soap opera music.

"Li Wenzhi—that was my Chinese name—comes from France. Nothing had prepared him for it, but now he's crossed the world to work with Chinese farmers!"

Then came the credits, including a photo montage of Ye Rong with past famous guests, and then the camera centered on the stage where she and I sat facing each other. She smiled and greeted me.

"Do you think you could be called a 'modern farmer'?" she asked, using the phrase xiandai nongmin, a term often associated with the government's initiatives to overhaul China's backward agriculture sector.

Somehow the directness of the question caught me off guard, so I fell back on a long preamble that I had learned by heart about not being a farmer but being as close as possible to them, throwing in buzz words like "cold chain" and "supply chain" that probably didn't mean anything to her audience. When I finished, Ye Rong deftly restated my ramble, making it sound more intelligent. I quickly nodded, grateful for the help.

As the interview went on, my gaffes piled up. In my effort to explain ideas and concepts—something I wasn't used to doing at work—I used terms that weren't appropriate in such a formal setting. For example, I kept calling farmers *nongmin* (agriculture people), which isn't wrong but has associations with poverty and sounds condescending. In her comments, Ye Rong used Old Hundred Names. I caught the difference when I watched later. But I failed to pick up on it during the interview.

Fortunately, it wasn't all mistakes.

"Well, we Chinese often describe ourselves as deeply rooted in our agricultural history," she said. "So how do you explain that no Chinese entrepreneur before you came up with the idea of selling salads?"

This one I nailed. I talked about how salads were foreign to Chinese tastes, yet they were a new form of healthy food that preserved more vitamins than stir-frying vegetables in the traditional Chinese way. I added that this trend was perfectly suited to modern young consumers like her.

She giggled, clearly connecting with me for the first time and giving me a chance to segue into how I had created salad dressings to win over Chinese palates, with flavors based on sesame oil and soy sauce rather than vinaigrettes or mayonnaise.

As the show went on, I looked and felt more relaxed.

"Half of all vegetables are lost between the farm and the consumers," I watched myself stating, while the statistics appeared on the screen with the shape and sound of a giant rubber stamp for emphasis.

"I started with foreign managers, but now everyone is Chinese," I continued. "I believe Chinese are just better managers in this environment." My interviewer nodded at this shameless appeal to her national pride.

When Ye Rong narrowed down to my own personal story, I opened up slightly more than I had wished to. I told her I had fenced for the French Junior Team when I was seventeen and had chosen to drop out to pursue my studies.

"Don't you have any regret about that choice?" she asked.

She had touched on a sensitive point. In my simple Chinese, I related a scene at the Frankfurt Airport that I remembered from early in my career as a young finance executive. Walking toward the gate on yet another business trip, I saw a newspaper headline and a photo of my ex-roommate from the national team. The night before in Cape Town, he had just won the gold medal at the World Fencing Championships; the photo showed him kneeling on the floor with his arms raised in victory, his faced suffused with joy and relief, a protective mask in one hand and a foil in the other. That day, I explained to Ye Rong, I saw myself wearing a gray business suit, reflected in the newsstand window, and I paused for a long time. My friend had reached a summit in his profession. "Where was I heading?" I wondered.

When the show aired, this digression turned into a transition between segments. As soon as I ended my sentence, the screen showed more pictures of me — touring my plants, standing in a field with a head of lettuce in hand while talking to a farmer — accompanied again by the vapid sentimental soundtrack and the male voice-over.

"Li kept looking for what his purpose should be. He never thought his calling was in the fields and farms of China," the voice said, making me cringe in front of my TV.

That evening, every Chinese person I knew called or texted me—even a maid I had fired several months before. During the commercial break, KFC junior managers grabbed their phones and called their counterparts at Creative Food, expressing a mix of awe and astonishment that the little supplier that they normally bullied in sales meetings had made it onto Ye Rong's show. As usual, nobody noticed my rough syntax, or at least they didn't comment on it. The "Fortune Time" producers had been careful to add subtitles too.

It seemed that people enjoyed the story of a foreigner who had seen an opportunity in a sector often neglected by the Chinese themselves. And because the show was then syndicated to several satellite TV channels, it got replayed in different regions for several weeks. For a brief period, in China, I was a true celebrity; people recognized me at shops and in airport terminals. I was Li Wenzhi—the modern peasant, the Frenchman working with villagers.

I have to say I enjoyed the brief fame that my TV appearance brought me. But there was a deeper reason for my unabashed self-promotion. A few months before, my company had launched a range of fresh salads packed in bags and bowls, to be sold in 600 supermarkets and retail outlets nationwide. For the first time I was dealing with Chinese consumers directly—a very different and much more complicated business. Mike and I could manage an account like KFC. But selling to supermarkets required large teams of sales representatives and promoters supervising how our products were displayed and marketed across multiple regions, just like those that established brands such as Coca-Cola and Mars had.

For my salad brand, I had chosen the name that the city of Paris had borne in Roman times: "Lutece." I hoped that the evocation of a European lifestyle would tempt consumers. Since I didn't have millions to spend on advertising, I followed up my "Fortune Time" appearance by taking every TV show and interview invitation I could get. By then, I had stopped wearing my wingtips and suits in favor of button-down shirts and neatly-pressed Dockers (I was still French, after all). As with "Fortune Time," everyone seemed to love the story of the Frenchman getting his boots dirty in the fields of China. And it gave me a chance to explain directly to consumers why buying my salads was actually safer than buying from street markets, even if it cost a little more.

The fact that my wife was Korean added a fascination I didn't anticipate. In the early 2000s, Korea, with its trendy fashion, glamorous soap operas, and flashy technology brands had become the hippest thing for young Chinese. Being European was fine, but the fact that a Korean woman had married me made me a far more attractive prospect. On one entertainment show, Jane and I appeared together, and we told the story of how we met while cartoon animations of us riding bicycles popped on the screen. Cropped pictures of us were mounted on anime-style bodies that tilted right and left as we pedaled up a hill. Meanwhile, Creative Food's team cheered in the audience, clapping when the cameras turned toward them. I even paid a few thousand dollars to make sure the cameras pointed at their T-shirts emblazoned with the Lutece logo.

I had many reasons to push for faster growth. The main one was that Yum kept opening restaurants across the country at a rate of nearly two outlets per day. If I wanted to stay relevant as a supplier, I had to keep up. Since 2002, I had built four larger and more technologically advanced plants in

Beijing, Wuhan, Shanghai and Guangzhou. That meant more investment, new rounds of fund-raising and nail-biting delays while health inspectors identified parts of our factories that needed to be redesigned before we could get all of our operating licenses. Meanwhile, Yum executives kept the pressure on. In confrontations that weren't very different from my dressing down with Sam Su a few years before, KFC's buyers threatened to give their business to others if I didn't meet their deadlines. For all the stress, the volume I won wasn't enough to get a good return on my investment. I desperately needed to find new ways to grow. Thus, the new bagged-salad line.

Why did I opt to get into an entirely new business when I could have sold to more restaurant chains? Chain restaurants were still a new thing for China, and the only substantial alternative to KFC was McDonald's. The problem was that the two chains were so fiercely competitive that serving one required forfeiting doing business with the other—and KFC was a far larger operator, though I always envied how loyal McDonald's was to its own partners. Starbucks at the time had big ambitions, but the salads we sold to their roughly 100 stores were miniscule compared to KFC's and Pizza Hut's 3,000 outlets. We did sell to some emerging Chinese restaurant chains, but they were still small, and few of them wanted to pay a premium price, especially for pre-cut vegetables. They mostly cut vegetables inside their own restaurants or operated small central kitchens. Each time I visited such facilities, I thought about all the food-safety issues. But no one got caught; that meant there was no real pressure on them to work with someone like me. So my only option was to tap a new channel.

In less than a decade, the bagged-salads category had exploded in the U.S., Europe and Australia, reaching $4 billion in revenues in the U.S. alone. One American in two was already

225

buying prepared salads; for them it was more about convenience than fear of eating something unsafe. But in China, I decided I would focus on food safety. Bagged greens and coleslaw mixes, in my vision of the future, would appeal to busy urban moms eager for fresh, safe and healthy vegetables in a sector plagued by scandals. My ability to wash and sort out the leaves in my plants would be a big competitive advantage; I offered anxious moms a level of safety they couldn't find elsewhere. We succeeded in getting our bagged salads sold in the largest supermarket chains in China, many of them global retailers like Wal-Mart, France's Carrefour and Germany's Metro.

I wasn't ignorant of the fact that the Chinese normally don't eat salads. But I felt that society was changing. People were traveling more and experimenting with new tastes. The Chinese middle class — a group that marketers defined as earning more than $5,000 a year — was still only around 100 million people in 2003, but it was growing at a rate of close to 15%; today, in 2020, it has already surpassed 700 million. That was big enough to build a significant business in salads. It wasn't the first time that Chinese people would change their food habits, I thought. Centuries ago, northern China had adopted yogurt from Central Asia, and in the past decade Chinese people all over had started to develop a liking for pizza. I wanted them to eat my salads not just because they were safe, but also because salad is full of nutrients that normally get destroyed in cooking. I made that point to anyone asking me for the reason I had invested in this new line of products. "I'm not selling salads; I am selling assurance, convenience and a nutritious food." That's what I told journalists, shareholders and employees.

The enthusiasm of supermarket-chain buyers for the product appeared to confirm my initial hypothesis. Many of the expatriates running the large foreign chains across China had seen how successful the new category had been abroad. Traditionally, the produce section of grocery stores was a loss-leader—a money-losing department you need to keep in order to attract people into your store, where they will go on to buy other, more profitable products. As Steve Wolfe, my lettuce mentor, had explained, lettuce breathes; that's what leads to decay in the heads you find exposed on the produce shelves. By flushing nitrogen into a bag and sealing the lettuce in with it, you deprive the leaves of the fuel—oxygen—that makes them wilt and rot. Thanks to that process, bagged salads last longer than normal vegetables, which means less waste for produce managers in supermarkets. A mix of leaves in a bag filled with nitrogen can last nearly two weeks, a much more economical model than whole vegetables. With the new category's sales surging, the produce section in the U.S. and in Europe turned from a loss leader into a profit center. Knowing this, foreign managers in international supermarkets in China were so enthused by my project that they didn't require me to pay the usual expensive listing fees to have my salads on their shelves. They all wanted them.

I chose a packaging that clearly stood out from the crowded range of *anime*-style labels lining the nearby shelves. Jane mentioned a group of young Italian designers based in Beijing, and I visited them on one of my regular trips there. This team had set up shop in a traditional courtyard house in one of Beijing's old narrow lanes, with the exposed beams and gray brick walls giving the space a stylish minimalist look. There, a dozen young designers from all over the world worked in front of large screens, sitting together at long wooden tables. I immediately hired the group and a few weeks later, they introduced their ideas for our new bags. The design they proposed was composed of geometric forms with a transparent bottom showing the contents of the bag and a top part made of changing shades of greens recalling dawn over a field. In the top right corner, Lutece, the name of the product, was boxed in a colored pattern; rice kernels made up the character strokes. A few weeks later, our new packaging was proudly out on the shelves.

My employees worked with a fervor I hadn't seen before. Until then, their company had just been a supplier to KFC. But now they arrived in the morning telling stories about friends and families calling them about their recent purchases of Lutece salads. There was a vibe of excitement across the organization, a new pride too. During recruitment interviews, candidates now made passionate expressions of interest merely because they had seen our products in stores.

Sales picked up quickly in supermarkets located in wealthier neighborhoods of Shanghai, Beijing and Shenzhen where expatriates and Chinese who had lived overseas resided. That confirmed my assumption that people who had been exposed to bagged salads would want to buy and try them again. But in other stores or in other regions we were selling as few as one bag a day—and those stores made up 90% of the market.

I sent marketing staffers to the slow-moving supermarkets to talk to consumers. They came back explaining that shoppers there, unlike in the big cities, weren't working professionals eager to try the salads they had discovered with a glass of chilled rosé on business trips in France or in California. Instead, most produce buyers were the grandparents or the maid who often lived with or very near the family, took care of the single child, and prepared meals at home. Two things we had not anticipated prevented them from buying our bags of salads. They didn't know how to eat a salad—whether they should stir-fry it or eat it raw—and they felt that a vegetable in a plastic bag wasn't fresh enough.

In China, salads aren't completely outside the conventional

diet. Every meal comes with a combination of cold and warm dishes. Often, a tender root vegetable like radish or taro serves as a base. First, it's cut into slices or shreds and rinsed in boiling water to eliminate impurities. It's then served with a mixture of vinegar, garlic and chili powder to further sanitize the dish. So I figured I just needed to show them how to eat my lettuce leaves.

To spread my gospel, I hired hundreds of promoters, whose role was to stand in the stores next to our products, offering samples of our Western-style salads mixed with dressing on a paper plate, using disposable forks. Kids tried it first; grandparents followed, and they usually liked it. While they chewed on their cabbage, mixed leaves or iceberg, the promoter laid out what she had been trained to say: The salad was fresh, it was safe, and it was full of nutrients—and by the way we had also been producing KFC's lettuce for years.

The promoters' presence inside the store was crucial in other ways, too. They manned the branded refrigerated cabinets we had bought to display our salads, guarding them against unscrupulous supermarket managers trying to place other brands in them and arguing against throwing our bags away at the end of the day, as was common practice for other vegetables. In addition, they dealt with the traveling crew of technicians sent to repair the chilled cabinets fast enough to prevent complaints and wasted bags. To support them, I hired sales representatives to negotiate terms with individual stores in every region, collect payments, check that bags were displayed nicely instead of crushed in a rusty corner of the fridge, and coordinate with our logistics team to make sure shelves always looked full. Aside from the promoters who were hired only for some events or for the best-running stores, I had expanded the team to around fifty full-time employees. That meant a lot of tasks to keep track of.

After each promotional campaign, I saw a quick increase in

revenues, which then fell back to a level slightly higher than before the event, showing that some customers had converted. But it was much slower than I anticipated.

I needed to expand so salads could become ubiquitous, but the more stores I managed, the more complex the coordination issues became. My research was correct—people wanted to eat healthy—but healthy eating for them didn't usually equate with eating salads. When a consumer had to choose a vegetable, they stuck to what they knew.

Also, wanting to eat healthy and actually doing so were two different things. "People don't buy foods because they are safe or good for them," said the CEO of KFC Hong Kong one day as I stood in front of a store counter with him, trying to convince him to add one of my salads to his menu. "When they stand here looking at the overhead menu, they'll look for what tastes good—and it's that spicy fried chicken!"

Under pressure to increase my sales per store to justify the large infrastructure I had created, I decided to expand my product range away from traditional Western salad. I had to find this elusive compromise between Chinese and Western tastes to convert more consumers, and do it faster.

"Here is my new sweet potato salad," said Wu Xiaolin, giggling and a little hesitant as she presented an orange mush of diced sweet potatoes in a mayonnaise sauce.

We had gathered a dozen of the company's managers at Mike's apartment to try new product ideas. Wu, a young graduate from Shanghai Institute of Technology, still looked like a student. Tiny and reserved during meetings, she tended to keep to herself. But when it came to new products, she blossomed into a poised executive, her voice steady, her comments clear and well-constructed. I had placed Wu under Su Hong, our technical director, to come up with new product ideas to suit local tastes.

We had started to sell cooked vegetable salads to Pizza Hut and KFC, so it made sense to capitalize on that trend. Wu knew that games were a good way of harnessing people's energy, so she asked everyone to come up with product ideas for one evening every two months, and she tracked their progress like a hawk. The reward for the best idea was symbolic—she didn't have much of a budget—but it was enough to send the entire company into a new-product-development frenzy.

That evening, Wu smiled with apprehension after distributing a scorecard she had designed, listing specific questions about each product's appeal, its appearance and its taste. Then we all picked up a disposable fork or a pair of chopsticks and tasted the product, filling out the document while commenting with a full mouth. Some stood around the plates, talking with animation about the current samples while others assembled the next set of products in the kitchen. Wu introduced her sweet potato salad and several variations of it. For the dressing, she had formed a partnership with a large Japanese dressing maker established near Shanghai, called Kewpie. It was typical of our process for promoting a new salad culture adjusted for Chinese tastes. Dressings, inspired by what worked in Japan, used sesame oil and soya sauce instead of olive oil and vinegar; some of the mayonnaise mixes were spicy. Wasabi replaced mustard in vinaigrettes.

Mike was as keen as everyone else. He introduced a cold soba noodle salad with shredded carrots and a vinegar dressing he had liked on a trip to Tokyo. Xu Shen, our supply chain manager, presented a cabbage mix that he emphatically connected back to his hometown of Lianyungang near Shandong province. His story was more compelling than the taste or the look of his creation; everyone laughed and made fun of his dried-up yellowish mess. It didn't matter. Xu cracked up and quoted

Chinese proverbs to defend his case. Wu Xiaolin raised her voice to bring some order back to the room.

It was already past nine in the evening. In the little guarded compound where Mike lived, people seemed to have gone to bed early. Ours was one of the rare windows casting light on the garden downstairs; the opposite block was all dark. Back home that evening, I shared with Jane how connected I felt to the team, proud that everyone's spirit seemed invested in my dream. She smiled and encouraged me with suggestions of Korean vegetables normally used to wrap barbecue meat. On such days, I could imagine a future where Creative Food would feed tasty salads to modern Chinese consumers.

But these evenings were just one step in the long process of launching new products. Wu was a food technician. Once a new recipe was short-listed as a strong candidate, her job was to check with the marketing department that it fit with consumer preferences and met concerns identified in research and then to perfect the recipe with the help of a professional chef. Then she had to test how the product held up over several days in a bag inside a fridge. If it still looked good and if microbiological results showed enough consistency to stay safely on supermarket shelves for several days without risking food poisoning, she had to file a report to get the product accepted by the Chinese Federal Drug Administration.

To address claims that grandparents didn't buy salads, Wu had already developed a line of diced carrots, celery and broccoli that she called "Ready-to-Cook." I didn't like the packaging very much. It was a cheaper product, vacuum-sealed in thick plastic with a bland sticker slapped on it. But it was an answer to a recurrent complaint our promoters heard from consumers. In these shoppers' view, the vacuum seal was a sign of freshness. In contrast, our elegant, flimsier-looking bags triggered a negative assessment. "It looks swollen, like the seal is punctured and the salads have turned sour," said a shopper when asked why she preferred the sealed bags to my slick packaging. I hoped Ready-to-Cook was a way to convert buyers, who would then graduate to our bagged salads once they trusted the Lutece brand.

It sometimes felt strange to hear consumers talk about such details. But that kind of scrutiny wasn't unusual. Nobody took anything for granted, whether government labels asserting quality, brand claims, or fancy packaging. Shoppers turned the bags upside down several times looking for damaged leaves, then they placed them back on the shelves and looked in the back of the display for untouched or fresher products.

Appearance wasn't the only issue. Labeling regulations didn't allow us to place a "best before" date on the packaging. We had to stipulate the exact date and location of production and the shelf life accepted by the authorities, usually just four days because standards were different from the U.S. So the first thing shoppers saw was that the salad hadn't been cut on that day. They sorted through the bags and picked the ones with the most recent production date, leaving the bags our promoter had loyally defended against rejection the night before to slowly decay until she had no choice but throw them away.

The mention of the production site on the label became another issue I hadn't anticipated. In Shanghai, I thought that making our bagged salads in our brand-new plant in Haimen would be a plus. But shoppers saw it as a negative. The reason? Haimen was a city located in Jiangsu province under the supervision of a different provincial government than Shanghai. Consumers knew enforcement varied between provinces. They believed factories under Shanghai's supervision were subject to closer scrutiny, so it didn't take me long to realize that the plant I was so proud of had turned into a liability.

You might think that shoppers are the same in their quality concerns the world over. In the U.S. and Europe, shoppers trust well-established food brands. If you shop at Safeway and buy Tyson chicken, you know that the USDA has vetted the product, that Tyson maintains standards that may be even higher than regulatory ones, and that Safeway has conducted a review of these systems.

But Chinese shoppers lack that confidence in brands or institutions. So they check quality themselves with an unparalleled intensity. Back when I launched my bagged salads, people checked labels, talked to my promoters, read the marketing material available with my products in stores, and paid attention to my advertising in cooking magazines. Some even went online to check my company website. Around a third of Americans will ask colleagues, friends and family about a product, check the company website, or read consumer reviews, but two-thirds of Chinese do this. Today's Chinese consumers review blogs, call companies and discuss products with peers on social media at a rate that is three times as high as in America or Europe. Nearly half of Chinese consumers interviewed in one research study even said they read a company's annual report.[5] Chinese moms I talked to often used the Wechat platform – a vast social media network equivalent to a combination of Whatsapp, Facebook, Instagram and Paypal – to check on foods they are considering buying and even to coordinate purchases of products they've deemed trustworthy.

Xu Yizhou, the mom of two boys at my daughter's school, explained how it works for her. "A friend of mine or another mom at school organizes a relative or an acquaintance to plant a few vegetables in Nanhui, near Shanghai," she said. "She

---

5   Cohn & Wolfe, China Skinny, Goldman Sachs

obviously can't consume all of them, so she puts together a group on Wechat and allocates the harvest among the families. The vegetables get loaded once a week on a truck to Shanghai, and we all gather in one place to collect the produce."

Xu knows that this won't replace the neighborhood market, but buying some of what she needs directly from a farm that has been vetted by acquaintances brings her comfort. "We Chinese tend to trust a close circle of friends more than any type of label or regulations," she said, making explicit her belief that her network of other moms might be her only true lever of control over the quality of what she buys.

I was betting that my salads could make their way into these tightly-knit communities—and they did, even in the pre-social-media world of the time. But it wasn't just the shoppers I needed to convince to expand my business. It was also the myriad of smaller, non-Western-owned supermarkets of China. In the U.S., Wal-Mart, Kroger, Albertson's and a handful of other chains represent close to 70% of grocery sales; suppliers can build a business with $500 million in revenues via only five supermarket clients. China, in contrast, has more than 250 supermarket chains with 100 or more stores, many of them based in one city or one region only. The five largest chains—the international buyers I had courted—represent less than 5% of the market. The senior expatriate managers in the main chains in Shanghai or Beijing supported my salads, but their buyers in regions far away were confounded by powerful regional chains who were better at selling what locals wanted at a lower price.

That made it hard to convince the local Wal-Mart buyer in a distant region to buy what he viewed as a hard product to sell— my salads were more expensive than traditional vegetables—so he simply rarely ordered our product, ignoring the agreement I had negotiated with his bosses. Worse, when I didn't have a promoter in his store, he went through our displays and threw bags of salad away, even when the salads were still consumable, and then charged us for it. If I had a staff person on site, such managers would pressure her to organize their entire produce display, taking her away from what I had paid her to do. I talked about convenient, fresh, safe and healthy products, but buyers and shoppers in smaller cities simply measured quality based on perceived freshness and lower prices. An expensive cut and washed salad in a plastic bag didn't measure up.

It didn't help that supermarket chains weren't scrutinizing their vendors as much as restaurant chains did. The qualification process usually boiled down to providing a few certificates proving we were a real company or that our products were registered with the relevant government agency. After that, supermarket buyers' focus turned back to price and to how much money I would spend in promotions and advertising to boost my sales.

Why were clients like KFC, Starbucks or Pizza Hut so much more involved in my operations than the supermarkets I supplied? I asked that question of an executive at Yum years later. He explained that if a restaurant or a coffee chain faces a quality problem, nobody accuses suppliers like Creative Food of delivering salads containing heavy metal or chemical residues.

"Instead," he told me, "you'll read that KFC is now facing a new challenge with its vegetables and betraying its consumers' trust."

Supermarkets, in contrast, had a more transient relationship with the food they sold. If a consumer had an issue with one of my salad bags, they weren't likely to buy it again, but they weren't going to take two subway trips and demand a refund from the store either. My quality complaints from supermarkets were always surprisingly few, and that opened the door to many excesses. A 2006 Greenpeace survey found that 90% of vegetables labeled organic in Chinese supermarkets contained chemicals—proof of the lack of control that retailers exercised over their suppliers. When confronted by reporters, retailers said they trusted the certificates which suppliers had provided during the qualification process. In their minds, it was enough to avoid legal liability and blame problems on someone else. In contrast, foodservice companies like Yum had dedicated teams to check their suppliers' claims.

In the years I sold salads to supermarkets, I never saw even one of their quality auditors visit my plants. But KFC's or Starbucks' auditors were involved in the most innocuous details, demanding, for example, the replacement of pierced wire mesh in a sieve used to drain vegetables so that no metal filament could end up in a bag of lettuce.

Meanwhile, the food safety issues I had noticed for years didn't go away; they now made headlines. The Chinese discovered, for example, that the cabbage they ate was often plunged in formaldehyde to keep it fresh longer, which allowed for longer transport times and thus lower costs overall. When I asked a vegetable trader I knew whether he realized this could cause harm, he dismissed the point.

"It's okay. Everyone does it," he said. "You just need to make sure you take off the outer leaves."

A Chinese blogger called Wu Jian started a website to report the types of food-related frauds that appeared and then vanished with each news cycle: vinegar diluted with glacial acetic acid produced synthetically, rather than from grains or fruits, to reduce costs; mushrooms and rice bleached to make them whiter; sulfuric acid applied to lychees to keep them bright red. His website was called "Throw It Out the Window!"

A white paper published by the State Council, the highest

advisory body to the government, highlighted the issue. In 2012, close to 80 percent of food companies in China had fewer than ten employees; that's more than 350,000 tiny businesses that regulators were supposed to monitor. And when unscrupulous businessmen did get caught, the law failed to punish them adequately. Penalties for food safety infringement amounted to only the equivalent of ten times the value of the defective product. For the cabbage dipped in formaldehyde, for example, there was a fine of around only one dollar.

I realized that it wasn't hard to get your vegetables listed in a supermarket. So, with thousands of suppliers competing with me without ever being checked, it was hard for Creative Food and our relatively expensive bagged salads to stand out as safer and higher-quality.

I've known Li Xiaoguang for a decade now. Our daughters went to the same preschool in Shanghai. As "Tiger Moms" go, she is in a league of her own. I've never heard the tall, introspective Shanghainese professor of design raise her voice at her daughter, but Youyou knew there wasn't any escape from the routine Mom had created for her starting in preschool. She had mastered the first year of primary school before entering kindergarten. After preschool, Jane and I sent our daughter, France, to World School, a Shanghai school we liked a lot but that wasn't considered particularly challenging. France was the only one in her preschool to attend our neighborhood school. Shanghainese parents often shunned it because there were too many students from poorer provinces studying there. Youyou entered the prestigious elementary school attached to Shanghai International Studies University (SISU), joining an elite crowd heading to top Chinese and U.S. universities.

Still, the two girls continued to go on playdates together. Li, always careful about how Youyou's choice of friends could benefit her future, told me candidly that she liked the way the two girls' personalities complemented each other. Youyou was quieter while France was more outgoing. On playdates, Li structured "breaks" for the girls during which she organized little math or writing contests; she would time the girls on mental calculation games or measure how many characters they could write while correcting the strokes' shapes and order. Jane and I laughed about it, but we were glad someone else was doing it. When I told her Li Xiaoguang had called to organize a playdate, Jane always answered enthusiastically, "I love Youyou mama's playdates; she's making our kid smarter and France doesn't seem to mind the drills at all!" My daughter had quickly learned that education issues don't follow a democratic process in an Asian family—even in a half-Asian one.

The family connection made it natural to ask Li Xiaoguang to help me understand how she and her family addressed their health. As in many households, her mother-in-law ran the kitchen and shopped for food while she managed her daughter's education, an occupation that left little spare time for anything else. Until two years ago, she hadn't really thought much about health in general, she said. But a particular event changed things.

"It all started when my husband's uncle, his mom's little brother, got diagnosed with cancer," she said. "His mom looked at the way he lived and decided that it came from his lifestyle." The uncle smoked a lot and ate mostly seafood. Like other consumers, Li wasn't blind to the fact that seafood was often tampered with. She had even told me how the family chose fish to buy. "Always sea fish. River fish is polluted; it's swollen and its color turns gold instead of the natural silver-gray blue," she commented.

When confronted with his uncle's disease, Li's husband immediately stopped smoking, then cut seafood from his diet.

At the same time, he asked his mother to buy beef instead of pork—the meat most consumed in Chinese households—because he felt it was leaner. At a university course he attended on weekends, he met a man from northern China who knew a good supplier of beef in Inner Mongolia, a region north of Beijing. The family started to buy from there, by-passing local markets and supermarkets for their beef supply. As with Xu and her Wechat vegetable network, Li's husband basically set up the family's own beef channel. And it wasn't the only food they bought through peers rather than through the traditional retail network. Li explained that she bought calcium-enriched milk powder from Australia through the school moms' Wechat group.

Li and her husband's experience might seem anecdotal, but statistics, even daunting ones, don't convince people to change their habits. It's when those closest to you get sick that you stop and reflect on what you might do to avoid the same fate. And this is happening at an increasing rate among urban Chinese. In the space of a generation, economic development caused people to drift away from a diet rich in vegetables and fruits to a deadly combination of sodium and sugar, heavy meat stews and other less healthy fare. The American Cancer Journal of Clinicians reported in 2015 that four million new cancer patients appear every year in China. There are no national surveys, but some regional studies provide more detailed evidence of the problem. Hebei Medical Hospital published a report in 2016, for example, showing that lung cancer occurrence had nearly quadrupled between 1973 and 2012. And in 2016, the World Health organization reported that China had the world's largest population of diabetics—110 million people, or 10% of the adult population—a figure that, if people don't change the way they eat and exercise, could climb to 150 million by 2040.

As with Li's family, there is a growing recognition by Chinese themselves that the way they live and eat has to change. Staple junk foods like instant noodles and sugary drinks have seen revenues drop consistently over the past five years, according to a 2017 McKinsey report. Instead, consumers are seeking healthier choices like 100% natural juices and herbal snacks.

When I read articles about China's food safety issues in Western media, I sometimes detect a level of condescension, an implication that the Chinese themselves don't know about their country's food-safety problem. That's not true. People like Xu and Li don't necessarily understand the specifics of pathogens and bacteria, but they know things aren't right. This has prompted creative ways of sourcing foods as well as changes in their diet. But the way Chinese increasingly watch their health can be very different from the methods of the health-conscious in the West. Traditional Chinese medicine, in particular, is never far away. "I am very careful to conserve *yangsheng* (vital powers)," Li told me.

Chinese medicine views the stomach as a vessel whose job is to transform the food we eat into the nutrients our body needs. A "digestive fire" made of the two "vital powers" — *qi* (which literally means "air" but translates as "life force") and *xue*, or "blood" — ensures the transformation. When looking at balancing health, Chinese focus on how each food affects the body, in particular cooling or heating it. Rarely do Chinese talk about proteins, carbs or other functional aspects of foods when describing their health benefits. "If nutrient quantity is gross revenue, then Chinese look at the net profit — or how much a food can increase the *qi* and the *xue*," says Alex Tan, a doctor of Chinese medicine in Beijing.

Imagine a stew pot slowly simmering on stove. If the heat is too strong, your stew is likely to dry up and stick, but if it's too weak, it will stay rather watery and may lack flavor. The Chinese try to balance the moisture in the body (the "yin") with the heat (the "yang"). Proteins are mainly "yang" and carbs are mainly "yin." But the mindset you're in and your environment both affect the digestive fire too. Stress and pollution bring "heat" to the body and dry it up. If you're too dry—you have too much "heat"— you need to eat "cold" foods such as rice, oats, vegetables, and beans or practice exercises like breathing or meditation that will help you cool down. If you don't, you risk inflammation, aches, and feelings such as anger and anxiety that lead to all modern diseases: cancer, cardiovascular disease and others.

Li explained some of the ways these principles guide her: "In spring, the change of temperature means that a lot of toxins will be released into your body, so we drink more green tea as a way to cleanse ourselves. In winter, we need to keep the warm inside, so we drink red tea."

There is also an interest in exercise that is quintessentially Chinese and not imported from the West. In Chinese medicine, exercise isn't about jumping on a spin bike or lifting tons of metal; excessive exercise, the belief goes, actually consumes qi and xue. Balance and longevity are more important than burning calories. You see this in the range of classes offered in Chinese gyms and fitness centers: Meditation, Qi Gong, Gong Fu or Taijiquan.

Even the government in its campaigns for healthier living tends to emphasize more traditional forms of exercise. On long-haul flights on Chinese airliners, a couple of hours before landing, a video shows some stretching and breathing exercises that aren't very different from the mindfulness practices many in the U.S. now advocate. Passengers of all ages raise their hands and practice Qi Gong as a way to cleanse the body. It all feels natural—except to the odd Western businessman watching it. Xu, the other mom, who practices meditation and floral arrangement as a way to rebalance energies, summarized these principles:

"We believe that all diseases connect back to our mindset.

For years, I've heard such comments with puzzlement, raising a Cartesian eyebrow at the mention of *qi* or the fact that Chinese friends and colleagues explained simple colds or throat aches with comments like, "You have too much heat inside." But I also noticed that none of these comments went away over the course of two decades; old or young, people tend to follow these principles.

The combinations of food choices to balance the season, the environment, your lifestyle and your current state of mind in Chinese medicine are infinite. Vegetables in particular hold a special place, one that is so taken for granted that most families fail to even mention them when talking about a healthy diet. In the West, a healthy person would eat some leafy salad greens, carrots, cabbage or sweet peppers and maybe some cucumbers, broccoli or squash. The Chinese eat all of these—and many more. In the U.S., we may hear of gailan, bok choi, yams and daikon as Chinese vegetables, but you've probably never heard of lily flowers, lotus roots, celtuce, chrysanthemum greens and bitter melon. Many vegetables are so local that they don't even translate into English apart from generic names like Guangdong greens or Shanghai greens. In every region, you have a plethora of varieties suited to the local climate and taste buds. Xu, Li and I together counted more than fifteen types of vegetables that they consumed in any given month—boiled, stir-fried or in salads. And this changes with the seasons. No wonder chains like Wal-Mart—which often favor a more standard range of food choices nationally—find it hard to compete with the local chains or the neighborhood markets.

As I thought more about it, I realized that in their approach to what it means to "eat healthy," the Chinese have something in common with the French. Both populations eat foods rather than nutrients; Chinese and French diet experts rarely talk about carbohydrates or proteins. I didn't even know what a "carb" was until I started to read English-language magazines. Instead, both nations' dieticians will talk about certain foods complementing each other for a healthy lifestyle.

Unfortunately, I didn't know any of this when I launched my salads. Looking back, what I viewed as a fancy product and a new hip Western lifestyle must have seemed pretty dull to the average Chinese shopper.

Watching my losses in my retail operations grow wasn't helping the business at Creative Food. I had to do something about it. So I withdrew from most of the poorly-performing supermarkets, keeping my products only where they did well—in supermarkets where I had full-time promoters. I also advertised in the buses people took when shopping and made sure my bagged salads were front and center in a wide range of refrigerated shelves. Next, I told supermarket buyers that they had to buy my salads outright, shutting down the option of returning products that didn't sell right away and forcing them to pay more attention to the way the product was handled inside the store. The number of stores I served quickly dwindled down to a hundred or so. But those were all profitable and the numbers started growing again.

To grow further, I decided to allocate more effort to a new type of grocery format entering China: convenience stores. A few months before, I had invited Mike on a trip to Japan, where the salad market was more developed than elsewhere in Asia. Decades before, Japanese investors had bought franchise rights for U.S. convenience stores like Lawson and Seven Eleven. By then, Seven Eleven Japan operated more than 6,000 outlets, and Lawson had more than 8,400.

Mike was impressed by what he saw. "More than half the

space in these stores is reserved for fresh foods," he said, looking at the range of not only fresh salads, but also cooked ones like potato, bean and corn salads, cold noodles, colorful sandwiches and bento boxes, a type of Japanese ready-meal.

In front of the Lawson store we visited—the logo still contained the old traditional milk cans from the original owner in Ohio—refrigerated trucks stopped and unloaded fresh deliveries three times a day, each order triggered by a cash register system digitally linked to the inventory to make sure the shelves always looked full and abundant. Japanese stores were smaller than in the U.S., but they had been so successful that they had outpaced their franchisors. In the end, Seven Eleven Japan acquired its American owner, while Lawson disappeared from the U.S. retail landscape entirely. Around the time I was restructuring my salad business, both chains opened their first stores in Shanghai. Mike was quick to recognize the opportunity.

"In Shanghai, only a fifth of the store is refrigerated," he said. "There is so much more we could do for them if we create a range of salads and fresh foods similar to what they have in Japan."

As part of the turnaround, we started serving Lawson and Seven Eleven and their competitor Family Mart, in Shanghai, Beijing and Shenzhen. This was a business much closer than big supermarkets to what we knew from working with KFC and Pizza Hut. We shipped our salads directly to a distribution center rather than to each individual store, taking advantage of the chain's growth without changing the way we operated too much. Because the Japanese retailers were very focused on managing the fresh section, there was no need—or space—for promoters or for our own chilled cabinets. Within a few months, our retail operations started to generate profits. Today each chain operates more than a thousand stores, and Creative Food's bagged salads, sandwiches and ready-meals are still sold in them.

While sitting at Xu's dinner table on a recent trip to China, I watched her thirteen-year old boy pick at a plate of stir-fried spinach with garlic, casually talking to his mom about his day at school as she brought green stems mixed with tofu and lily flowers to the table. All these years, I had viewed the microscopic farming plots as a barrier to the modernization of China's agriculture. But after a few hours with my Chinese friends, I was beginning to see things differently. Where would all these seasonal foods come from if there were fewer farmers? Would there still be regional differences? If China follows the development path of the West, the number of farmers will shrink while operations increase in size. Farms will focus on scale and productivity, specializing in fewer crops, breeding the most productive ones and neglecting some that may have higher nutritional content but lower returns per acre. Is that really what Chinese consumers want?

The sheer number of small farmers is the toughest hurdle to controlling the safety of the food Chinese eat. But they're also the reason you can still buy tens of different varieties at the neighborhood market, helping the Chinese to eat healthy according to their beliefs — modernizing without Westernizing. For the first time that night, I realized that the family farmers weren't necessarily just an obstacle on China's path toward modernization; they might actually be its cultural gatekeepers, protecting the local food industry and underpinning a renaissance of Chinese beliefs that will be key to the health of both the Chinese people and the safety of the foods they cherish.

12

FAKE COMPANIES

BETWEEN KFC's brutal price-lowering tactics and my campaign to turn the Chinese on to salads, I thought I had enough to worry about. Then one morning in 2004, I opened an email from one of Creative Food's German investors. Attached to the message was a glossy presentation about a company called Chaoda Modern Agriculture, which had recently listed on the Hong Kong Stock Exchange.

"This is what you should be doing," my investor had typed. There was no salutation or polite preamble.

I opened the attachment and found myself reading a superbly professional description of this rival company. Chaoda's sales had doubled every year since its inception less than five years before; now it turned profits so high it was embarrassing to compare it with Creative Food. The company had sales of $50 million and net profit was well above 50 percent.

Chaoda, the presentation explained, leased large swaths of land from local governments, re-hired local farmers to work according to professional agriculture practices, and sold vegetables directly to customers, bypassing all intermediaries. Anticipating any questions, the report went on to explain why margins at Chaoda were so high. There were too many intermediaries between farms and consumers, so Chaoda sold directly to supermarkets in China or importers in Asia and captured the difference. Then, the report detailed how the company, with all the money it planned to raise, would expand its own chain of produce stores across China, avoiding the very supermarkets I was now betting on.

I had known of Chaoda before that email. But this was the beginning of a period of constant—and always unfavorable— comparisons with it. Everywhere I went and everyone I spoke to—my investors, friends in the business world, even Jane's journalist colleagues—wanted to talk about Chaoda.

"Oh, you're selling vegetables?" people said when I introduced myself. "I read an article about this amazing company listed in Hong Kong."

Though part of me was envious, and the repeated conversations rankled, my deepest reaction was first doubt and then irritation that few others shared that doubt. Sure, I would have loved to show 50 percent net profit. But it was too far-fetched. I knew my suppliers didn't make such profits, and neither did produce traders. Large professional farms struggled to turn any profit at all. It was very sensible to sell directly to clients but delivering perishable foods to them took more than a few words on a presentation. Most supermarket chains didn't have centralized distribution centers; you had to deliver directly to each store. Shipping around China would require an army of refrigerated trucks and billions of dollars of losses before you could ever get to the scale you needed to make a profit. As for overseas buyers, I knew too well from my broccoli debacle how hard it was to meet their quality requirements. Shipping overseas would require full control of your farms and an impeccable system to track the produce from field to end user across multiple seasons and regions.

How could someone start from scratch and suddenly

overcome challenges I had wrestled with daily for years: the ever-changing continental climate, the stubborn villagers, ruthless wholesalers? How could someone turn a world of uncertainty into such a predictable profit machine?

The acerbic tone of my investor's email was in tune with general conversations I had had with our shareholders over the past few months. When I turned my first full year of profit, I naively expected to be praised. Instead, people got more ambitious and more demanding of me. Looking at companies like Chaoda, many questioned whether I was the right man to lead Creative Food in its next phase of development. I heard from some directors that the board was discussing the option of hiring a professional CEO. I didn't help by showing outward annoyance at comments that directors made during our formal meetings.

"Would it make sense to engineer a veggie burger for McDonald's?" said one of them in 2004, as we considered new ways of expanding the business.

"This isn't India," I said. "The Chinese want better meats. They're not turning vegetarian any time soon."

Five years into the venture, I was turning a profit but one that was much smaller than what I had promised. The German bank even complained I had deliberately misled everyone to get funding after I stopped the Japan export program. By now, I had confidence that I was running the company pretty well, but I did feel disappointed at their impatience after what I thought had been a wild ride away from the brink of disaster. Now came Chaoda. Even the company's name was annoying: *Chaoda* means "super large". And it was, supposedly, doing everything I said I would do. Bigger, better and faster.

By 2005, Chaoda had raised hundreds of million dollars on the stock market. Some analysts questioned the lofty margins that appeared unsustainable. But an increasing number of my investors conducted reviews of the business, then came back and confronted me with questions during board meetings. Some were even looking to invest in Chaoda's new bonds.

The fact that Chaoda, in all of its presentations to investors, identified the right challenges made it even more credible. It explained how intermediaries caused vegetable prices to increase with every step in the chain. None of them made a lot of money; they added only around a five percent markup to cover their costs and profits. But they created a lot of waste. Each intermediary unloaded trucks and stored vegetables at often ambient temperature to save cost. Then, they simply peeled away the outer leaves of the vegetables to improve appearance. The peeling itself was a waste, but without refrigeration during storage and transportation, vegetables also lost a lot of moisture, causing more weight loss. On paper, it made total sense to try and bypass that system.

But there was a problem that Chaoda didn't explain clearly in any of its reports. I knew from our model farm experience that it wasn't easy to manage the villagers once you had hired them as workers on your farm, and even harder to train them to do things differently. Also, leasing land and employing workers meant an increase in costs that wasn't always matched by rises in productivity and quality. Chaoda claimed to have somehow dealt with all of that successfully on a large scale from day one.

Another issue I didn't understand: Chaoda claimed that it had several farms in different parts of China, and a planted area twenty time larger than mine, even counting all my suppliers' farms. Yet, for all that, I had never heard of them as a potential supplier. I asked wholesalers too. They knew the name, but they didn't see Chaoda's produce in the market. In fact, the largest wholesaler in Beijing put it this way: "The only time I hear about

Chaoda is when they dump a large load of vegetables at prices below the cost of growing and disrupt the entire market." That didn't sound like a good way to generate high margins.

In my mind, the issues were clear. I was already one of the biggest vegetable buyers in China so, one way or another, and it felt logical that Chaoda, with all of its reported acreage, should have dealings with me or at least my suppliers — but they didn't. I suspected that Chaoda used "creative" accounting to show high margins. But I could prove nothing and struggled to convey all of this to others. The comparisons between Creative Food with Chaoda didn't stop, and my answers made me sound increasingly defensive.

I now believe that one key to the Chaoda riddle lay in the role government subsidies played for most agricultural businesses in China. Every year in January, China's State Council issues a report called "The Number One Document," offering reflections on the policies and initiatives that authorities consider a priority. Traditionally, the document focuses on rural and agricultural issues, emphasizing the importance of the sector to Chinese leaders. In 2004, China waived all taxes on farmers, in a strong signal that after years of using the countryside to support the cities, it was time to protect and modernize agriculture. In my meetings with government officials, the word "modern" kept coming up, just as it had in my TV interview with Ye Rong. The term acted as a code word, an expression of commitment to change things for the better, and also an "open sesame" to the magic kingdom of government subsidies. The fact that Chaoda's full name included the word "modern" showed that it knew which buttons to push.

The stakes were high. The government's plan to modernize would bring financial benefits for companies who were working to improve the country's agriculture. I had received some subsidies myself. In exchange for investment in a new plant, hiring local workers and bringing some cachet to a rural district, I could negotiate for some of the money made available by the province or the central government. The subsidies took the form of a combination of tax exemptions, direct cash toward investments and interest-free loans. Local officials backing my investments also benefitted. Their promotions up the government hierarchy depended on a combination of indicators measuring the region's GDP growth, jobs created in their towns and the amount of foreign currency generated If I could help a local official improve in at least two out of those three areas, my project had a good chance of winning some cash. Whether the project made money in the end didn't matter too much. Every player of a certain size in China's agriculture industry received some government help. I had watched my old traders convert into farmers by tapping into these pools. And if I was doing it, it made sense that Chaoda would be too.

So why weren't they disclosing any subsidies in their annual report?

I wanted to know more about this competitor and its mysterious and outsize success. So, in 2005, I asked Mike to reach out to the newly-built Chaoda farm near our Wuhan plant to see whether its manager could help arrange a meeting with Chaoda's owner. A few weeks later we had an invitation from Kwok Ho, Chaoda's mysterious billionaire CEO. The name sounded like someone from Hong Kong, but Kwok was a former government official from Fuzhou, a coastal city in Fujian Province across from Taiwan and a one-hour flight south of Shanghai. At the airport, Mike and I hired a taxi and drove to Chaoda's headquarters downtown. It didn't look ostentatious. In fact, the non-descript white-tile building resembled what you would see anywhere in China's modern sprawl.

Once inside, it took a while to get to Kwok Ho's office. First, we had to go through a receptionist, who then passed us to a secretary, who in turn made us wait in a room. Mahogany wood panels darkened the space, creating a library-like atmosphere. This room connected with others, a bit like an airlock between chambers, as if it were designed solely to block intruders.

As Mike and I were led through more dark corridors and handed over to more assistants, our voices and steps bounced against empty walls. That, too, felt strange. In my office, clients' orders — or complaints — churned relentlessly out of the fax machines while loud conversations took place in cubicles. The way I saw it, my company culture was like others which traded fruits or vegetables. People working with such highly perishable commodities developed an acute sense of urgency — and as a consequence there was a lot of activity. But there was none of that at Chaoda's headquarters, even though this was a company that was now reporting sales of $1 billion in fresh vegetables across China and Asia.

Before we met Kwok, one last assistant made us sit in a windowless conference room where we watched a video introducing the company. Once again, it was slickly done and, even to a professional like me, it made total sense. If I had had enough money to produce a film back when I started, it would have looked much the same. However, some images seemed out of place. There was a vegetable processing line that looked eerily like ours, even though Chaoda's business was to trade raw vegetables, a less-processed product than my salads. Did Kwok plan to enter my market? I wasn't sure, but the prospect was daunting. Even as an outsider, Chaoda's large cash pile could make it an attractive alternative for my clients, who were concerned I was too vulnerable already.

When I raised the question with Mike, he noted that the

equipment in the video looked exactly like that of one of our competitors in Shanghai. I later learned from one of the investors in that business that he had been talking to Chaoda for a few months before my trip to Fujian. The discussions had fallen apart after he accompanied Chaoda to a provincial government meeting in Nanjing and felt that Chaoda was using his company's name and clients to negotiate more subsidies.

Finally, we got to Kwok Ho's office. It was almost bare, with a couple of books on the shelves, more mahogany furniture and a few black leather armchairs assembled in a horseshoe. The arrangement recalled any Chinese government official's office. There was no computer. When Kwok entered, he greeted us with the ease of someone who has been hosting such meetings all day for years. Three assistants in their twenties sat next to him, notebooks in hand.

In his fifties, Kwok Ho had a pockmarked face, gelled hair combed back and small eyes that made him look shrewd and alert. He wore a black suit with a black shirt and had the look of someone who had seen many battles and relished the thought of another one.

"President Li, I've heard a lot about Creative Food," he said to start the conversation. "My team in Wuhan sends me weekly reports about the status of our farms, and they've described your operations there in detail,"

Chaoda's new farm in Wuhan was just a mile away from my own factory in Zhangduhu, where Doug had built his model farm. The Zhangduhu secretary had told Mike that the Chaoda farm had been heavily subsidized by the local authorities. I was flattered that Kwok knew about Creative Food—but hearing how he had gotten his knowledge left me with an uncomfortable feeling. The reports he mentioned sounded more like intelligence gathering than the data-focused spreadsheets I received about my own operations. Mike said later that such reports were the usual way senior government officials received updates. "You don't run a business by writing such reports," he added.

For half an hour, Kwok and I talked in general terms about our two companies and ways in which we might cooperate. I tried to understand how he managed the inherent uncertainty associated with crops.

"We have our own ways," he said, smiling but refusing to divulge details. "You know, we Chinese do things differently."

I bristled at this. Apart from me, everyone in my company was Chinese, and I knew that the only Chinese secret was hard work. But the message was clear: Kwok judged me an outsider.

I was also a potential client for him, and a big one at that. But instead of looking eager to cut a deal, Kwok sounded more like a government official promoting his region. In the end, he gestured to one of the twenty-somethings and ordered him to follow up with a list of prices for vegetables we might be interested in buying from Chaoda. We then headed out the door, back through the many chambers and outside, where we joined another assistant tasked with showing us Chaoda's farms.

The car drove for an hour until it reached what the assistant described as Chaoda's core farm. For a long time, we rode among fields of pumpkins, then cabbage, then Chinese greens. Chaoda's empire seemed limitless. Yet to yield such high profits, I presumed it did something special, something that no one else was doing in China.

The assistant repeated his lines as he must have done with many visitors. "This is a 1,500-acre farm," he said proudly. This was a giant figure in a country where average farm size is less than one acre. He seemed to genuinely believe he was working for a company that was changing the ways of China.

But what I saw told a different story. I spotted a couple of smaller gardening-type tractors I assumed were used inside greenhouses. But for the most part, the furrows inside the field weren't deep, a sign that they were made by hand. This "1,500 acre-farm" looked to me like hundreds of small plots operated by small farmers, just like everywhere else in China. Chaoda might be nominally leasing the land, but all indicators showed villagers were farming it as they had done for decades. There was no way that such humble plots could achieve the levels of productivity that Chaoda claimed.

A few minutes later, the car stopped at the packing house. I had seen many similar operations; they were often just sheds but usually very large so hundreds of workers could fit inside to clean and trim vegetables before wrapping and packing them in cartons. They were usually very busy places. Here, I walked the empty premises, wondering how the narrow concrete building could accommodate more than a handful workers. The refrigerated cold storage was so small it wouldn't even hold one day of my lettuce inventory; it certainly couldn't contain the thousands of tons per year that were supposed to be harvested from the surrounding farm.

When I asked why the facility was deserted, the young man explained that it wasn't yet harvest season. That too didn't make any sense. By nature, a vegetable grower staggers his planting so he won't have his entire crop ripening at the same time. And when the season ends, savvy farmers rotate crops to make the best use of the land.

What I saw in Fujian. — the empty office, the casual neglect with which Kwok treated a potential client, the unimpressive farms, and the inadequacy of the facilities — was a long way from what was described in the slick presentations.

On the road to the airport, I checked one last thing: one of Chaoda's own retail vegetable stores. There was one in downtown

Fuzhou, a nondescript white building the size of a convenience store. A lot of shelves were half-empty, a few plastic crates were piled in a corner, and the staff calculated the bill with a wide plastic calculator with giant keys. It wasn't digitally integrated like the Seven Elevens and Lawsons I served in Shanghai and Beijing. The sparse shelves betrayed poor planning and bad store management, and the vegetables looked the same as in any mom-and-pop store down the street.

To Mike and me, all of this screamed of a scam. We had no proof. But I was an educated insider who could see through what financiers may not have noticed.

Mike was blunt. "This isn't a farming business," he said. "Obviously, Chaoda is making money from other means."

For six more years, Chaoda continued in this manner. Twice its auditors resigned, causing temporary declines in the stock price. But the accounting firms never explained the reason why they refused to certify the books, and in each case, the stock recovered quickly, and Chaoda hired another accounting firm, arguing that they had had disagreements on fees. The company seemed invincible and Creative Food continued to be compared to it.

By 2011, Kwok had raised $1.4 billion from investors. Jane sent journalists from different newspapers to me, telling them there was a story there. She saw how affected I had been by the constant references to Chaoda and its "superior" model. Jane has a natural tendency to turn protective when she sees her loved ones hurt, so Chaoda—and many of my investors—were on her list. When these reporters contacted me, I would share my doubts, but no one seemed to have the time or the resources to investigate in detail. And I watched what I said carefully because the more I raised issues with Chaoda, the more it sounded like an excuse for my own less-than-stunning performance.

Finally, a short-seller who published reports under the title Anonymous Analytics put out a piece detailing a lot of what I had observed with Mike in Fujian. The report mentioned inflated capital expenditures and asked why the company needed to raise so much money since its impressive profits should have been enough to fund its expansion. It also accused Kwok Ho of funneling cash out of the company through other businesses he had a hand in. Anonymous Analytics pointed to $500 million worth of fertilizer bought by Chaoda from a company controlled by Kwok. The fertilizer manufacturer had no equity, no employees and only one client.

After that report, Chaoda's stock price collapsed and never recovered, though it still trades on the Hong Kong exchange.

I felt somewhat vindicated, but something continued to nag at me. Other companies involved in agriculture had followed Chaoda's steps onto the Hong Kong's stock market with equally unlikely profit margins. Investors continued to pile into these businesses. I was too busy to spend time investigating, so my only hope was for someone else to uncover what I guessed was a giant Ponzi scheme leveraging government subsidies to boost profits.

Mine is an educated guess, but one that was validated again and again by people I met in the industry. It all started with subsidies, the ones Chaoda didn't account for in its annual report. I knew most agricultural companies in China received government help. I also knew that Chaoda had received public funding in Wuhan and in other provinces. But subsidies are usually made to offset large capital investments. They shouldn't affect profits.

So, assuming I was right and that Chaoda was taking subsidies and not accounting for them, where did they go?

My hypothesis is that they probably got hidden in the accounts through a complicated shuffling of invoices aimed at overstating capital expenditures and reducing costs. Anonymous Analytics had flagged such practices in its report.

Sales could be manufactured too. In China's value-added tax system, sellers pay a percentage of sales invoices to the tax authorities. The state keeps track of these tax liabilities by issuing sequenced invoices called *fapiao*. The problem in agriculture is that most farmers or small traders couldn't issue *fapiao* because they lacked a legal entity registered at the local tax bureau to do so. They did most of their business in cash. So, when they were requested to provide a *fapiao* to Creative Food's accountants, many simply bought the invoice on a thriving black market. Companies behind the *fapiao* were real, but they weren't my suppliers. The same practice potentially allowed Chaoda to issue *fapiao* to document fake transactions. The tax authorities didn't check whether the transaction was real. As long as the tax was paid, you could issue as many invoices as you wanted and buy invoices for the corresponding purchases—making it look like you had made sales you hadn't.

The only way to uncover such a masquerade would have been to check the actual volume of vegetables moving through Chaoda's warehouses: literally counting the trucks as they came and went and comparing their loads to the invoices in the books. The tiny warehouse I had seen in Fujian looked very suspicious. My guess is that the two auditors who refused to certify Chaoda's accounts caught whiff of the fraud this way. Like any Ponzi scheme, such combinations also required a constant inflow of cash to fund projects and tax payments. That too explained the incessant fund-raising on the stock market.

A couple of years after my visit to Chaoda, and years before the Anonymous Analytics report came out, an investment banker I knew introduced me to Kwok Ho's wife, Chiu Nalai. She had just divorced Kwok and, the banker said, was looking for new business opportunities. On a trip to Hong Kong, we arranged a meeting with her and the banker. I was curious to understand why she wanted to talk to me specifically; I remembered how Kwok had dismissed me as an outsider.

That morning, I took the subway from my cheap hotel to the luxurious Grand Hyatt. In the breakfast room overlooking Hong Kong harbor, Ms. Chiu, a trim woman in her fifties, stood up when I entered. As we proceeded with the usual greetings and name card exchange, I noted she was wearing a white pair of jeans with expensive Italian loafers that contrasted elegantly with her black silk top. She looked much more stylish than Kwok.

After a polite exchange, the banker started. "Look, the reason we want to talk is because my client wants to launch her own venture on the model of Chaoda," he said.

I nodded approvingly.

"Any company listing in Hong Kong needs to shows a track record of three profitable years, but Ms. Chiu doesn't want to wait for so long," he continued, then paused to see how I was taking this.

I of course realized why she wanted to meet me. As usual, things were expressed indirectly. Creative Food did have three years of profitable audited accounts, and my story provided a good narrative that might attract investors. I smiled, indicating that I grasped where he was heading.

The banker continued. "We could merge Ms. Chiu's new business into Creative Food and list together in Hong Kong."

I didn't think for a minute that I would partner with anyone associated with Chaoda. But I can't say I wasn't flattered. Maybe this was my chance to uncover the Chaoda story, I thought. So I faked interest and asked a few questions about how the common business would expand. That's when Chiu finally spoke.

"We just need your agreement to merge the two companies," she said. "As for the figures... we'll take care of that."

I raised an eyebrow, prompting her to continue.

"You've seen what we did at Chaoda," she continued with a bright smile. "Showing growth and profitability won't be an issue, trust me."

I had my answer.

In 2020, Chiu was Chairman of Le Gaga Holdings, a Nasdaq-listed company operating vegetable farms in China. In its latest available report to investors, the company announced operating profit in excess of 45 percent of sales.

13

SELLOUTS AND HEARTBREAKS

PROTECTED FROM the wet summer heat by powerful air conditioners, twenty managers slowly filed into the meeting room of a three-star hotel in Zhenjiang, a two-hour drive from Shanghai. They had come from all over China to hear me explain the strategy for 2005. Every summer, we met for two days to focus our year-end objectives and negotiate work plans and goals. The places we chose for these meetings weren't fancy, but they always had a slight tourist appeal .

I usually asked Mike to select a city. He knew what the team liked, and I trusted him to keep costs down. That year, he had chosen Zhenjiang, because it was famous for its cuisine featuring a sweet balsamic-style vinegar. In this annual ritual, our managers spent a day and a half in meetings and half a day on sightseeing. People working together separated by hundreds of miles but talking daily on the phone loved to get together and share war stories. For meals, we grouped around large round tables, and after dinner, parties formed naturally, usually playing cards while drinking tea or warm beer and munching on salted melon seeds. I usually retreated to my room; my presence made everyone more formal. Mike would keep me posted on what went on.

At the meeting that morning, tired heads were nodding due

to the late-night card games. Then I pulled up a slide with my strategy for the next year featuring the slogan: "GET BIG FAST."

For years, our common goal had just been survival. I now wanted to shift to a more aggressive and expansionary strategy. For that, we needed to build up our management capabilities. I illustrated my new slogan with a miniature picture of me controlling a diamond-shaped kite balanced in the wind, with each corner labeled with a different goal—fast growth, new products to stay ahead of competitors, improved quality controls and beefed-up management procedures. And, I said, performance of managers would from now on be assessed based on these four criteria.

I knew it would look daunting, stretched as my team already was. So I also offered a new pay structure to reward the best performers and keep them loyal. People could earn incentive pay of up to half a year of their salary if they achieved their goals two years out of three. China's GDP was growing at a rate exceeding 10 percent each year. Creative Food had grown fast too. But so had many other companies who courted my managers in daily phone calls, asking them to jump ship. I wanted everyone feel motivated and valued at the same time.

I was met with silence and expressionless faces.

It wasn't a language issue. By then, all my managers were familiar with my variety of Chinese, with its grammatical mistakes and sometimes inappropriate vocabulary.

"No questions?" I asked.

I couldn't believe I was back to the same blank reactions I had seen five years before, especially after what we had been through together. The story I told myself about being at the center of a tight-knit group of dedicated employees was crumbling with every second that passed in silence.

Then Mike stood up and turned to the group. "In China, we

have a proverb for what Xavier just explained," he said, and switched to Chinese: "*Bing dong san chi, fei yi ri zhihan.*"

I had no idea what it meant, but suddenly the grim faces opened, and people slapped their thighs and laughed. Mike looked at me with a disarming smile. I could have kissed the guy.

He explained to me later that the proverb meant, "Three feet of ice don't get formed in one day." With one turn of phrase, he had made it clear to everyone that the company needed a broader and stronger managerial base, and that I couldn't be at the center of everything any longer.

In the past months, I had created new decision-making processes, and Mike had been answering questions raised by the team, helping to turn the new rules into practical tools. For example, if a manager wanted to travel, she first had to fill out a form and get approval from her boss, then the finance manager had to sign off on it after checking that the traveler's department had sufficient funds for the trip. For every decision, we introduced this kind of triangulated review, where the employee's direct manager and also the one indirectly responsible participated. Many long-time employees resented the increased scrutiny and the loss of direct access to me that they had enjoyed when the company was small. There was some grumbling, and some passive resistance too. People were frustrated that decisions didn't happen as fast, even as I felt relieved not to be the ultimate decider on everything anymore.

In my outline at the meeting, I had been trying to explain why I had made these changes, but the ideas evoked no emotion until Mike spoke. He connected my concept of faster growth and more bureaucracy with something deep and familiar. I was indeed still an outsider; I would always be one. But with Mike, I felt I stood a chance of taking the business we had saved from oblivion to the next level.

My employees weren't always happy about change, but now they understood why it was necessary.

From the moment I took on the day-to-day running of the business, I made decisions without ever getting used to the accompanying anxiety. Before each choice I made, I agonized, and as soon as I had acted, that feeling would be replaced by hesitations about the choice I had just made. To hide my gnawing inner doubts, I often acted too fast. My judgments about people or my views on the company's strategy were generally sound, but when it came to implementation and organization, I pushed everyone around without taking the time to listen or convince them of why my direction was the right one. The fear that people would spot my lack of experience drove most of my choices. The goals I communicated were often unclear, certainly too ambitious, and left my managers confused.

Ignorant of what it took to run a plant or a farm or to sell a product, I would rush and huff, recasting the problems that managers brought to my attention in needlessly broad terms, always seeking an optimum that didn't exist.

When the new plant in Beijing was still in its planning phase in 2003, Su Hong, our technical director, came into my office with Mike and laid a blueprint on the small meeting table I used next to my desk.

"We've gotten approval from the local authorities for this layout," she said. "But I can't see where to fit KFC's new hot kitchen without creating cross-contamination between fresh and cooked products."

KFC was offering to give us the new business—a range of potato and corn salads—providing we could retrofit all our plants with a small cooking area. I wanted the new sales but had no idea how to modify the plan to add a kitchen without affecting the flow for our fresh vegetable processing.

"It's not just a kitchen we need to add," Su added. "Because the new hot salads will have ham and eggs, we also need to have separate storage for these proteins or they will contaminate our fresh vegetables."

I hated such meetings. When I looked at a blueprint, my brain went blank. Adrenaline coursed through me, and I felt incapable of figuring out the connections between doors, corridors and walls, and how all this would affect the production flow.

"Maybe we should hire an industrial architect," I ventured, mentioning a couple of Australian companies I knew.

Su nodded politely, taking notes.

Mike, meanwhile, had been studying the drawings. Now he spoke. "Here, you can knock this wall down, adjust this door and put the new inventory here without interfering with the flow of fresh vegetables."

I could see that he had answered Su's most pressing concern. She was immediately at full attention.

"And you can position your fresh lettuce inventory here, so it's located at the north part of the plant, less exposed to the sun's heat when you unload in the summer," Mike added.

Su gave him a radiant smile. She had a solution to her problem—and more. She could move forward without acting on my idiotic idea to call on an expensive architect.

I then tried to make up for my poor practical decision-making by obsessing over all the tiny details of the plant-building schedule, calling Su and other managers every day, pushing my own fears and stress onto everyone.

I had done the same thing with Doug in Wuhan.

"How is the rain today?" I asked him on my daily calls, trying to goad him into the fields.

Doug had said on one such call, "It stopped for a day—but the soil is still very wet."

"If we can't get into that field soon, we're going to miss the season," I said, stating the obvious.

"I know, I know," Doug said.

"How many days without rain do you need for the soil to dry up?" I pushed him.

Under pressure to give me an answer, Doug made a reluctant commitment. "Three days, I guess..." he said.

It was two days later that a frazzled Doug drove his tractor into a field packed with protesting villagers, fearing that if he didn't, I would terminate him.

Mike's presence reassured me. His attitude toward operational issues was the mirror opposite of mine, the *yin* to my *yang*. Carefully analyzing the ins and outs of every point, he formed a view by first immersing himself in the details. His familiarity with Chinese culture and language meant that he could tap into a vast pool of resources that remained out of my reach. He talked to vendors, engineers, and other specialists to seek advice when he lacked experience.

But it was more than that. His character was more inquisitive and less defensive than mine. He didn't look at every issue as a challenge to his own competence, which created an atmosphere that made it easier for people to express their views. When he reported to me on problems, he outlined options, always careful to let me make the final call, keenly aware of how sensitive I had become when it came to my grip over the chain of command. Mike never forcefully advocated for one solution when he spoke. But working closely together meant I had learned to read his body language. A tone of voice, a choice of words and a certain tilt in his figure were enough for me to guess what he really thought. Our relationship brought peace to my tortured soul, his pragmatic suggestions an ointment on the burn of my endless questioning.

Over the years of Creative Food's growth and transformation, Mike's mediation and management talents meant he went way beyond his job description. He officially ran sales. But I delegated many other tasks to him; he checked on construction budgets, closed a difficult supplier contract, and talked a resigning manager into staying, among other things.

Our relationship wasn't always easy. If we disagreed on an issue during a meeting with other managers, he would ask a pointed question, usually a "What if" that forced everyone to consider the implications.

During one sales meeting, I brought up a plan to launch salads under a retailer's own label. I had met the French management at Carrefour, and they were interested. I envisioned the new range of salads as selling below my Lutece price, in effect increasing exposure for the salad category in general. Mike didn't see it this way.

"What happens if you have a quality problem?" he asked. It sounded less like a question and more like the start of a lecture.

"I'm not sure. I guess it is our product, so it is our problem," I said.

But Mike turned forceful. "It's their brand, so it should be their liability," he said.

Clearly, he didn't like the idea at all. I knew that if I raised this question with the client, it would immediately nip the project in the bud. How could the retailer accept responsibility if I was manufacturing the product? I resented Mike for making the point, not because he was wrong, but because my lack of experience meant I had little idea how to deal with the issue. When I raised the point with the French executive at Carrefour, it looked like he hadn't thought of it either. The project fizzled after that.

In other instances, if Mike didn't like my decision, he

would simply stay silent for the rest of the discussion, sending a clear passive-aggressive message to everyone that he wasn't supportive—and, I felt, undermining my ability to create unity and momentum. In those situations, I could feel the negative tension building in the room as other employees watched the dynamic between us.

When we agreed, there was a very different pattern. He coordinated, dispensed advice, caught slackers, and alerted me to potential problems. The contrast between having Mike engaged and not was striking. He always followed orders and never challenged me publicly, as Kevin had done. But for everyone in the company, the message was clear: If you wanted anything done, you had better have Mike on your side. And so, over the years, I became more and more dependent on Mike's views of any new idea.

While our arrangement worked well despite these occasional tensions, I also wanted real friendship. On our epic Creative Food journey, I longed for the bond that Ulysses shared with his sailors, or the connection that bound Huckleberry Finn and Jim. I also wanted insurance against a potential betrayal. Yet, while I spent more time with Mike every day than I spent with my wife, he never acted as if we were personally close. There was always only the deference of an employee toward his boss.

Once, I accompanied him on a pilgrimage to a Buddhist sanctuary on Putuoshan Island—one of the five sacred sites in Chinese Buddhism. We climbed hills, kneeled together and talked about life during walks along the beach. That's when Mike shared his childhood experience of serving tea for his father's guests. But it didn't change his demeanor at work.

Only on rare occasions did I get a fleeting sense there was more between us than just a contractual agreement. On a visit to an industrial bakery in Shanghai, the Taiwanese-American manager showing us the plan addressed Mike as *Gemen'r*, a word in the Beijing dialect that you might translate as "buddy." I knew that in most business settings, Mike would be addressed with the more formal "Director Chen." As we followed the manager into the yard, I looked at Mike in surprise. "You know that guy from before?" I asked, always suspicious there was some hidden deal going on.

"Nope," Mike said.

"So why does he call you *Gemen'r*?" I asked.

"A lot of people call me their friend," he said. "But my real friends don't call me anything. They don't need to." And he gave me a cryptic smile before walking on.

As our salad business struggled through 2005, I became obsessed with the success of other bagged-salad companies in Australia, Europe and the U.S. I spent a lot of time tracking Scalime Technologies, the French consultants who had initiated the boom in the category. Their main client in the U.S., a company called Readypac, already operated a business exceeding $400 million in revenues. I convinced myself that getting access to Scalime's high-tech packaging and processing lines as well as their new recipe ideas was the secret to our future success.

As usual, Mike was less impressed. His years in sales, he said, had taught him that success in Chinese supermarkets came from making sure you've got clean and good-looking products on the shelves every day—and that you got paid for it.

"Of course, you've got to do all that," I said dismissively, when he questioned the opportunity to spend hundreds of thousands of dollars to get nicer-looking salad bags and better machinery.

To try to convince him that I was right, I asked him to accompany me to France, where I planned to sign a five-year advisory deal with Scalime Technologies.

After two days in Lyon, a large city which is about 300 miles south of Paris, during which we negotiated with Scalime's executives, visited their clients, and argued the fine points of the legal documents, I asked Mike what he thought, certain he had been blown away by the chance we had ahead of us. Mike hadn't spoken much for two days, which wasn't surprising since our talks had been in French or in English (like many educated Chinese, he understood English well but was less comfortable speaking it). He leaned over and spoke to me in Chinese.

"Have you checked their fax machine?" he asked in a conspiratorial tone. While I had been expounding on my dreams for China's new salad culture, Mike had been roaming unnoticed around the office.

"Why should I check the fax machine?" I asked, sensing I wouldn't like what he was going to say.

"For two days I haven't seen a document on their fax machine and, look, they've received few phone calls," he said. "These guys aren't busy."

I was angry with him for being so stubbornly distrustful. But I was angry at myself too, for not paying attention to such details. My senses lulled by the familiarity of dealing with French people, I had taken their claims at face value, while Mike, struggling to understand everything, had looked deeper.

He came from a world of shrewd and opportunistic Chinese sales managers and distributors, and from his days in government, he understood intricate political maneuvering. In his world, things were never straightforward.

I had to acknowledge that I had seen the owner pick up his phone only twice, and one of those times had been to answer a request from someone who sounded like his wife.

In the end, I didn't sign the agreements laid out in triplicate in front of us. Scalime's consultants weren't happy. But a few years later, the company went out of business. When I later reached out to the entrepreneur behind the successful American salad businesses, he told me that the decade-long cooperation with Scalime had been fruitless for him; he had just waited for the contract to expire and didn't renew it. It wasn't about products and packaging, he told me during a two-hour conversation. His success was based on a strict system of store inspections and payment collection. That had always been Mike's point.

I liked that Mike alone had the temerity to oppose me and protect me from my own rash decisions. But it still annoyed me when he pulled me back just as I wanted to rush forward. He seemed genetically unable to get excited.

Creative Food grew rapidly in 2004 and 2005, and I added more senior executives to beef up my management team. I liked people who had held big jobs in big-name companies, but Mike looked more at cultural factors.

"This guy can work within a multinational, but he's used to a very large structure with many people under him and a very established system," he said after meeting one candidate I liked. "It's likely he'll suffer at Creative Food because he'll have to do a lot on his own. I'm just not sure that's the right guy."

This disagreement got to the root of our difference in outlook. Mike was smart enough to understand we needed stronger management discipline. In fact, he was instrumental in creating a lot of the new routines and procedures that we implemented. But our approaches to leadership were vastly different, rooted in aspects that were not personal, but cultural.

I came from a world of predictability, where the rule of law underpinned business decisions, making it easier to take risks and partner with people you didn't know. In the U.S. or Europe, you as the leader outline a vision for the future and you work toward it within the trusted, deeply-rooted capitalist system, moving as fast as you can. In contrast, Mike, like many Chinese, believed that the overall system was flawed, or at least imperfect. In that context, individuals in business can't navigate alone. They need a tight group of trustworthy people to advance but also to protect. In Mike's view, reinforcing the team of employees we had was the only secure way to keep growing sustainably. Change needed to happen, but without breaking what we had — and that meant moving more slowly than I wanted to.

In China, collectiveness as an instrument of protection for the individual starts at the village, with families and clans. Later in life, classmates and companies — the successful ones — will provide a similar network of support away from the village. This network of *guanxi* — connections — is both emotional and practical. People will call on these relationships to get a job, a promotion or any practical favor with the understanding that it will need to be returned. Yet within the group, there is an incredible faith in and reliance on each other that I have never encountered elsewhere. I have a Chinese friend, educated in the U.S., who invests millions of dollars through a long-time associate without a contract or an agreement to document the partnership.

"One day, I tore up a piece of paper and handwrote a two-paragraph note that he signed so my wife would have a claim if something happened to me," he said with a smile.

His view was that the history of trust he shared with his friend protected his family much better than any legal agreement.

The perception of individual rights and freedoms in China is also different from the West's. The safe environment provided by the group comes with requirements, but mostly empowers rather than limits individuals. It's very different from the American view, where personal rights and liberties come before the group's. In trying to build such group loyalties, many Chinese companies operate on the principle that if you take care of employees first, results will follow.

In Chinese businesses today, American management styles are slowly diluting some of these attributes. But some very successful foreign companies in China have embraced the old beliefs in order to tighten the sense of collectiveness among their employees. TNT, the global logistics provider, hired their drivers' wives to run the dormitory and canteens located at its distribution centers so the men could enjoy a sense of community during late night shifts. Starbucks offered to cover healthcare costs for some of their employees' parents because the company found that this was a deep source of anxiety for their staff. A maker of Ikea sofas covered tuition in private schools for workers from outside Shanghai who couldn't send their kids to local public schools because they weren't meeting the strict residency rules. At Creative Food, I sponsored some employees, allowing them to obtain Shanghai residency and opening the door for them to local schools or apartment purchases.

The downside of such a culture, if not managed, is that a tight group tends to be too internally-focused; this happens often in work units in state-owned companies. I could feel that happening at Creative. I thought I should increase the pace of change by stretching our team. Mike worried I might break the team instead.

He believed I was underestimating the implications of the changes I wanted. So he evolved into the protector of our employees, arguing for incremental changes while I clung to the vision I had for the future. The tension never ceased. But it worked — as long as I kept pushing and incorporated feedback in a positive way.

For example, I wanted to bring in experienced managers trained in disciplined organizations so they would build the same framework at Creative Food. Mike, ever the pragmatist, saw things more simply: he wanted to hire personalities who were competent, but mainly who could work with our existing group.

He had a point; we had seen a few recruits from big companies fail. They knew how to operate in a mature corporate environment but could not apply the same principles in our company, where they were pressed for both time and resources. After a couple of months at the Creative Food, one operations director I had recruited from GE outlined his plan to train our plant managers on how to improve quality.

He then turned to me, asking, "What's my training budget?"

"We don't have the money for an extensive training program," I said. In my view, I had hired him to teach these skills himself.

He looked at me bewildered – disgusted, even. Two days later, he sent me his resignation.

Despite countless such examples, I was bothered by Mike's attitude. In my eyes, he was protecting the old Creative Food culture that I was trying to get away from: the one where getting things done was the primary goal with little attention to processes. I felt he was resisting my efforts to bring new talent into the organization. With every candidate I introduced, he was quick to identify potential problems, failing to see that meanwhile, he was becoming overwhelmed by his status as the person everyone relied on.

Sometimes he admitted that the incessant requests for his advice took a toll. "I don't have all the answers," he said to me one evening as we both sat in my office to hash things out. "I just think about things carefully and form a view. I am never completely sure." The pressure on him was intense from inside too. Mike was a protector, but as the main bridge to me, he was also the main channel for people to convey a sense of loss, fear or confusion in the face of my pronouncements.

As a result, he believed newcomers should first "prove

themselves," so they wouldn't confuse everyone with misguided decisions. In meetings, he often challenged their ideas and methods, clearly undermining them in front of everyone. I felt it was unfair, and that people needed time to adjust. What he feared most was that newcomers would bring a different culture, one that was more bureaucratic and political, robbing ours of its positive attributes without adding much. Many of the new managers resented him for that, creating a rift that was hard for me to reconcile. An assistant buyer called Guo Xiangceng, whom I had let go after a few months into the job, texted me one night, probably harnessing the courage to share his feelings after one too many beers.

"You think you're the CEO of this company?" he wrote. "You're fooling yourself; the real CEO is Mike!"

I knew there was some truth to this. I had become over-reliant on him. The balance worked if I kept pushing, but I too was starting to feel worn down. As the organization grew more complex, our focus on preserving the collective spirit meant long periods of time spent in meetings. Every new idea required extensive debate and explanations to convince the team of its worth. That wasn't what I wanted. In addition, I still lacked the language ability to convince or to express nuances. I wanted to be Caesar crossing the Rubicon. Instead, I was tied down by the need to negotiate the operational implications of every new idea. As I began to understand more of the operational details, I too started to focus on risks rather than opportunities, increasingly agreeing with Mike's views and leaving a vacuum that the organization was quick to regard as a power shift, allowing rumors and manipulation to flourish.

Sensing that something was off, I sometimes tried to assert my independence by making decisions without consulting Mike. One day, I hired an operations director without having him interviewed by him and the rest of the team.

"Enough," I told myself. "If Mike can't see we need new ideas, then I'll do without his opinion."

When Mike heard about this, he didn't pick up his phone for three days. The fourth day, he sent me a long resignation letter in Chinese explaining that since I didn't trust his advice, it was better for him to leave.

Beyond the first feeling of shock, I wanted to understand what was behind the words he had written, the linguistic nuances that I was sure he had included as clues to how he really felt. Since I couldn't share its contents with anyone at the company, I called a friend from Hong Kong and asked him to read it and share his opinion.

Edward, who normally was busy with his own issues running a real estate firm with thousands of employees, called back within minutes of getting the letter.

"There is a lot of sadness in the words Mike chose," he said after reading aloud parts of the letter having to do with me detaching myself from him and the group. "If you want to keep him with you, you'll have to make up your mind whether you trust him or not. He's clearly got the sense you are wavering, and that you have lost some trust in him. It's an honest letter, not a power move."

That's the feedback I needed to make up my mind. When I finally managed to get hold of Mike, we met in my office and sat together for a long time. As usual, he picked a proverb to express his view.

"Confucius once said *Yi ren bu yong, yong ren bu yi*," Mike said. This translates as "If you distrust someone, don't use him, but if you use him — then trust him."

I sat back and looked him in the eye. My gut told me to trust him despite my resentment of how dependent I had become on him. He wasn't the problem; my idealistic view of how I should run the company was. The bond I had aspired to build between us did exist. It wasn't the type of overt commitment I had imagined, so I had failed to value it, blinded by my romantic ideal of what it should be.

"Often, you think the solution to our problems will come from outside," he said to me. "While I agree we need to change and reinforce discipline, I don't believe the solution will come from one person, not even from me. That's why I've been reluctant to hire a senior manager to fix all our operational issues."

I understood what he meant. In a way, I had let him and the rest of the organization down as I promoted new initiatives without always securing what we had built together. That day, we agreed he would stay on and that I would recruit more on character and less on skills and hire more managers and fewer directors.

Characteristically for me, I wasn't sure it was the right choice.

I had a hard time assessing the depth of my connection to my managers too. We had spent a lot of time working together through tough times. But there still was a deference and formality that I found disconcerting. During our offsite management retreats, I often entered the dining room to find that at my table, the two chairs on each side of mine were empty while all the other tables were packed. Few managers wanted to sit next to me because I was the boss. When we traveled in group, they joined me in talking about work or practical life details like the purchase of a car; all of them had bought their first vehicles after 2003. But such conversations were a long way from what a Westerner would call a bonding experience, the sharing of one's life purpose or of some vulnerabilities that signal your trust in the relationship. From a Chinese point of view, the ruler distributes power and authority. As such, I wasn't expected to mingle with everyone else.

But beyond the formal respect for my authority, there remained the deep commitment to the collective. It didn't take the form of ostentatious declarations of loyalty to the team. Such proclamations existed, but nobody took them seriously. It bubbled up mostly in small game-like events, like the contest we held to choose the Lutece name, the competitions to create new products, and annual rituals like Chinese New Year celebrations. On such occasions, people lost their usual formality and started to act playful, releasing incredible creativity along the way.

At the annual dinner to celebrate Chinese New Year, Creative Food, like other companies, hosted its entire management team and workers in a large banquet hall, where everyone played games, performed songs, acted, and celebrated in a raucous and boozy atmosphere. For these managers and workers, the time of year meant renewing their commitment to the company, similar to the choice farmers make at that time to either plant a new crop or leave farming to go work in a factory. Every year, I traveled to each of my plants to celebrate this immutable ritual. I knew it was a sensitive period, a moment of change in Chinese life.

At each plant, I made an official speech but then quickly got down to participating in the games the team had prepared. One year in Shanghai, Old Li, my driver, taught me a tongue twister in Chinese that I proceeded to recite in front of an audience of two-hundred people, factory workers included. Of course, I stammered after a couple of lines. The room erupted with laughter, but also with recognition of how hard it was for the poor foreign boss. Some stood up and joined me on stage, but they stumbled not much further on in the tongue twister than I did, causing even more laughter and teasing in the clamor that followed. For these events, employees also prepared elaborate shows, designed costumes, and rehearsed late after work for months in anticipation of a performance that only lasted a few minutes over the course of a meal.

Towards the end of dinner, I went from table to table to thank them for their hard work during the past year. "*Nimen xinkule* (you have worked hard)," I repeated, offering a toast to all workers. Each table's occupants stood awkwardly, denying that they worked too hard and trying to find the words to express formal gratefulness, uncertain whether I would appreciate return praise from them.

After that, it was their turn. A lower-ranking supervisor, sometimes a worker, would gather his courage to address me, face flushed by excitement and alcohol, sometimes hesitating a little, retreating to his own table until his colleagues pushed him forward with words of encouragement. Once next to me, he would approach discreetly, waiting for me to finish a conversation, standing respectfully with two hands around a glass held at waist level. I would then get up and say a few words to him as he blushed and probably wondered why he ever had been foolish enough to place himself in the limelight. He would then place his glass well below mine as a sign of deference and say, "Thank you, boss! You have worked hard," before tapping my glass gently with his and then calling for a straight shot while the crowd cheered.

On such nights, I could physically feel the energy running through the audience, the folksy playfulness finally liberated as my managers and workers reconnected with the games and traditions of life in the village and celebrated being together.

The kind of intimate sharing of experiences I knew back home may not have been common among my Chinese colleagues, but the bond was there, maybe deeper than what I had known in the West because of the knowledge that the company and I represented a safe space in which they could finally express their creativity. This closeness was expressed on certain occasions only, and always in that collective sense, within the limits of a trusted community.

One Sunday afternoon in December 2004, I reluctantly left my home in Shanghai. Jane was a month away from giving birth to our first child, a girl, and I wanted to spend as much time with her as I could. I had just completed a new round of fundraising, bringing in an investor from Japan. So, when investment bankers from Islemount Partners called to set up a meeting, I nearly turned them down. New to the investment-banking business, they didn't seem like people who could add much for me. But Roger Marshall, my old ally and supporter, had made the introduction. Roger had been such a stalwart since the ABN Amro days that I took the call and set up the meeting, although I didn't expect much from it.

Alex Hill and Wayne Farmer, both Canadians, met me at a cafe downtown, where I took them through the presentation that I normally used to introduce the business. The way I explained it, my future had three possible strategic paths. I could move toward becoming the best lettuce supplier in China, expand my farms, and reduce my cost of production. The comparison model I used was Dole and their banana plantations.

Or, I said, I could focus on the business with supermarkets and build a brand synonymous with fresh salads, as had LA-based Readypac or Fresh Express in Salinas, California — both giants in the industry.

Finally, my third option was to expand my range of products beyond mere salads and focus on providing a range of fresh foods to large corporate chains like KFC, McDonald's and Starbucks. My model for this was a British company called Geest which produced fresh foods with a short shelf life. Their products included bagged salads like mine, but also fresh sandwiches, wraps, chilled pizzas, soups, sauces, and ready-meals that looked like Blue Apron meals ten years before Blue Apron existed. Geest made these foods for major British retailers, including Tesco and Marks & Spencer, who stuck their own labels on them. It was an innovative business model. I had contacted Geest to discuss a potential partnership in China, but received no response.

The meeting ended on a friendly note, with no commitments on either side. But a few weeks later, Wayne called.

"I've just come across an article in the *Financial Times*," he said. "It looks like a small company from Iceland called Bakkavor is launching a take-over bid for Geest. These Icelanders sound very ambitious. Would it be all right if I introduced Creative Food to them?"

I told him to go ahead. Wayne used the "Contact Us" button on Bakkavor's website and within two hours, Bakkavor's chairman, Agust Gudmundson, replied that he was interested in talking about an investment in Creative Food. Wayne asked him to sign a confidentiality agreement so we could send him our business plan.

On a conference call a day later, Agust struck me as being spare with words but a straight shooter. "I'm interested in talking about acquiring your company to expand in China and diversify away from the slow-growing European market," he said. "But give me a couple of months until I hire someone to take care of business development in Asia."

And with that, negotiations to sell a stake in Creative Food began.

I continued to struggle with the organization I envisioned — and with my right-hand man. I had made my choice by trusting Mike, but it didn't make things between us any easier. For every change I planned to make, every manager I wanted to bring on board, Mike presented a list of risks and potential consequences that were scary enough to make me pause. I was worn out. Our recruitment efforts stalled. And when I did manage to hire someone, Mike made a point of repeating to me the mistakes and missteps each new manager made. None of the three operations directors I hired to keep an eye on the plant managers across the country made it in the end. One left because I didn't provide him with the training budget he wanted, while I pushed the other two out because they couldn't seem to grasp what their subordinates were doing. Meanwhile, we all got increasingly busy running a complicated business.

Six months after my introductory call with Agust, I was invited to speak at an international retail conference in Budapest. Executives from the world's top chains gathered once a year to network and review the state of the industry. They asked me to share my experience selling salads to Chinese consumers. That alone represented quite a recognition of what I had accomplished. The conference invited Jane to accompany me, so we both flew to Paris, left our newborn daughter with my parents and took off for a romantic two-day trip to Eastern Europe. The founder of Doctors Without Borders spoke just before I did. I was on edge. The room could hold a thousand people, and two giant screens behind me would play a video about Creative Food that Jane had helped produce.

As I waited backstage for the keynote speaker to finish, Bakkavor's chief negotiator called me. I stood behind a black velvet curtain on the side of the giant stage, peeking out at the Doctors Without Borders founder, now France's Minister of Health, giving his speech. Surrounded by the noise of stage technicians pushing carts and talking into their walkie-talkies, I learned that, after weeks of haggling, Bakkavor had agreed to my terms and wanted to buy a forty percent stake in Creative Food with an option to buy the remaining balance three years later. A few minutes after that, I stepped out for my presentation. The audience of executives laughed at my jokes, applauded in the right places, and rushed to introduce themselves to me afterwards. I was on top of the world.

The following day, Jane and I did what we usually did when we wanted a romantic time together: we went running at 5 am. As we reached the top of the hill overlooking the Danube River, I spotted the tents in the castle courtyard being set up in preparation for our black-tie dinner that night. We ran on, and I began to ramble aloud about issues at Creative Food. Despite my sense of triumph from the day before, doubts about Creative Food always crept in. Insecurity was my default mode.

"Your business is dripping all over our lives," Jane said.

I knew she was right, but I couldn't help continuing. I complained about the company's inertia, my inability to take the business into new areas, Mike's stubbornness.

Jane listened for a while, but she had heard my complaints one too many times. "It's annoying to hear you constantly refer to what Mike thinks," she said finally. "I believe the company's inertia reflects your own."

For several years now, Jane had been on my side, accepting constant traveling and late nights alone while I met and negotiated with suppliers or clients. All along, she had been a steadfast believer in my ability to see this venture through. But she couldn't stand the way I was now second-guessing myself.

I looked back at her, shocked, bruised and angry. Then I blew up in a defensive rant. But the truth was that she was right—and I hated to hear it.

In some dark corner of my soul, I knew that bringing in a partner like Bakkavor would help me weasel out from my reliance on Mike. I would be able to push new ideas and resources. Selling highly perishable foods to demanding customers was what Bakkavor did every day—and in volumes much larger than ours. Mike wouldn't be able to say they didn't understand the business. I would no longer have to listen to his objections.

In September 2005, I flew to London and met with Roger Marshall. We planned to meet a few of Creative Food's oldest shareholders to explain why they should support me and vote in favor of the deal with Bakkavor. It was not a sure thing yet. Many investors felt that after so many years of struggle, we were now on an upward trajectory and that we should wait for a better deal. I disagreed. I feared the next food safety scandal, I feared losing Mike and other key employees, and I feared not being able to raise more money. In short, I feared that the castle of cards I had built could collapse at any moment.

After taking the high-speed train from Paris, I met up with Roger in front of a stately Victorian building overlooking Hyde Park. We were scheduled to see one of my oldest investors, Jeremy Paulson, whom I had known since my days at Asiafoods, when he was a shareholder there. His emerging-markets fund managed more than a billion dollars in listed companies around the world. But his investment in Creative Food was his and his partner Richard Carss's own money. Since the inception of my company, they had been amazingly supportive, sending me cash each time I asked for it. The deal with Bakkavor would make a handsome return for the risks they had taken. I couldn't wait to tell them about it.

Roger and I waited in the boardroom of their investment company. A mix of traditional oil paintings and framed pictures of Middle Eastern scenes decorated the walls. Jeremy and Richard entered the room and greeted us in their posh British accents.

"Nice to see you, Xavier. How are you?" Jeremy said, as we stood up to shake hands. "I suppose you didn't access your emails this morning on your way from Paris."

I said that I had not.

"You might want to take twenty minutes and read this carefully," he said, handing me four pages that he had printed out. "Here is what we received this morning," he added, very formally, while Richard looked on. "Read it and tell us what we should do with it."

Roger looked at me, wondering what the atmosphere of secrecy was about. We both nodded politely and watched the two men leave the boardroom. Then we sat down and read the documents.

The emails contained shocking allegations accusing both Mike and me of embezzling money from the company for our own profit. There was a lot of accurate information, with a level of detail that most employees at Creative Food wouldn't be able to provide. They stated, for example, that assets were missing on the books of our Shanghai company, alleging that I had stolen them from the business. But these assets had been physically moved to our Guangzhou plant. In the scramble to start the plant fast, I had neglected to check that the ledger reflected the transfer. It was bad accounting, but it certainly wasn't embezzlement. Likewise, other facts were twisted to show intent to defraud the company. The senders' email addresses were in former employees' names. The domain name was @163.com, a service offered by Netease, a portal similar to Yahoo, where people create free email addresses. I immediately believed they had been created by someone for the sole purpose of making these allegations using other people's names.

I shuddered when I saw that they weren't addressed only to Jeremy and his partner but to all 25 of my shareholders. Jeremy could make an assessment and decide what to do with his own money. But the banks were represented by managers who might worry that they could be incriminated for hiding potentially embarrassing information. I feared they would overact to protect themselves.

In my mind, the accusations were easy to dismiss. I knew they all came from Winnie Wu, the finance director I had let go six months earlier. No one but Winnie could have written at this level of detail about issues inside our company.

I had hired her two years before to build up our internal control systems and improve cost management. She had butted heads with Mike on several issues and I didn't intervene at first, thinking the two needed to work it out. But I didn't like how dismissive she was of everything we had built, and unlike with operations, I knew something about financial procedures.

I encouraged her to listen more, to adapt what she knew to our organization. I even hired a consultant to help her set up the systems. When I saw that Winnie remained aloof, political and abrasive, I started looking for someone to replace her. She probably sensed that danger. So she coerced our IT technician, I learned later, into automatically sending copies of all my emails to her account. When I began to notice that certain employees knew things they weren't supposed to know, I hired a forensic expert from Kroll Inc., the international investigation agency, to go through our server and check whether someone was monitoring my emails. The man identified links to Winnie's computer, proving she had read my communications. But she had been careful never to download any messages.

There was too little evidence to prosecute her. "Without the physical presence of a document on her computer," the forensic expert said, "you won't get a judgment in your favor in a Chinese labor dispute."

Over the next few weeks, I pushed Winnie out—but I didn't do it in the spectacular manner I wanted to. Dismissing an employee in China wasn't just business as usual, it quickly became personal. The issue of "face" in Chinese culture means that people can feel humiliated to the point of seeking revenge in all sorts of ways. I had learned to let people go in the gentlest possible manner, after a long talk about how much I valued our relationship and pointing at outside factors to justify the decision: a change in organization, a difficult financial period, or a shift in strategy.

Moreover, I made sure to pay fired employees more than the legal termination payment, holding for a few additional months the extra amount that wasn't bound by law to be paid immediately. As I had done with Kevin, deferring payment was meant to dissuade disgruntled employees from sending allegations of misconduct to other employees, customers or government agencies. Even if they were false, such allegations were sure to disrupt our organization. So, I gave Winnie my fakest smile, parted with her as best friends, and sent her away with a generous payment that I partially delayed until six months later.

The meeting in London happened exactly one week after I had signed her last check.

After half an hour, Roger and I met the two bankers for lunch. I was upset. But Jeremy played down the issue. He had seen it before, he said. But he warned me that this could disrupt our company's sale to Bakkavor. Anything casting doubt on my integrity would be a red flag, providing ammunition to opponents of a deal inside Bakkavor. Many of the company's employees, who had come from the old Geest business, already openly questioned the wisdom of investing in China, so far away from the company's British roots. Roger agreed with Jeremy that this could be a problem. It wouldn't look good if the emails surfaced again a few months after Bakkavor's investment — and I didn't put it past Winnie to find Bakkavor's owners and write to them directly.

In Roger's view, we needed an independent investigation leading to a report that he could disclose.

I cringed. Having a report on this issue might give it more credence than it deserved. I had seen it in Roger's eyes already. Much of it was my word against Winnie's. Roger probably trusted that I hadn't done any of the things she accused me of doing, but it looked bad and messy. By relying so much on Mike and failing to assert my authority inside the company, I had created a power vacuum that allowed rumors and conspiracies to flourish, and for schemers like Winnie to have the freedom to manipulate others.

As usual, it was all my fault.

It took a few months to get a report from the agency that Roger had hired, delaying the closing of our transaction with Bakkavor. In the meantime, auditors found more mistakes in the books that Winnie had managed for two years, forcing me to accept a reduced price for the business. I was comforted by the fact that Agust didn't really budge when I told him about the allegations. He assured me that he had a vision for what we could do together and that this wouldn't change it.

In the end, the report stated that the investigators couldn't find any proof to back up Winnie's allegations. The firm contacted the former employees who supposedly had written to the shareholders, but none of them responded. It reviewed my actions and Mike's, which also yielded nothing to back up the allegations. The only detailed facts mentioned in the report referred to a memo I had written in my defense. For the board, that was enough to move on. But for me, the stain remained. Mike and I were cleared, but I knew that there would always be someone recalling these allegations and wondering whether they were true. A truly thorough forensic investigation would have shown the allegations were all false, but there was no time to conduct that kind of detailed inquiry. In the end, it was still my word against Winnie's.

Still, Roger sent the report to Bakkavor. Our deal then moved forward.

A couple of weeks before signing, Chiquita contacted me. The banana company had just acquired Fresh Express, the leader in the U.S. bagged-salads category. They now had ambitions to expand in China. I wavered a little, but chose to stick with Bakkavor; I liked Agust and his people. The last-minute appearance of a second suitor had the advantage of making us look sought-after. I had to disclose their interest to Bakkavor, which helped overcome the tense haggling that usually takes place before the completion of a sale. In April 2006, Bakkavor bought forty percent of Creative Food with an option to buy the rest of the company if it hit a certain size at a valuation nearing US$20m.

What should have been a celebration for me turned out to be strangely anticlimactic. After being diluted by successive rounds of financing, my shares turned out to be worth a little less than two million, which isn't the type of wealth that allowed me to retire on a private island. But it was more than I or anyone in my family had ever made. So, I felt incredibly grateful. Other investors doubled their investment, some tripled it — a fair result, a credit to my persistence, but not a home run either. But the sudden wealth I acquired upon selling a chunk of my company to an investor whom I respected and liked only partly made up for the wounds, accumulated over the years. I didn't share my feelings with him, but Winnie's allegations helped bring me closer to Mike, because I knew for a fact that he hadn't done what she alleged. The death from cancer around the time of my former expat lettuce expert, Steve, cast a shadow over the success. Steve and I had kept in touch over the years, and he had continued to invest in the company. I was touched that he still trusted me and had looked forward to proving that trust was justified. I missed him.

Back in 2001, I had on one occasion laid down on my office floor, fearful and overwhelmed by responsibilities while still full of dreams for my fledgling start-up. Five years later, I sold a stake in a business with six factories, a thousand employees, and $30 million in revenues, but with mixed feelings about it.

14

MORE CHINESE THAN THE CHINESE?

EVENING WAS coming when our car pulled into a maze of warehouses and workshops crammed together under plastic roofing that cast a surreal greenish halo over everything. Sitting in the back seat, I finished my phone conversation and looked around, wondering where we were.

"Old Li, are you sure this is the right address?" I asked my driver, the man who for the past seven years had been guiding me through the most remote places of the Yangtze River delta.

Outside my window a dozen women sat at a long wooden table under one of the green sheds, working their sewing machines.

"Unh," Li said, grunting assent. "It's here, just straight ahead."

In front of us, a dark alley led us past a couple of fire escapes, puddles from an afternoon shower, and gutters draining water one drop at a time. I was sure there were rats scurrying in the shadows; I listened intently for squeaks and hisses. I had seen many scruffy factories, but this one didn't look anything like a place where you would make food. Yet this was where the great-looking frozen pizza slices I had seen in dozens of convenience stores around Shanghai were put together.

This visit was part of a wide search for companies for Creative

Food to acquire. Our understanding after I sold a stake in Creative Food to Bakkavor was that I would stay on to grow the business. In exchange, they would provide me with unlimited funds, ending my years-long struggle for cash. With their firm backing, I had a $30 million credit line from a Japanese bank, and I was under pressure to put it to work.

Old Li got out to guide me, and together, we skipped over the puddles and climbed a stairway. Strangely, nobody was there to greet us. Upstairs, we entered a kitchen like many I had seen in local canteens while I was at Asiafoods. Grease had permeated every wrinkle of the walls. On tiles that used to be white, there was now a permanent yellowish stain that congealed into a thick layer of grime at every corner. Kitchen pots, blackened by the gas-powered flames, were piled by the side of the stove while a lonely wok, equally black with filth, lay on the floor under a leak in the ceiling. Every drop of water from that leak echoed through the deserted space. On the formica preparation table sat a large wooden chopping block covered in blood stains.

In my mind, I heard the voice of Denis, the French operations director from my Asiafoods days, yelling, "I hate wooden blocks! They keep bacteria inside even after you clean them thoroughly. They're the single best way to contaminate your clients."

Beyond the kitchen was an empty office filled with dark fake-mahogany furniture and black leather sofas of the type favored by a certain grade of Chinese government official. Nobody was there. Li had seemed sure of his navigation, but I still wondered if we were in the right place.

When a kitchen worker finally appeared, Old Li told her we were looking for her boss. She disappeared for a minute or two, and soon a man came up another stairway, this one leading directly into the office. I don't remember his name, but his face has stayed with me. He had a look of utter neglect. Baggy black trousers that were too long fell on dirty shoes, while his shirttail hung partially out of his pants. He had tried to comb his greasy black hair, but like everything about him it was sloppy. Strands fell across his face.

"We're from Creative Food," I said. "We called you to see if you were interested in a cooperation." The term was a Chinese euphemism to avoid saying, "I want to buy your company."

The man smiled a bit too eagerly, revealing a couple of badly decayed teeth.

"Sure, I am very happy to cooperate," he said. He pondered for a second. "And you can buy my business too," he added. It was uncharacteristically forward for a Chinese entrepreneur.

From there, we proceeded outside his office onto a steel grating and down the stairs to visit his workshop. As soon as we arrived at the entrance, the stench of urine overwhelmed the smell of baking dough. The toilet was located two steps to the side of the entrance and clearly had a sewage problem.

Inside the small but efficient workshop, everyone wore white clothes and hairnets. It looked at least like the production complied with sanitary rules, but the details were damning. Strands of hair peeked out from under every worker's hat. One of the two small rooms was dedicated to preparing the pizza toppings; the other was used for baking. There was no separation between unwashed produce, raw meat and the area where the baked pizzas were sliced and packed in individual boxes. In the preparation room, ham, chicken and vegetables like tomatoes and peppers were cut next to each other before workers spread them on the dough. That too was a contamination risk. Obviously, the plant had gotten its production license through back channels; there was no way such a place could pass a formal inspection.

After a few minutes, I realized I was uncomfortably warm. "Aren't you supposed to keep the room at 40 degrees?" I asked the owner.

"Yes, but it's the end of the shift and they probably switched off the air-conditioning to save money," he replied.

The air conditioning units being used to cool down the room were the same as those I used in my apartment. Even if they were on, I knew they would not maintain low enough temperatures to prevent bacteria from growing when the temperature outside exceeded 100 degrees.

The boss either didn't care or didn't know about such details. But to me, it was shocking that his pizza slices were being marketed everywhere in Shanghai, and even in fastidious Japanese convenience store chains. Assuming the entrepreneur had bribed a local official to get his licenses, I wondered why no client's audit had uncovered the issues I was observing.

It angered me. For years, I had jumped through hoops, constantly under pressure to provide the best price and constantly fretting about safety — all the while competing with businesses like this, with leaky toilets right next to tables where food was handled.

The pizza entrepreneur was an extreme case, but he wasn't very different from many of the companies I began visiting at the end of 2006. Many were growing fast, making profits and selling their foods to large supermarkets, where, I reasoned, they could complement my salads. But they were usually tiny operations that did well by operating below the radar — and certainly below the quality standards of a company like Creative Food.

If I invested in such companies, I knew they would resist any changes I might want to impose. Even if I bought the business outright, the price at which it sold its products would likely be so low that upgrading it to meet China's regulations would turn it into a loss-maker. The separation of low-risk and high-risk processing areas, for example, required a larger plant, one that would stay cool all day. I didn't want to buy a seemingly profitable business for a high price because it didn't operate in line with the regulations and see it lose money as soon as I took over and began implementing costly but vital improvements.

There was another reason shopping for investments wasn't as easy or fun as I had dreamed when I was broke. The day I visited the pizza entrepreneur, I was alone. But on most trips, I traveled with my new boss, the man Agust had hired to run Asia for Bakkavor. A six-foot-five man in his late thirties, Einar Gustafsson towered over me and acted the part of the gregarious Viking. He had short curly blond hair, gelled every day to give it undulating waves, and a stubble that suggested a rugged sailor ready to take China by storm. Einar was interesting because he was much more sophisticated than first impressions implied. An Icelander raised in the U.S., he had been a management consultant before joining and successfully turning around a small seafood processing company in Boston. After that, he joined Agust and his brother in London to help them acquire companies in China and Asia.

With a brashness that made me cringe, he would ask up front in every meeting how much the owners wanted for their business with a directness that translators often struggled to express in Chinese. During these awkward meetings, I realized that I myself was now embarrassed by this Western bluntness. The Chinese always turned to me, tongue-tied but eyes filled with questions. Some of them avoided Einar's query, while others blurted out a figure that was so high it bore no link to reality.

Several times, I confronted Einar about this, but he continued unabashed. In his view, the Chinese roundabout way of building relationships was a disguise, or a preparation for what would turn out to be a shrewd negotiation in the end. He wanted to unmask them right away.

When I tried to explain that process matters in all things Chinese and was a way to build trust and show respect, he dismissed me with a laugh. "Your problem is that you've got Stockholm syndrome," he replied. "You've been here so long that you're becoming more Chinese than the Chinese themselves!"

Einar had grown up in the U.S., but he was deeply immersed in the Icelandic business culture of the time. Companies from the tiny country were acquiring businesses around the world. They moved fast, and like Bakkavor, they bought companies many times bigger than their own. Brashness had made them successful, so why change?

But deals in Europe and Scandinavia worked because you could assume some shared values and a stable legal environment. I had learned over and over that this wasn't the case in China. What protected you here were personal relationships, not a set of contracts or values — and that meant building these relationships first. That was too slow for Einar. I had made the mistake of buying him a copy of *Mr. China* by Tim Clissold, the story of an American businessman's investment mistakes during the Roaring 90s. Now he thought he knew all he had to know. I couldn't convince him otherwise.

We butted heads constantly. I found myself defending the ways of China, repeating clichés about the country exactly like the people who used to annoy me.

"You don't understand, China is different," I would say without any effect.

Some of the companies we considered buying were much larger and better organized than the pizza business — often many times bigger than Creative Food. But of course, that didn't bother Einar, but I couldn't help but worry about all the things that could go wrong.

In fact, on our long list of targets, there didn't seem to be a decent business that was not too small or too big for us to swallow. Any business in China comes with a maze of fealties ranging from local officials to employees and clients, all of whom have personal relationships with the entrepreneur. The larger the company, the more complex those connections. That's how people make up for weak rule of law.

One way to deal with it was to leave the business alone after you acquired it. But that was risky because, as with the pizza business, it probably did things well outside the code of conduct of a company like Bakkavor. Or you could move several of your own executives into the new business and gradually take over management. But there was a problem doing that, too—and it wasn't just the issue of language and culture. I was sure the web of personal relationships wouldn't simply transfer to a new executive; it would stay with the founder, creating more risks. Einar heard all this from me, but he didn't take it seriously.

On one occasion, we traveled together with our investment bankers to Zhengzhou, a city in Henan province in central China. The goal was to visit Synear, one of the largest and most successful frozen dumpling brands in China, a company with $300 million in annual sales that was listed on the Shenzhen stock exchange. Given that prices in China were still a fraction of what they were in the West, the business was equivalent to a billion-dollar revenue in the United States.

When our car stopped at the entrance of the humble headquarters, Li Wei, the company's chairman and founder, was standing on the porch, waving goodbye to an American equipment supplier. As everyone emerged from my vehicle, Einar continued chatting with the bankers, but I watched and listened to the American supplier on the steps. I noticed with a twinge of awe and envy that his Chinese was impeccable. Old China Hands like him—people who had studied Chinese formally at university—sprinkled their conversations with proverbs I didn't understand, literary and historical references I had never heard of. That impressed their Chinese counterparts—and it never failed to make me feel inadequate. I relied on Mike for that kind of cultural context.

As if to reinforce this, the American made bowing movements, retreating from the entrepreneur, his two hands clutched over the boss's right hand, his mouth flowing with elaborate praise in Mandarin, showing deep respect for the decorum that usually surrounds a high-level executive in China. Li Wei stood there, looking down at the much taller man a few steps below, smiling gently but disengaged. He seemed accustomed to such courtship.

A few minutes later, Li Wei joined everyone in the meeting room and sat with his team on the opposite side of the large oval table from our group. We all were served burning hot green tea in porcelain cups, and I started the conversation with general questions about the business, the history, the company strategy. It was my way of trying to build a personal rapport with Li. Einar sat next to me. The exchange in Mandarin prevented him from participating, and I could sense he was getting restless. Li answered confidently, seemingly unaware of my colleague's internal agitation. Then the conversation slowed down a little.

Einar used the chance to interject in English. He turned to me with a mischievous smile before returning his intense gaze to Li Wei.

"How much do you think your business is worth?" he asked in English. And before the Chinese entrepreneur could respond, he added: "I want to buy you out!"

Despite his bluster and occasionally embarrassing behavior, I did like Einar. He had my back when it mattered. Within a few weeks of Bakkavor's investment, I decided to stop working with the remaining supermarkets where we sold bags and bowls of salads, coming to terms with what had been a mediocre run in China's retail sector. Lutece's profits from the stores were enough to cover the cost of a promoter on site and the refrigerated trucks delivering the salads daily. But it was a lot of work for a small return. But I decided to keep serving the fast-growing convenience store chains.

As had been the case with our doomed Japanese exports, my stubborn pride had made me slow to recognize the problem. I had also delayed a decision to retreat for fear it would raise a red flag in the middle of my negotiations with Bakkavor. When I finally made the decision and explained it to him, Einar didn't hold it against me. To him, it made sense to shut down a poorly performing business. He even defended the retreat during acrimonious meetings with other managers at headquarters in London.

Creative Food was still growing and was increasingly profitable, but once again I had failed to reduce our company's overreliance on KFC. So when Starbucks, at the time just a small client for Creative Food, contacted me with a plan to grow from 100 to 1,500 stores in China over the next five years, it sounded like perfect timing. Starbucks needed more than my salads and fruit cups. It wanted a whole range of foods, sandwiches and wraps mainly, to put in coffee shops wherever they opened — and it wanted the same range everywhere in China.

The problem was that the coffee chain wanted a commitment fast, which meant building new workshops in every plant — and those workshops had to be fully separated from where I cut my salads to avoid contamination between meats and vegetables. This was an entirely new adventure, one where Creative Food was unproven. I would have to learn how to deal with risks specifically associated with meats, such as nasty bacteria like e-coli, listeria or salmonella.

The tight timing, it turned out, wasn't a problem. A year before, I would have had to fly around the world to raise the necessary funds to expand in this way. Not anymore. When I told him about the opportunity, Einar jumped at it. Bakkavor sold $200 million worth of sandwiches, wraps, and burritos to large U.K. supermarkets annually, and that was exactly the type of business he wanted in China. In one call, he convinced Agust to fly a whole crew of sandwich production experts from England to design the new workshop and train my workers on all aspects of food safety and productivity. I watched in delight as so many resources—money, people—poured in. Within a few weeks, I was ready for production next to my plant near Shanghai.

Starbucks approved us as a new sandwich supplier, even after the whole deal was almost derailed when we inadvertently embarrassed their technical director, a stocky former pastry chef from England, as he tried on one overcoat after another in the changing rooms, finding each of them so tight he couldn't even close the front. I had to give him a second coat that he wore in front, like scrubs. In the rush to finish the workshop, we had ordered only one size—the one that fit our local workforce.

Einar and Agust could have asked me to pay for their people's time and travel; after all, Bakkavor owned only 40 percent of Creative Food's shares. But they never even raised the subject. Creative Food's other shareholders proved less magnanimous. The Starbucks project made business sense, but the new sales caused losses before they added to profits. People worried this might affect Bakkavor's buy-out of the rest of Creative Food. Once again, I was perceived as not making enough money. Some of my investors wanted me to slash costs and increase profits. I pushed back, arguing that it wasn't a smart strategy now that we had a chance to build a good long-term business with Starbucks. A few shareholders insinuated I had sold them out and switched my allegiance to Bakkavor.

That hurt. I, too, wanted to sell Creative Food to Bakkavor for the best price; after all, I also had a large stake in the company. But I wanted to do right by everyone: Starbucks and our other clients, Einar, myself and the other shareholders. In the end, Einar sat down with Roger Marshall and me one evening. Over whisky, we negotiated a new price—and an agreement for Bakkavor to buy us out earlier than originally planned.

One year after I had sold a minority stake in my company, I had finally gotten a profitable exit for those who had trusted me and, in the process, cashed in more money than I ever thought I would—and so did the people who had been there all along, starting with Mike. Looking at it from outside, it all sounded great. With the sale to Bakkavor, I was transformed into a sort of in-house entrepreneur, independent but with far more resources than before, and without the isolation I had experienced for years.

But instead of feeling triumphant—or even just relieved—I felt dispirited. During the worst period of Creative Food's short life, I had drawn energy from the belief that one day I would prove my naysayers wrong. But even as I accomplished that goal, it felt meaningless. I didn't feel emotionally attached to Creative Food as entrepreneurs can be to the companies they have built. Instead, I was drained, empty, and exhausted.

I could have left then and there. But I had been so good at outlining the vision of a bright future for Bakkavor and Creative Food together that, against my better judgment, I found myself driving the new expansion plans. It took me some time to realize that, just as I had finally freed myself from the duty I felt toward one group of people, I had created another unwelcome role for myself: cheerleader for a goal I wasn't sure I had the energy to tackle.

Around the time of the sale to Bakkavor, I joined an association of successful businessmen in Shanghai, hoping to share my story with others who had been on the entrepreneurial journey. Many in that exclusive club had started and sold more than one company, and much bigger ones than mine. Instead of feeling at ease among peers, I felt like a kid among adults. So, in a challenge to myself, I pushed down my negative feelings about staying on at Creative Food. It was just a step, I told myself. I, too, would build and sell several businesses.

Jane didn't compare herself to others like I did. She was annoyed by this "new me" and my sudden pretentions to serial entrepreneurship. One Sunday, after we had lunch with the founder of a company making digital screens and his family, she called me on it.

"Today, you once again offered to invest in his company," she said. "He didn't ask for anything, but you just aggressively offered anyway. Can you stop doing that? You sound like a jerk."

And then she said words that made my heart sink: "There is an arrogance in you since you sold Creative Food. I don't like what you're becoming."

What she saw was our two kids growing up and being raised by nannies while we both got increasingly busy. Abruptly, she decided to resign from her role as Shanghai Bureau Chief for Dow Jones Newswires. Instead of letting it be a wake-up call, my reaction to her decision was to think, "It's okay; I make enough for both of us."

Tensions about what we each wanted from life multiplied. As Jane built a rewarding freelance career, writing on interesting topics for *Forbes Magazine* and *The Wall Street Journal* and transforming herself into a video journalist, I was dismissive of her efforts. Still measuring everything and everyone against my own standards, I complained to her that the money she earned didn't reflect the quality of her work, projecting my own greed and insecurities on someone who was much better anchored in life than I was.

Meanwhile, my own plans weren't exactly working out as expected. In the vision I had developed for Agust and Einar, I was building a juggernaut, gobbling up businesses and aggregating complementary lines of products, and turning myself into an indispensable partner for all restaurant chains in China. Like Bakkavor in Europe, I would soon sell sandwiches, soups, ready-made meals, and salads to Pizza Hut, McDonald's, Starbucks and many others.

The foreign restaurant chains were my main clients because the foods I made for them were sold under their own brand names, and only they would value the systems and processes Creative Food and Bakkavor were bringing. KFC, McDonald's and others weren't naïve foreigners trying to replicate the same standards of quality as in America out of moral purity. They were as focused on earning a buck as anyone in China. But making sure their foods were safe was non-negotiable. They were selling KFC or McDonald's burgers, not Creative Food lettuce. The fact that they needed suppliers with strict quality standards eliminated from the race thousands of cheaper but non-compliant competitors. With them, I could work toward providing safe foods and get paid a decent return for it.

To get to that point, though, we had to keep expanding — and expansion meant buying existing Chinese businesses. Einar and I built a database of nearly 1,000 companies, big and small, that we could potentially acquire. As we worked through the list, visiting and vetting these companies, I noticed a pattern exemplified by the pizza maker. The competitive nature of China's retail industry meant that many of them had designed an attractive product at a competitive price: specialty frozen dumplings, pizza slices or small savory snacks. But because most of them sold to supermarket chains, which were much less concerned about brand reputation than my restaurant clients, the elements of quality control that were critical to me were not part of their processes.

When I asked them about quality-control measures, entrepreneurs usually answered with a list of equipment they had recently bought—a new packaging machine or a new pesticide residue tester. But the implementation of a food safety system to check quality from the farm to the customer required people, software and experience. Supervising farms and certifying key suppliers costs more and slows things down. It also requires a different company culture where every employee pays attention and stands for quality, like the bearded man in England who had yelled at me when I almost entered a clean production room without first putting on a hairnet.

Like the pizza slice maker, these companies got all the necessary operating licenses, but they did so because they were a critical employer and investor in their district, town or village, not because they met the requirements for cleanliness and safety. Profit and protection of the local community—the villagers, the local officials' ambitions, the money from tax collection—took precedence over everything else. Without clear food safety rules and little pressure from government inspectors to comply, the responsibility toward the ultimate consumers of their foods remained a relatively unimportant factor.

I knew that if I decided to acquire such companies, their business models wouldn't work for me. And changing those models meant investing in people, training and equipment to improve quality control—which usually required more money than it made sense to spend. I didn't see how this would change, unless the supermarkets decided to send their own teams of quality auditors to check on suppliers, as restaurant chains did.

When I suggested this to the director of quality at one of the large international supermarket chains, his answer was candid. "I don't even have time and resources to train my own in-store inspectors on how to handle our fresh foods safely," he said. "Sending them out to check on our suppliers is just not realistic." He could have added that he was himself dealing with fierce competition from local retailers who didn't do that either.

As our search progressed, it became obvious that I faced an ugly choice with every acquisition: either forget about profit until I could set up quality-control measures at each company we acquired or rely on the integrity of entrepreneurs I barely knew and let them keep doing business the way they always had.

Months passed after the Bakkavor deal without us making a single investment in an outside company. All the money in the world wouldn't change the fact that many Chinese food businesses prioritized keeping costs low and turning profits over quality and food safety. Everyone talked about partnership, yet nobody meant a word of it. It remained every man for himself. And none of the actors in the plot—clients, government, or food manufacturers—felt the solution should come from them. They were all, they said, just doing their jobs.

I changed tactics, turning my attention to companies that could help me supply frozen foods in addition to fresh foods to restaurant chains instead of brands selling their products to supermarkets. The big restaurant chains were building far-flung networks all over the country. KFC alone already had stores in more than nine hundred cities, and many of those cities were too far away from my six plants to even consider selling them fresh foods. I reasoned that if I could supply them with frozen foods from my existing plants—think panini, pasta sauces, and soups—I could make inroads in these new cities while also cementing my hold on key clients by controlling a larger portion of their ingredients. When their business in these new regions grew enough to justify the cost, I would then build a fresh-food plant there. Like Bakkavor, I thought that being a fresh-food producer made me different from the hundreds of frozen-food producers that existed already, mainly serving export markets. In addition, few had developed a strategy for China's domestic market. So, I began to focus my acquisitions efforts on regions with the best frozen food manufacturers.

One such region was Shandong Province, located roughly between Beijing and Shanghai on the coast opposite Japan. Working with a company there, I reasoned, I would be close to several fast-developing cities where Starbucks, KFC, Pizza Hut and McDonald's were all desperately looking for suppliers — and I would also be near many of the farms that supplied me with produce. I stopped looking for big and famous businesses, much to Einar's disappointment, and chose instead to focus on companies roughly half the size of Creative Food that were already exporting frozen foods. Because quality requirements for exports were stricter, I wouldn't have to teach them the basics of food safety, I thought. If I was lucky, I would find a company with a good management team and an existing business shipping to overseas clients. In exchange, I would bring new sales channels by helping it develop new products for my network of restaurant chains. I could even add a workshop to make salads for the nearby regional cities at a lower cost than setting up a new plant.

I had been visiting companies in Shandong for days when I arrived in Layang county, an hour north of Qingdao, the region's main port city, to visit Henong Frozen Foods. That afternoon, I met with Hu Xuemin, the company's owner. Flanked by the government officials who had been escorting me for many such visits, we sat in the board room to discuss how we could work together. An affable large-framed man with intelligent eyes and a face reddened by a long life spent outdoors, Hu had started from poverty to build a frozen-foods empire. Henong was one of his many companies; he also owned a hog farm and an ice-cream plant. Henong had been exporting frozen vegetables and strawberries to Japan for several years; the company had sales of $10 million and showed a consistent profit each year. But as the Chinese currency appreciated in value, Hu now faced more competition in Japan. And China's labor costs were increasing too. Hu sensed that his future markets were no longer abroad and that being a cheap commodity exporter wasn't a good long-term strategy.

As I had anticipated, he calculated that by working with me, he could pivot his business toward fast-growing domestic restaurant chains. Hu was already well into his fifties, so when he explained that his daughter studied music in Beijing and that his son attended a university in Arizona, I guessed that neither of them wanted to come back to the village and run his businesses. When I toured Hu's plant, I noticed that it didn't have any fancy equipment, but it looked spotless. The business appeared solid: simple because it needed to stay lean to compete, but tightly-run so it would appeal to diligent Japanese inspectors. Unlike many factories I had seen, there was no graveyard of rusty materials in the back, and the workers' uniforms were basic but clean. He even had a room showing a map of his supply sources, color-coded by region and varieties.

Hu himself looked the part of the sober entrepreneur. His blue suit and red tie were not so fashionable that you wondered whether shopping in luxury boutiques in Shanghai distracted him from the business, but classy enough to set him apart from the masses of small-town entrepreneurs with sloppy haircuts and sometimes stained and mismatched suits.

I didn't always understand Hu's heavy dialect. He didn't speak any English, and his Mandarin was basic. But I felt a connection with him. He was a man from a farming village who had started out by pushing carts of vegetables alongside the fields during harvest, then risen to become a team leader during the Cultural Revolution. During China's economic opening in the early 1980s, he had traded vegetables, and with the money he earned, he had invested at the right time in his frozen-foods company. The local mayor told me how Hu had built subsidized housing for his workers and recently paid to renovate the village's main square, where people gathered to exercise and dance at night. He had also bought a pond, just behind the square. He planned to turn it into a park where villagers and workers could fish and relax on weekends.

As usual, the banquet the night following our meeting quickly turned boozy. Officials were well-soaked already when I found myself standing side-by-side with Hu at the bathroom urinals. Hu had followed me when I left the private room where we were all sitting. Since I was the guest of honor, and a foreigner, it seemed normal for Hu, as a dutiful host, to usher me around, even to the bathroom. As we stood there, away from the bustle of the party, I suddenly sensed that he had something to say.

"You know China well for a foreigner," he said slowly, not looking at me but straight at the tiled bathroom wall.

I didn't respond, partly to express my humility; I felt far from understanding the place even after a decade there.

"That's why I need to confess one thing: my company's financials are not all that transparent," he said.

This wasn't a surprise. Hu was a small-time entrepreneur, and cutting corners was part of life.

"I can't say that in front of the officials at the table," he continued. "But I want you to know and to tell me if you're willing to deal with that."

What he was essentially telling me was that the profits on his books were much higher than stated. And I knew that by revealing to me that he was making a higher profit than he was paying taxes on, he was already jockeying for Creative Food to pay a higher price for his business. But I liked that he addressed this on the first day, at the risk of putting me off a deal with him, instead of waiting until later when I would be more deeply invested in negotiations. Right there at the urinals, I decided I would do business with him. Rarely did local businessmen — almost all of whom had something to hide — come clean up front. I smiled, washed my hands, put my arm around his shoulder, and walked with him back to the banquet.

Einar wasn't a big fan of buying into frozen-food businesses. Bakkavor was a fresh-food specialist and viewed large-scale frozen-food manufacturers with some disdain. But I argued that from my Henong base, we could design all sorts of frozen foods that could be shipped to smaller cities and reheated inside restaurant outlets. For my clients, it would eliminate the need to find, train and monitor hundreds of new suppliers, one for each far-flung city. In the end, Einar trusted me enough to convince London to do the deal. We bought seventy-five percent of Henong and made a loan to the company so it could buy the raw materials for the Japanese frozen strawberry season, a profitable and well-established business that we believed would generate the cash to pay for our plan to manufacture frozen ready meals.

But a few weeks after we sealed the acquisition, Hu, who had been ramping up his production of frozen sliced strawberries for the season, reported that prices in Japan had collapsed. We were stuck with warehouses full of the fruit produced at an average price now 50 percent higher than what the market was offering. If the market didn't recover, I would have to take a write-off approaching $1 million.

Hu was resourceful. At the meeting where he broke the bad news, he quickly explained that he could mitigate our losses by reducing the price he would pay for the fruit to the local farmers—because he did not have formal contracts with them.

I was shocked. Firm contracts with farmers known for safe practices had been a major reason I had chosen Henong as our partner. Now, on top of not having contracts with them, he was ready to renege on his promise to pay those farmers the agreed price. Surely this would alienate them for the next season.

"But I remember that room in the factory," I said, "where all your growing areas were plastered on the wall, each bearing a code number to identify the origin of the products. Don't you have firm agreements with these growers?"

Hu smiled patiently and explained how the room I had seen was for his Japanese clients' visits. He knew exactly what they wanted to see and hear, so he had set up a false documentation scheme to support his claim that he could make safe food.

"Look," he said, "clients don't want to commit to a price and a volume for the season. They all want to wait and see. So why should I make a commitment to the farmers on my end?"

Here was a man who kept a spotless factory and genuinely cared about doing the right thing. But even he was not ready to invest in farming or to take the risk of formally contracting with farmers. Instead, he had junior quality-assurance staff put together cross-referenced files mapping out farm plots before clients came to visit so it looked like such contracts existed. Our auditors had seen these bogus documents, and they had been fooled too. This was such a common practice in the industry that Hu had not viewed it as a serious matter that he should disclose up front.

Despite my disappointment—until that day, I believed that

Hu had been completely honest with me—I could sympathize with his reasoning. From my own experience at Creative Food, I knew the intense pressure Henong felt to do whatever it took to compete. I also believed Hu's clients weren't fooled themselves by all the professional-looking documentation but used it to convince higher-ups in their own organizations that they had been rigorous in their choice to buy from him. It was an elaborate and never-ending game of poker, with no one willing to call anyone else's bluff.

A few days later, after we had met Hu in one more contentious board meeting about our strawberry issues, I was riding in the front seat of a black Audi from Layang to Qingdao, where I would catch a plane back to Shanghai. A plume of dust disappeared behind us. The road wasn't busy, and I vaguely noticed a public bus that we seemed to be passing again and again. In the back seat of the car, which belonged to Hu, Mike and Wu Qingsong, our new finance director, hashed over the meeting. Hu's driver, Mr. Zhao, looked straight ahead.

The weather was hazy, common for an early spring afternoon in Shandong. The road was lined with fields of fertile black soil slowly recovering from winter. Wheat and corn hadn't yet sprouted, and vegetables were still sheltered in red-brick greenhouses in preparation for being transplanted outside. These greenhouses were typical of the region. The red-brick walls absorbed the sun's warmth during the day to release it at night, providing an ingenious way of generating heat inside as the region transitioned from its brutal winter.

Suddenly the car slowed to a halt. That bus that we had been passing had stopped twenty yards ahead of us, next to a construction zone on the left-hand side of the road, and it was now blocking our way. Zhao was still looking ahead without a word, but I sensed the atmosphere tensing up. We all stopped talking, wondering what was happening as we followed Zhao's gaze toward the bus.

The bus driver climbed down in slow motion and stalked toward our car, carrying something in one hand. As he approached, I saw it was a metal bar. His face full of rage, he shouted a couple of invectives at us until he reached the front of the car. And there, without another word, he swung the bar and started smashing every one of the Audi's windows. We hunkered in our seats, hands over our faces.

Zhao blubbered out words of apology.

"I...I am sorry, I apologize," he stuttered to the man outside.

Through the cracked windows, I heard the bus driver answering. "You bastard, here is what we do to bastards like you," he said, pointing his free hand's index finger menacingly at Zhao.

He then walked back to his bus, started up and disappeared into the dust ahead, leaving us alone in the battered car.

I was tense but not scared. The bus driver never threatened me personally; whatever had precipitated the incident, it was all about Zhao. I was surprised that the driver had not stopped in his tracks when he saw me. After so many years in China, I was used to seeing people change their behavior when they saw a foreigner. They could be nastily bickering with each other but switch to smiles in a matter of seconds when I appeared. This time, my presence did not matter in the least.

Fortunately, the angry bus driver had taken his road rage out only on the windows; the car still ran fine. With or without windows, we had a flight back to Shanghai. Mike reassured Zhao that we wouldn't rat him out with his boss. That made him relaxed enough to explain things.

Busy with our talk and my own thoughts, I hadn't noticed that our car and the bus had become embroiled in a race which neither driver wanted to lose. The road often narrowed to one lane; both drivers wanted to be in front when it did. "The bus driver lost his temper," Zhao said. "But he also knows he can get away with that type of behavior because he has protection in town."

"What do you mean?" I asked. "Protection?"

"Yeah, in Shandong, most bus lines are controlled by the *heibang*," he answered, using the Chinese term for the local mafia. "They own the buses and they make sure there is no competition because they also have influence over local government officials."

His voice was unemotional, as if this were common knowledge. Mike nodded when I looked at him to confirm.

Then Zhao added with resolution, "But I also have some *protection*, and as soon as I get back, I am going to take care of this. This will not stop here."

He picked up his mobile phone and made a couple of calls, plotting some revenge for the same night.

The wind coming through the now-open car pressed against my face. I remembered the hostage situation in Linhai, the riots in Hebei. Here was a world most foreigners never saw. We were just months away from the start of the 2008 Beijing Olympics. Qingdao was the place where all the sailing events were scheduled. Shandong Province's infrastructure was world-class, with modern airports and high-speed railways already in place in the main cities. The Chinese food sector, of which I had become an unlikely part, was changing, and at a fast pace. In all my plants, inspectors were getting stricter and more knowledgeable, not least because there was an increasingly vocal demand from consumers for safer foods.

But the effort wasn't consistent across the country. I don't think any one person or group was at fault. The habits and culture of an entire people are simply slow to change. I had spent that afternoon arguing with Hu, whom I still liked and respected. I told him he needed to treat the farmers he worked fairly. I said *responsibility*. He answered *profit*.

The violent bus driver helped cast a different light on that conversation. I had assumed, yet again, that I shared a set of values with Hu, and so I was upset when we failed to connect as I expected. But the mistake was mine. Hu had grown up pushing vegetable carts in communal farms, surviving the conflict-ridden and sometimes murderous years of the Cultural Revolution. I had grown up in France, a stable wealthy country with clear moral and legal guidelines governing business relationships. Who was I to judge Hu? His was a culture of survival in a world where many traditions had been obliterated and where connections and personal history mattered more than being right or wrong. Both he and the bus driver had grown up in a place where upheaval was the only constant. That didn't mean I couldn't work with him. But I couldn't assume we shared the same values.

My surprise at Hu's actions, my car ride to Qingdao: it all exposed how little I still understood about China's inner workings. Bakkavor's deep pockets hadn't changed that fact. I had learned that given time, I could build deep loyalties. But my car ride that day reminded me of how vulnerable I still was — and would always be.

15

DAYS OF RAIN

FOR MOST BUSINESS people, when thinking about 2008, the global financial crisis will be the first thing that springs to mind. For many associated with China, it would be the Beijing Olympics. For me, the year evokes something else: the Sanlu scandal, which erupted when a trusted infant formula brand was exposed for using a toxic chemical called melamine in its products which, according to official reports, sent 300,000 babies into kidney failure and killed three (a surprisingly low number).

When news of it first broke, I saw it as just one more food-safety fracas. I was still reeling from my own "near-miss" scandal—Henong and its strawberries—and I was busy working on my second post-Bakkavor acquisition. One month before the Sanlu news broke, in August 2008, Einar had flown to Beijing with some of our customers to attend celebrations related to the Olympics. I stayed in Shanghai to close a deal to acquire a plant in Guangzhou much larger than my own ramshackle factory in that city. So I wasn't paying a lot of attention in September when the television media started airing interviews with tearful mothers and angry fathers whose babies were gravely ill.

I now see that what happened to Sanlu, its customers and its foreign investors was something I evaded only by luck. Any day during my tenure at Creative Food, a KFC customer—or hundreds of them—could have ingested life-threatening e-coli bacteria or toxic chemical residues from our lettuce. Sanlu was my worst nightmare, happening to someone else.

Sanlu, one of the largest makers of infant formula at the time, was based in Shijiazhuang, the provincial capital of Hebei province, near Beijing. Its brand was known for quality and its ability to rival foreign competitors. Its reputation among families was good. It was thus a proud symbol of emerging China. Fonterra, a company owned by New Zealand dairy farmers and the largest milk processor in the world, had a 40% stake in Sanlu, placing the company at the center of its China strategy. It had invested $165 million. Before the scandal broke, that stake was valued at close to $500 million.

For months, leading to the summer of 2008, blogs, social media posts and articles across China reported that hundreds of babies were hospitalized with kidney problems after ingesting infant formula. Sanlu's name was often mentioned, but the company denied its products had any connection. On August 2, 2008, that changed. Sanlu called Fonterra's executives in China to tell them that out of a batch of sixteen samples of infant formula brought to a Shijiazhuang lab, fifteen had come back indicating the presence of melamine, a plastic normally used in laminates like formica.

Why was melamine in milk in the first place? Under pressure to compete, intermediaries who bought milk from the villagers and aggregated it before selling it to processors like Sanlu, diluted milk with water to save cost. Then they added melamine because it could pass as a protein in the processors' quality checks. Among the villagers, it was widely known as "protein powder." When milk was delivered to the factory gates, it was tested for protein and fat content—but nobody tested for melamine.

The day it found out, Sanlu called an emergency board meeting, including Fonterra's representatives. When briefed,

Fonterra's head of China, Bob Major, a thoughtful white-haired New Zealander with a research background, made his view very clear: "If you have any doubt about the quality of your product, call it back immediately," he said during the conference call.

But his Chinese partners didn't see things in the same straightforward manner. They were worried about repercussions. A public recall one week before the start of the Beijing Olympics would seem like a slap in the face—not merely for Sanlu but for China itself. The Beijing Games had been carefully designed to place the country on the world stage on par with developed Western economies. It would look very bad to disclose that a flagship formula maker was jeopardizing children's health.

That summer, Games-conscious health inspectors slept in my Beijing plant to make sure everything we produced was safe to eat. Fearful that a food safety scandal could happen under their watch, my minders went overboard. Every trifling operational issue turned into a drama that got increasingly tense as the Olympics approached. As during SARS, I feared I would get shut down any day. Few foreigners understood that environment. But I'm sure that Sanlu's executives feared that the company and its thousands of employees would be in deep trouble if they went public with the news.

By the end of the call, Bob Major told me later, he believed that his view had prevailed: Sanlu's board had agreed that all products would be publicly recalled and that authorities would be notified. But the meeting minutes took time to arrive, and when they did, Major realized that the Chinese version—the only one legally binding—didn't mention any public recall. Under pressure from the local authorities, Sanlu had initiated a limited "trade" recall. That meant taking infant formula off the shelves but leaving the tainted formula in the homes of consumers who had already bought it. The company was bringing back thousands of tons of formula from hundreds of cities without giving a single explanation to anyone.

For three weeks, in multiple meetings, Major tried to convince Sanlu and the Shijiazhuang City officials that it was in their interest to come clean. But the city stonewalled all efforts, arguing that foreigners didn't understand the implications of going public.

"I couldn't believe what Shijiazhuang officials told my team," Major said, reading from a document on his laptop:

"Sanlu should provide treatment to sick children."

"Sanlu should keep things confidential."

"Sanlu can do a trade recall but is not allowed to publicly communicate it."

"Sanlu should be patient with journalists and find ways to neutralize them." (It was common for companies to pay bribes to journalists or search engines to eliminate negative stories.)

For Major and Fonterra, it was about babies dying. For Sanlu and its Chinese executives, it was about the livelihood of thousands of local workers and companies associated with it. Major recounted how one city official laid it out to him during a closed-door meeting: "In New Zealand you think of individuals first. In China we think of preserving harmony in the society first, even if individual interests sometimes get damaged or passed over."

By September, Major was done with the stalling. In coordination with the New Zealand Prime Minister, Fonterra contacted the China Ministry of Foreign Affairs and the Ministry of Agriculture to formally put them on notice that it would go public on September 9. The same day, the story that Sanlu's formula contained melamine broke in the *Lanzhou Morning Post*, a newspaper in the remote Gansu province. After that, media coverage raged uninterrupted for days. The Chinese people were incensed; everyone wanted the culprits punished.

Under the instructions of China's Premier, Beijing moved in swiftly to take control of the situation. Investigations found that, unknown to Fonterra, the Sanlu board had decided to reprocess the formula collected during the trade recall. The company then resent it to the market with a melamine dosage that was deemed safer. Police arrested the executives involved in that decision. Meanwhile, Major and his team conducted a number of tests on milk bought from supermarkets. The tests revealed that all but one brand contained melamine — many at levels as high as Sanlu's. By November 2008, three months after the first disclosure to Fonterra, several senior executives at Sanlu were sentenced to life in jail, while the intermediaries who had marketed the melamine as protein powder were executed. A fund to indemnify victims' families was set up, funded solely by the sale of Sanlu's assets to a state-owned company. As far as Fonterra was concerned, the police couldn't find any evidence of wrongdoing.

People will debate forever whether Sanlu knew the contents of the milk it was buying, whether Major and his team should have known earlier, and whether the scandal should have been branded a China milk crisis rather than a Sanlu crisis. Regardless, the case matters because it highlighted a common mistake among Chinese and foreign business people operating in China: assuming that on morale issues, both sides think alike.

Bob Major had formed a view about his counterpart at Sanlu, Tian Wenhua — just as I had about Henong's Hu. Because she seemed a good person — Tian was known to treat common folks in her company with respect and care — he assumed she would do business his way, the Western way. When the truth came out, Major trusted that Tian, a grandmother, would think as Westerners would if babies' lives were at stake.

But Sanlu was a former state-owned company owned collectively by its employees, and the local authorities were powerful stakeholders. The town mayor got promoted if the city's taxes and employment increased. In exchange, companies gained contacts within the government who could resolve red tape problems. The system worked because regulations and laws were unclear or immature. Even private companies like mine operated in close coordination with local officials. Ignorance of that fact meant missing part of the reality of doing business in China.

Tian's loyalty was to her employees, her city and her country — in that order. She knew that coming out publicly with the truth on the use of melamine would rock the entire system, and that was just not done in her culture. It's quite likely she made erroneous assumptions about Bob Major too, believing that he would never undercut his own company's interests by going public with the issue. Both of them were wrong, simply because they assumed the other shared their own business and moral priorities. Fonterra lost its entire Sanlu investment due to the scandal.

Operating a business in China, or simply investing in a business, requires an intimacy with the industry and its stakeholders that is hard for foreigners to achieve. Unable to communicate effectively due to language or cultural issues, executives become dependent on a tiny cohort of English-speaking people in their organizations: managers, counsels, or assistants. They live in large cities like Shanghai, Beijing or Hong Kong, shielded and isolated from daily operations. Slowly, they become disconnected from the wider network of allegiances every Chinese businessman depends on to operate. Not everyone is trying to deceive, but very often, even the more honest advisors will say what they think you want to hear or what they would like you to believe is true rather than the actual truth.

It took me a long time to learn these lessons. But over the years, I've noticed a pattern among successful Chinese businesspeople that I try to emulate. Because it's so hard to know whether your interlocutor shares your beliefs, because it's impossible to grasp who the person is loyal to in the end, you want to first assess from what position a person is speaking: what he or she knows and how he or she knows it. Then you determine whether the person may have a reason to share this particular information, all along questioning whether the interlocutor has a potential bias or incentive. And you do so by talking about the same issue to different people with different biases and incentives, constantly triangulating information—including independent reports about market conditions—until you form a view that becomes your own.

In such a paranoid environment, staying alert and critical is key. At Creative Food, my way of averting potentially nasty surprises was to monitor quality complaints personally every week and meet clients regularly. This helped me bypass company politics and any temptation to cover up problems. As I learned with Henong's traceability system, reports can be falsified, but keeping an eye on many different sources of such information, including perusing independent satisfaction surveys, monitoring of blogs and online posts, and regularly conversations with distributors and retail clients—can close gaps. As a foreign investor in China, you can't rely solely on your board meeting disclosures.

A consultant shared a story that I find illuminating. A few months before the melamine crisis, he was visiting a new plant owned by the massive dairy products maker, Mengniu. Founded in 2000, Mengniu had become the number-two player in milk behind Yili and had recently listed on the Hong Kong Stock

Exchange. The giant factory was spotless, with fifteen processing lines running in parallel, entirely operated by robots imported from Sweden. High up on the wall hung a digital screen that displayed the total milk production since the beginning of the year. The curve went up exponentially.

As the small group of foreign visitors this consultant was a part of made its way across the factory floor, executives commented in awe about how far China had come in its modernization. The man, familiar with the structure of milk supply in China and the millions of farmers with one skinny cow chained to the wall in a concrete backyard, pulled out his notebook, wrote down the numbers highlighted on the digital board, and circled the figure.

Just below the circle, he wrote: "WHERE THE FUCK IS THE MILK COMING FROM?"

When the milk scandal was unfolding, I didn't have time to fully comprehend its impact. By October 2008, the global financial crisis was roiling the world, including my part of it. Bakkavor was still operating profitably, but the debt the company had incurred to acquire businesses in Europe and Asia came back to bite Agust. He and his brother were forced to sell billions of investments in Iceland and Europe at fire-sale prices just to hold on to the company they had founded. To stave off bankers and avoid foreclosure, Agust agreed to "ring-fence" Bakkavor's UK business. That meant that all the cash generated by the $3-billion corporation went toward repaying debt. No dividends got paid to shareholders. No cash could be sent to Asia.

Suddenly the $30 million credit line I had negotiated to expand in China was rescinded. The British banker who had taken me out to dinner to talk me into borrowing more disappeared. In his place came someone from the "Special Projects" team — otherwise known as "bankers-who-don't-take-you-out-to-dinner." In the space of a couple of weeks, I went from actively looking for large companies to buy to simply fighting to find enough cash to pay for the businesses I had already bought. Luckily, I had been there before.

From running the acquisitions business, Mike and I stepped back into running Creative Food's day-to-day operations. Not wasting time, I cut half of Creative Food's overhead, closing down a newly renovated office and eliminating positions that had been created to integrate the new acquisitions. By the end of 2008, everyone including me was once again doing three jobs. The pressure was intense, but it still didn't compare to the early years when I was bleeding cash from all sides. In fact, I felt strangely relieved. Creative Food was a business I knew inside out. Running it to earn cash wasn't a big challenge compared to acquiring complex Chinese food businesses.

A few months into 2009, I sensed that there could again be investment opportunities. Valuations for many of the businesses we had looked at had come down. Still strangled by the banks, Bakkavor couldn't act. I set up a separate investment fund into which Agust put his own money. But as CEO, Acting Finance Director and Acting Operations Director for Creative Food, I was pretty busy already. The fund's money sat there for months while I struggled to extract myself from the day-to-day running of what was now a business with eight factories, four farms, 1,200 employees, and more than 3,000 restaurants and coffee shops to serve every day. Tired and overwhelmed, I again considered leaving.

Eventually, Agust refinanced Bakkavor's debt and ended the ban on sending cash to Asia. When Einar showed up for a board meeting at the end of 2010, he sounded as if the past two years had been a mere parenthesis.

"Let's go out and buy companies again," he said. "What's the plan, Xavier?"

I turned defensive, thinking the man had no idea of what I had just been through. And he must have sensed that I didn't have it in me any longer. He asked openly if I should look into hiring a new leader for Creative Food while I focused on acquisitions for the company.

I never thought I would be emotional about the idea of giving up control for good, but I was. Even though I had sat on the investment fund for the past year, I thought I was the only one who could do it all. I called Einar the same night to tell him it was time for me to leave Creative Food to focus on my investment fund.

My right-hand man wasn't weathering the changes much better than I. In 2006, after Bakkavor's original investment, Mike had looked deflated almost constantly. He didn't complain—and he denied being depressed—but I could discern from his comments that he wasn't comfortable with the company's direction.

He often asked questions: "Why such a rush to buy companies?" "Do you realize the risks you take on by acquiring large local businesses?" He had a hard time watching me and Bakkavor's British experts add new processes that required more investment and jobs, probably feeling again that all this change was diluting our sense of collectiveness and slowing down our lean organization. I wondered aloud whether he was able to envision a future that wasn't an incremental improvement over the past. We talked for hours. I grew frustrated and told him so.

"I don't have an issue with change itself but with the way Bakkavor is changing things; they're just not thinking things through," he said. I knew he wasn't really talking about the Icelanders. Mike had taken to saying "Bakkavor" instead of singling me out.

"When you add more management layers without clear

needs and goals for each new position, you'll have a hard time avoiding a drift toward complacency," he said.

I understood what he meant. It was easier for people to find excuses when roles weren't completely clear in a new organization. But I believed it was a necessary transition if we wanted to create a larger business that wouldn't depend on him or me.

Gradually, he grew distant, and less interested in solving problems. "Here are the pros and cons," he would say when we had to decide something that involved complex trade-offs. "Now you need to make the decision."

I didn't seem able to convince Mike—whose lack of commitment I resented—that the benefits of change were greater than the risks. And the fact is that he was probably looking at things with a clearer head than I because he wasn't tied to the promises I had made to Einar and Agust. I felt the same sense of dilution, the lack of meaningful purpose. Clearly, after years of fighting for survival, I hadn't been able to formulate a compelling mission beyond making the company profitable.

Soon after my own decision to leave, I asked Mike if he could step aside from running day-to-day operations at Creative Food to help with the new acquisitions fund. I had always wanted him involved in acquiring new businesses, but until then Creative Food had sucked up all his time. Mike had occupied many positions at the company, from sales to operations, depending on where I needed him. His orientation toward operational minutiae would help get new companies in shape from the start, I thought. I failed to appreciate that he accepted probably more out of duty than out of any enthusiasm for becoming an entrepreneur. With Mike involved, I felt confident enough to invest some fund money in a small pizza chain start-up that he would lead. My vision was that while Pizza Hut focused on the high end of the market, my restaurants would make $2 pizzas and dominate the mass market.

On a Saturday morning in November 2010, a month after I had decided to leave as CEO and run the investment fund, I was in Taipei with a group of entrepreneurs. When the phone rang in my hotel room at 6 am, it woke me up. I grabbed the device on my night table and sat on the edge of the bed looking at the screen; it was flashing "Zhang Jianwen," the name of our Haimen plant manager.

Haimen, ninety minutes away from Shanghai, was our largest plant. Zhang, a stocky man from Gansu Province in northwest China, had been working at Creative Food for five years, starting as a lowly production manager in Shanghai. When I opened our Wuhan plant, he spent eight months there to supervise construction and to make sure the plant met our customers' quality standards. Back in Shanghai as regional manager, he had built one of the best-performing teams in the company. Zhang was direct and sometimes abrasive, but he was respected and had dealt with his share of emergencies during the start-up phase in Wuhan. He didn't need much hand-holding. If he was calling me at 6 am on a Saturday, I knew it wasn't good news. A surge of dread replaced drowsiness as I picked up the call.

"Zhang Jianwen, *ni hao*," I said.

"*Laoban* (Boss) — (pause) — there is a problem," he immediately said in a somber voice. "At 5:15 this morning, the Haimen plant burned down."

Once he had made it clear that no one was hurt — the workshop had been empty — I cleared out of the hotel room and jumped on the first plane back to Shanghai. By noon, I was in Haimen.

The damage was extensive, but firemen had contained the blaze before it reached the brand-new sandwich-making workshop we had built for Starbucks. To my surprise, Mike was there too. Watching him report the sequence of decisions he had made while I was on the plane reminded me how much I had missed him over the past few months. He had officially resigned and was due to leave the company to run the pizza business a few weeks later so he didn't have any precise role in our operations department. But Zhang had begged him to come and help.

"Our sales manager notified KFC; they have agreed to buy from our Wuhan plant starting today until the Shanghai plant can operate again," Mike reported. This would cost us, I thought—we would need to airfreight lettuce daily from Wuhan to Shanghai—but it was better than losing the business to a competitor.

Mike continued: "Zhang is currently with the town mayor, who is working his network to understand what steps will be required by local authorities to restart the part of the plant untouched by the blaze."

I could sense the positive energy among the staff as each manager then described what he was doing in Mike's bullet-point style, dutifully following up on the tasks he had assigned.

The technical manager reported in the same voice, "First, I have already called two contractors who are scheduled to visit this afternoon. Two, we are assessing whether we can re-use some of the untouched cold panels and air-conditioning units. Three, our accountant contacted the insurance company and scheduled an inspection for Monday."

My next stop was the Fire Bureau. "Your panels weren't fireproof," the chief said when I showed up at his office. "You're in breach of the regulations. That's why the fire spread so fast."

There was no emotion in his voice. "Please sit in the room next door and wait for me."

Hours passed while the chief and his team investigated the fire's cause. It looked like a short circuit in one of the office's air-conditioning units had started it, and it then took only 45 minutes for the fire to spread. Under Chinese law, I was personally liable for the accident. I also knew that the fact our panels weren't fireproof had resulted directly from a decision I had made to save money during construction. The electric wiring in the small plant office where the fire had started wasn't in line with the code either because I hadn't bothered to use a licensed electrician. I could be in serious trouble even though there weren't any victims.

From the empty little room with white walls where I was assigned — basically under arrest — I called Mike, and asked if the mayor could help with my release. I wasn't the only businessman in China cutting corners with fire regulations, and Creative Food employed close to 300 people locally, so she should be able to help us, I thought.

"It's not going to be that easy," Mike said. "The Fire Bureau is under the Defense Ministry; our mayor has no authority over this agency."

More time crawled by. I felt increasingly powerless. Life is funny, I reflected. For years I had lived in fear of a food safety scandal that had not materialized, but now that I had decided to leave, old decisions totally unrelated to food safety were catching up with me. For hours, I avoided thinking about it by continuously engaging Zhang and the team by phone. When I wasn't calling, I watched the bare white walls, wondering if this was the way it was supposed to end, occasionally spacing out and noting innocuous details like the black stripes left by chairs rubbing against the poor-quality primer on the walls.

After a long day of waiting, Mike finally called with good news. "You're free to go," he said. I asked what had changed the mind of the chief. "We're lucky. The mayor's husband was the former police chief; that agency, like the fire bureau, falls under the Defense Ministry. He knows the chief and vouched for you based on what his wife told him," he replied. "He also promised that you wouldn't leave the country until the end of the investigation."

Leaving the country was out of question for me. I thought about my employees and the local officials supporting us in the reconstruction. But no sooner was the worst fall-out from the fire behind me than a new crisis arose. Later that year, as construction for the new plant was ongoing, the Chinese IRS audited the plant I had acquired from my competitor in Guangzhou, exposing millions in liabilities.

As with the fire, a shortcut I had taken had come back to bite me. Two years before, I had discovered that our company hadn't paid the right tax rate on some of our cooked products, specifically potato salads and corn salads. Because they went through a cooking process, tax authorities viewed them as "foods" rather than "vegetables," and taxed them at a higher rate. When the accountant told me, I made what I thought was a reasonable compromise. I decided to comply from the day I found out. But I didn't volunteer to make up for what I hadn't paid over the past five years. That would have been too costly at a time when I badly needed cash.

A few months later, the accountant didn't get the salary increase she expected, so she resigned. In revenge for what she felt was an act of disrespect, she went straight to the tax bureau with piles of documents proving my misdeed. The initial calculation by the authorities showed that I could be liable for $500,000 in unpaid taxes, but the sum could increase to $2.5 million if the authorities could prove intent to evade tax.

Busy with the post-fire reconstruction in Haimen, I searched for a quick solution. I met with a lawyer who claimed he knew the local tax bureau chief well enough to make it all go away for a minimal payment. Of course, the lawyer asked for a cut of the money I would be saving—and I assumed the local bureau chief would too. It was a new tight spot for me. I had entertained many officials in banquets over the years, but this was straight-out bribery. I argued with myself that the audit was triggered by a denunciation, so I shouldn't stay passive in the face of it. I needed to quickly manage the fall-out of it. I called Mike at the pizza chain to bounce it off him before deciding.

"How are you going to pay this lawyer?" he asked when I explained the situation.

"I guess he will give me an invoice for legal advice," I said, a bit sheepish because I knew what he meant.

"What will our Finance Manager Zheng Xiaoping think when he sees this invoice with a firm we've never worked with?" he continued, the pitch of his voice rising. I regretted calling already. Once again, Mike was raising hypothetical questions to make his point.

"Soon enough, everyone will know or suspect what you've done," he said. "The message you're sending to everyone at Creative Food is that it's okay to pay or receive bribes—and you're not even solving the problem because this can surface again later if the corrupt official gets caught."

I knew he was right, but I wasn't prepared to follow his advice and wait passively for an outcome because I feared the financial implications could be dire. And I felt guilty that my poor choices in the past could now damage Einar, Agust and Bakkavor, who had earnestly backed me up since the takeover.

So, I called a Chinese friend who ran a large industrial real estate business. The property sector is plagued with corruption, I thought; he will have experience dealing with issues like this. My friend was even more forceful than Mike. "Listen, you never want to pay bribes," he shouted on the phone. "It makes me so angry to hear you even consider that. It will tie you down in lies forever. Once people know you pay, it will never end."

To show his support, he offered the help of his head of taxation, a woman with considerable knowledge and connections. With her, I managed to create a backchannel communication with a retired tax official in Guangzhou who, once convinced I wasn't a miscreant, acted as our sponsor with the local office of the Chinese tax department. My friend's executive was an incredible professional. She helped draft explanatory letters that addressed the officials' concerns and passed on good words about Creative Food's honest behavior in all other aspects. In traditional Chinese fashion, I had tapped into someone's network to solve a problem — and thus stayed clear of any bribery scheme. In the end, I paid the part of the tax I owed, plus delayed interest, but I avoided a much larger fine.

Meanwhile, at the burned plant in Haimen, Zhang, the local mayor, and the Creative Food team rebuilt the entire workshop and obtained all the necessary licenses in less than four months — a process that should have taken at least double that time. The fire chief cleared me of any responsibility but made sure that this time, our company used proper materials and licensed contractors. By April 2011, the new Haimen plant opened.

The two disasters had hovered for months over our company, both with the potential to put Creative Food out of business. Bakkavor was still very much under the gun with its creditors, I didn't have the cash to pay a multi-million-dollar fine, and without the Haimen plant, a third of our clients didn't receive the salads and sandwiches they needed to operate unless I airfreighted them daily from Wuhan to Shanghai. In both cases, my choices to operate outside the law had come back to haunt me. But a loyal network of people inside and outside the company had helped mitigate the impact.

For the sake of stability amid all the upheaval, I had decided to keep the news of my resignation as CEO confidential until I found a successor. But the recruitment process was moving slowly. Watching everyone's commitment during the reconstruction made me feel increasingly guilty about my still-secret plans to leave. In meetings where I was supposed to make decisions about recruitment and investments that would affect the company well after my departure, I procrastinated on purpose, leaving everyone confused about my sudden indecisiveness. All along, I was an emotional wreck, feeling like I was betraying the team I had relied on for so long.

One night late in April 2011, Jane fell to the floor of our bathroom, overcome by an agonizing headache. She had never been susceptible to headaches, so I at first thought it would pass.

"What's going on?" I asked at the bathroom door after she called me with a faint voice. She lay on the cold tile floor, eyes closed, in an effort to control the pain.

"I....I...I don't know," she said, wincing. Every word seemed to cause her more pain. "Can...can you switch the light off? It hurts."

Minutes later, she tried to stand but quickly had to crouch back on the floor because the pain was intolerable. I knew it was serious when she started to sob. Jane doesn't cry. When she gets upset, she turns analytical, and when she is in pain, she sucks it up. A few years before, she had biked 180 kilometers during an Ironman race, enduring a stabbing spasm in her lower back that made her limp through the twenty-six miles of the marathon before finding out the following morning that the brakes on her bike wheel had been stuck all along. That night, watching her crouching in the dark bathroom, weeping silently, face in her palms, generated fears I hadn't experienced before.

After an hour, the pain hadn't receded, so I decided to take her to a hospital. She clenched her teeth, stood up and put her arm around my shoulders. Slowly, we took the elevator downstairs; a taxi took us to the emergency room of one of Shanghai's best international hospitals, where an American doctor looked at her. He wasn't sure what the issue was, but he sounded concerned, mentioning a possible brain hemorrhage or meningitis. The doctor gave her some morphine to alleviate the pain. After a brain scan showed no hemorrhage, he suggested a lumbar puncture to check whether there was any blood in the spine. He did explain that there could be complications, but I decided to go through with it. Jane agreed, but she was already only half-conscious under the influence of the morphine. Watching the doctor plunge the needle into Jane's lower back, I couldn't help but notice how gigantic the instrument looked. The syrupy yellow spine liquid he extracted showed no trace of blood. Yet the doctor recommended that the hospital keep her until she could see a neurologist.

The next day, the Chinese neurologist advised bed rest until the headache passed. Two days later, Jane became paralyzed by pain, unable to raise herself without screaming in agony. I turned restless and angry at the doctor who wouldn't act.

Always practical, Jane asked if I could bring our kids to the hospital; she hadn't seen them since we left home in the middle of that first night. When I arrived with them later that day, they entered the room carefully, conscious that something serious was going on. France, my six-year-old daughter, looked concerned, but she stood next to Jane's bed without saying anything, caressing her forehead. Leo, my five-year-old son, standing on the other side of the bed, asked the question I couldn't bear to articulate aloud: "Is mom going to die?"

Jane turned her head slowly and looked him in the eyes with

a tired smile. "We all die one day," she said.

When your loved one is in trouble, friends and family try to express support and concern by texting incessantly for news, which is exhausting for the care-giver. But our friend Josh did something I'll remember all my life. Instead of texting for news, he took a taxi to the hospital and quickly explained that I needed to get the digital files of Jane's scans. His brother-in-law, a neurologist at the Mayo Clinic, was waiting to give us a second opinion. It was midnight in Minnesota as the doctor looked at Jane's files on his home computer. When Josh and I called him, his diagnosis was clear: the lumbar puncture had caused fluid to leak from her spine, creating a vacuum that sucked her brain down, a condition which had caused a subdural hematoma. The suction also caused bleeding inside her head as vessels popped. Untreated, a blood clot could form in her brain and cause seizures, and could be fatal. We still didn't know what had caused the original headache, but the hematoma was now the main problem.

Josh and I scrambled online, searching for "subdural hematoma," and soon saw that there were specialists in Hong Kong trained to patch such holes. In China, the neurologist still felt that bed rest was the only option. He warned against moving her to Hong Kong. But Jane's condition was getting worse and after hearing from the doctor at the Mayo Clinic, I wasn't going to stay put and wait for the worst. Despite the risks of a three-hour flight, I decided to evacuate her.

Confronted with the possibility of losing the woman I loved, the angst that had possessed me for years while running Creative Food suddenly seemed irrelevant. I flew to Hong Kong and stayed at the hospital with her.

I told Einar about the illness and asked if he could come to China to take over my role at Creative Food until the successor we had identified together could join. Einar came a week later and ran the operations for a few weeks.

On May 23, 2011, sitting alone at Jane's side in the Hong Kong Canossa hospital, I wrote a long email handing over my duties to Creative Food's new CEO, Woody Guo, a tall man from Shandong who had led the China operations of Hormel Foods, the maker of Spam. I heard later from Mike that the team felt I had let them down, but I was past caring about that.

In the stark white room, silence replaced the cacophony of the last months. Outside, the spider trees blossomed with fragrant white flowers, the peaceful atmosphere disrupted only by the "tap tap" of my two awkward fingers on the keyboard. My neck hurt from hunching over the laptop, so I paused a little and listened to Jane breathing peacefully in her sleep.

Both the pizza chain and the fund I had used to acquire it didn't last much beyond my departure from the post of Creative Food CEO. A few months into the start of the pizza chain, I had fired two general managers (Mike, who went willingly, being one of them). After that, the natural course of action would have been for me to step in and run it. I guessed what my backers were thinking: "Xavier did it once; he can do it again."

Jane fully recovered after three weeks in the hospital, but her illness and recovery, instead of being just a passing scare, had focused me on what was really important to me. Despite what my colleagues and former investors believed—and what I had briefly deluded myself into thinking—I had never liked being an entrepreneur. I was unable to distance myself from the daily avalanche of issues that comes with running a business; with me, everything became personal and emotional. The years at Creative Food had drained me, and I wasn't ready to start again. Rather than step in to run it myself, I shut down the pizza chain, liquidated the fund, and returned most of the cash to investors.

Some appreciated the honesty; some were less happy. But for the first time in a decade, I could choose what I wanted to do.

I embarked on an intensive course in learning to read and write Chinese. I had run a company entirely in Mandarin, but I was still illiterate in Chinese. For all those years, I had felt at worst like a cheat and at best like I was missing a large part of what it meant to live in China. With my children now attending local public schools, learning to read and write Chinese was the challenge I most wanted to take up. There was no university program for my particular level, so I rented a desk in an office and dutifully showed up for my studies every day for eight hours, as if it were a full-time job. I did this for a year, alternately studying alone or working with a tutor. Initially, I figured that since I knew a lot of words, I just needed to associate character images to these words. But written Chinese is a whole new world.

Today, I have reached a level that I still find inadequate. I can sometimes read newspaper articles at a snail's pace. But more often, I manage to decipher every character in a sentence only to find out that I still have no clue what the author is trying to say. A few years after my push, I have forgotten how to write most of the characters and mainly rely on word-processing magic to express myself in emails and chats. I've just subscribed to a character-writing app and still hope that someday a switch will flip, and true understanding will come.

During this year of study, companies began to contact me, asking me to advise them on how to grow their businesses in China. First, I saw it as a distraction. But soon I realized I enjoyed the intellectual stimulation and the pressure to understand in a short period of time how a new-to-me industry worked. Today, I partner with a strategy consultant friend, and together we advise multinational companies on a range of complex business issues, mostly in the China food sector.

Mike is never far away, sometimes working alongside me on projects but mostly taking time to travel, to read, and to care for his mother now that his father has passed away. Even though I moved to the U.S. in 2015, Mike and I still talk nearly every week and, when I am in China for work, we travel the country by bus, car, and train, watching how things have changed and debating how they will evolve in the future over our favorite meals. He still insists on ordering for me at restaurants, looking at me with his kind smile each time I compliment his choice.

Creative Food struggled for a few years until Einar was finally able to impose the focus on quality that Bakkavor was known for. In the meantime, some managers left, including Zhang Jianwen, the Haimen plant manager who alerted me to the fire, but most have stayed on. It is now a thriving business with more than $150m in annual revenues.

With every consulting project I take on, I get better insight into the ways China's agriculture continues to evolve and modernize. The situation is still complex. China remains a huge grain producer. It would be cheaper for the country to import, but the government subsidizes farmers in planting grain crops for the sake of maintaining a degree of self-sufficiency in staple foods. In most food categories, China produces at least half of the world's supply. So, it's fair to assume that however China evolves will affect the rest of the world.

Changes in diet have caused an explosion of dairy and animal farming. And there are 700 million farmers still trying to make the best of the little land that is left to them as rapid development eats into farmland, new generations emerge, and cities call. Once in a while, a food processor gets caught with tainted materials and argues that he didn't know what he was buying.

But the Sanlu crisis of 2008 became a turning point in China's relationship with food safety. For the first time, it wasn't possible anymore to claim that the incident was an isolated one at a rogue company or that overseas nations didn't understand the ways of China. Sanlu was a Chinese company, selling milk formula produced in China for Chinese babies. It had received all the badges of honor that a corporation can claim from the authorities. In fact, its management was deemed so good that the company had been exempted from a number of lab tests other companies had to comply with.

There were no more excuses. Chinese consumers were angry and distrustful of the authorities. Even if nobody ever said it officially, industry insiders knew it wasn't just a "Sanlu incident." It was the illustration of a structural imbalance between a fast-increasing demand for milk and a supply anchored in a different age. No spin would make up for the increasing realization among Chinese mothers that something was wrong with the foods they were buying. If they weren't sure anymore that the milk that they fed their children was safe, then a fundamental pact was breached. For the Chinese authorities, that meant social stability was in real danger.

Beijing reacted with force, blasting out a series of changes that bypassed normal processes involving regional governments. Throughout 2009, the central government issued new rules to increase supervision and modernize the dairy supply chain. It pressured dairy processors to get more control over the milk they bought, forcing them to invest in their own herds. In some dairy provinces, peasants were banned from milking their own cows and instead had to take them to milking "stations", or else house them in supervised "cow banks." Modernization was becoming more important than protecting the livelihood of China's farmers.

Ten years later, thousands of non-compliant dairy processors have been shut down, many peasants have left the industry, and millions of cows have been culled, replaced by imported heifers from Australia, Uruguay and New Zealand. Even more important, these cows are now housed in large modern farms that are professionally managed. Today, you can safely estimate that twenty percent of China's dairy cows can be found in operations that have at least five-hundred cows on what would generally be considered modern-scale dairy farms. Another twenty percent can be found in establishments with a hundred cows or more. That's up from nearly zero before 2008.

These modern farms are easier to supervise. As a result, cows inside are better treated and more productive, and the farms themselves are better at recycling the effluents that used to cause huge environmental pollution. Today's modern farms control less than half of China's four million cows, but produce close to two-thirds of the milk in circulation.

A process of modernization that took a century elsewhere has been achieved in less than a decade. Arguably, it was the fastest modernization of any food supply chain in the world. With compulsory white overalls and sanitary masks, computer-controlled feeding and vaccinations, China's new farms — the largest ones house several thousand cows — look more like space stations than any farm you've seen before. Each time I drive through the stench of manure oozing from the ranches north of Bakersfield, California where I now live, I am reminded of what someone said during a visit to such a farm in China: "If you smell manure on a dairy or cattle farm, you can be sure that effluents aren't recycled properly; the operation is outdated."

But the tremendous changes don't hide the fact that sixty percent of the cows in China are still managed by family farmers. And even inside modern farms, many workers still lack experience when it comes to taking care of the animals. There is a reason it took a century to modernize European and American supply chains. You can mobilize capital and technology to accelerate the transformation of an industry, but people take more time to adapt, highlighting just how complex it is to create a reliable and modern supply of any food in China.

With moms increasingly worried about the safety of Chinese-made foods, imports have risen in the post-Sanlu years. Until 2008, China was a net exporter of mostly low-value pre-processed foods like frozen and dried vegetables and fruits going into canned soups and yogurts in the U.S. and Europe. Since 2008, it has turned into a net importer of high value dairy products, wines, meats and boutique olive oils.

From 2004 to 2008, China's food imports grew at a healthy rate of 9.9 percent annually. Since then, the growth rate has jumped to 33.6 percent per year. Food imports in China are already as big as in the U.S., but they are growing four times as fast.

In the face of such changes, Chinese food companies aren't staying idle. With consumers increasingly willing to spend more for better quality foods from abroad, many companies have moved away from old practices focused on reducing costs to business models that aim at building trust. Changes in the dairy sector have caused adjacent industries like poultry and pig husbandry to modernize too. Investors are plowing cash into large-scale integrated meat processing operations that control all stages, from raising chicks or piglets to slaughter. The seafood industry at the center of the EU investigations in 2001 is changing too. New regulations issued since 2015 have increased compliance costs for Chinese fishing boats, bringing them closer to international standards. At home, domestic aquaculture is under new environmental scrutiny with "zero growth" policies until the level of compliance improves.

The Chinese government seems to have clearly understood that reforming its agriculture sector is now required by its citizens. For the growing middle-class, economic growth isn't enough as an indicator of prosperity.

With twenty-five million rural dwellers migrating to the cities every year, the countryside of China is changing too. There are fewer farmers, and they're getting older. But that doesn't mean they're still operating as they did a decade ago. The farmers who stayed in the villages are often the best ones. They can afford to stay because they manage to extract a good return from their land, and over the past decade, they have typically taken over the management of the land left fallow by villagers who moved to the city. Kong Xiangzhi, an expert in Agriculture Economics at Beijing People University, quantified this change for me:

"The proportion of farm land transferred – that is, the land leased by someone other than the original family with rights to that land – has grown from less than five percent in 2008 to close to thirty percent in 2016," he said.

That's a fundamental change for buyers like Creative Food: the emergence of a larger pool of professional and like-minded growers, people who tend to listen more to their clients because they have much more at stake than the farmers do. These new entrepreneurs – *dahu*, or "big households," as they are called in the countryside – need to earn a return on their investment, pay other villagers for the land, and sell an amount of produce that is far too large to just feed to the family in case of disagreement with clients. These types of operations didn't exist when I first started growing my broccoli and lettuce.

While that's a significant change, it's unlikely that these big-household entrepreneurs will expand to build operations similar to California's giant farms, taking over China's countryside. A big household often operates a farm ten times as big as a peasant farmer – around ten acres for vegetable farmers – but it can't compare with a U.S. farmer. Even when Chinese cities have absorbed around seventy percent of the population, a figure similar to developed countries, close to 500 million people will remain in the countryside, with far too little arable land for all of them to operate at an efficient scale.

But I like it that the "big household" operators seem to have surprised most of Beijing's policy makers. After the 2008 milk crisis, the government tried to promote the grouping of peasants into "cooperatives" or, alternatively, it encouraged the establishment of large corporate farms funded by private capital. But the cooperatives often turned out to be mere marketing organizations, leaving farmers to till individual plots as they always had. And I have yet to see a large corporate farm growing fruits or vegetables turn a profit. Such farms require large investments and carry costs that the peasant farmers don't have, including leasing the land from the village and hiring local laborers. Meanwhile, their crop yields are similar or inferior to individual farmers. This may change over time, but it's not guaranteed.

The Big Households have more flexible arrangements with their fellow villagers. When they operate someone else's land, they may simply do it for free until they know how much it can yield. For the villager living in town, it's a way to keep the family rights to a piece of land in case they lose a job. Over time, the two sides work out lease arrangements that are mutually beneficial. Beijing, catching up to the already-underway formation of Big Households, recently started to promote a simplified legal structure called "family farms," allowing farmers to issue invoices so they can sell their produce to companies and retailers directly — and also online to anxious moms in the large cities.

It's a proven model in European countries, where family farms remain the dominant structure outside of the animal husbandry and grain sectors, in which highly-automated corporate farms dominate. And it's a trend I've seen in several parts of China.

China's family farms are starting to invest in smaller agricultural equipment to improve productivity, exchanging innovative ideas with peers in social media groups that help accelerate the propagation of innovations. In 2014, in the mountains of Sichuan in southwest China, in a region which a decade ago had been devastated by a terrible earthquake, I visited Big Households that had converted rice fields into kiwifruit orchards. The average household income for kiwi growers in the region was three times as high as that of the average farmer in China. Several Big Households in that isolated Sichuanese village had made so much money that their farmers were driving luxury German sedans.

Yao Zhiqiang was waiting for me at the exit gate at Wuhan airport, grinning and waving.

"*Laoban* (boss)," he called reaching for my bag with a large smile. "*Ni hao!*"

Yao, a sturdy man in his mid-thirties, spoke rapid-fire Chinese with a Hubei accent. It was June 2016, and he was now the manager in charge of logistics at Creative Food's Wuhan plant. It was also five years since I left the company for good. But I was back to pay a visit to the Xinzhou region of Hubei Province east of Wuhan, near Doug's old model farm. Einar, who still oversaw the company for Bakkavor, had given me his blessing to return and talk to some of my former colleagues and workers.

Leaving the airport, I walked with Yao toward the parking lot where he had left the company shuttle bus. Yao talked to me like an old friend. He had never been so friendly before, though he was part of the original team of employees who started the plant in 2003. I was relaxed, no longer the boss, and he seemed to be at ease too. I actually looked forward to the ninety-minute ride in the rickety old van. The Wuhan sky was gloomy as we entered a modern, mostly-empty highway that didn't exist when I first built the plant.

"It's going to rain today," said Yao, leaning forward over the wheel to look up at forbidding clouds. I didn't respond, but I was suddenly thrown back to those tense days of waiting with Doug for a Hubei rainfall to stop so we could start planting our lettuce.

Yao's cell phone rang constantly. I could hear him giving instructions related to deliveries for the evening. "My drivers are tired," he said after getting off one call. "They're not bad people, but they tend to forget things, and for me one bag missing can mean a lot of trouble with customers."

As we passed through Yangluo Town, once barely an overgrown village and now a place with a growing population of 600,000, Yao explained that he had bought an apartment there. Back when I traveled to the plant, I used to stay in the one and only hotel. "You remember, boss, when we all used to sleep in the dormitory at the factory?" he said with a proud smile, recalling the early days when I alone slept outside the plant's communal housing.

Today, he owned not only an apartment but also a car. And with increasing demand from rural folks looking for housing in town, his flat has already increased in value by fifty percent over two years. With a steady job and growing assets, he was clearly feeling pretty confident about the future.

As the car negotiated the country roads, we talked about his wife, who is an inventory clerk at the same plant, and their baby daughter. "Are you worried about the safety of the foods you buy for her?" I asked.

"Well, we're careful. I try to buy my vegetables from the village where I was born," he said. "I don't really trust the wholesale market in Yangluo. And for the fish, I know the farmers put fertilizer in the ponds to accelerate algae growth and save money on feed. So, I try to stay away from fat carp."

The bus passed by the Chaoda farm. Between yellowish plastic tunnels, weeds grow everywhere. Curious to know how the company that used to be my nemesis was performing, I asked Yao about it.

"It's still operating," he said, "but nobody is really managing it."

Yao remembered that Chaoda sub-contracted some land to local strawberry growers to make ends meet. Later in my visit, someone at the plant told me that another part of the land had been covered with asphalt and was being used for driving lessons.

After slightly more than an hour, the bus turned left onto a road that led to the factory. I reminded Yao how this used to be a dirt track. Part of my negotiation with the Secretary Wu was to get this road built. "We were so cheap," I recalled, remembering the haggling over every contractual point at a time when the company relied on every penny to survive.

He smiled back at me, nodding but with some pride. "I have a story for you!" he said. "For years, the local authorities have asked us to spend 10,000 renminbi (about $1,500) on a large advertising sign at this cross-roads. They tried everything. Cajoling didn't work so they put more pressure. In the end, Creative didn't spend the money, but Chaoda did — and after Chaoda stopped paying, a large cotton grower put his sign there. But now they're both bankrupt! And we're still alive and growing!"

Chaoda wasn't bankrupt, but it was a shadow of itself, limping along as a penny stock on the Hong Kong exchange. Like Yao, I couldn't help but feel a bit of pride. We *had* made it while so many others had not. And people like him had benefitted. Creative Food now supplies Mc Donald's too, and Bakkavor keeps investing in larger and more modern facilities.

At the plant, Li Liyong, the factory manager, was waiting in the yard as the bus came to a stop. I had promoted Li from his Guangzhou job as a quality manager a month before I left the company. Like Yao, the round-faced manager seemed joyful and proud to show me his work. Secretary Zhao from the nearby National Farm where Doug operated the model farm was there, too. Secretary Wu had retired a long time ago, so I had asked Secretary Zhao if he could help me trace Old Xia, the head of Village Number 9 who had worked with Doug to try to change farming practices.

The Wuhan plant hadn't changed. It was not fancy, but it was brimming with activity, crowded with workers in white protective clothes, cutting, packing, cleaning. There was none of the scruffiness I used to complain of but never did much about. Clearly, Li had a dedicated budget to keep rust and mold away. Inside the workshop, brand new signs in English and Chinese reminded workers of what they were supposed to do:

"Clean hands after bathroom time"
"Knives' sanitary bath time compulsory"

There was even a stop watch and a bell to indicate when it was time to sanitize hands and tools.

Bakkavor had introduced a few practical solutions I had seen in the UK, including small magnetic rulers attached to the wall that could be grabbed at any time to check whether the cut lettuce met size specifications. But what impressed me most was how the culture among workers had changed.

After a quick tour, I sat down back in the changing room, pulling my boots off as Secretary Zhao and his small group caught up. "President Li, you won't believe what happened just now," he said with a laugh. "I was walking through the plant, and one of the workers told me I wasn't allowed to be inside the workshop without a protective sanitary mask."

Zhao didn't seem upset, though it was clearly unusual for him to be called out like that when visiting one of his tenants. Li Liyong looked a bit embarrassed, confirming he should have made both of us wear masks as well. A few years ago, I would have laughed in disbelief if someone had told me that a Chinese worker, like the red-bearded man in England so many years ago, would ever call out a Communist Party official on sanitary procedures.

On our way to Village Number 10 where Old Xia had been transferred, I asked Secretary Zhao about the changes in the local economy. The National Farm still grew a large amount of cotton, but that crop's share of production was down significantly from the 80 percent it represented in 2003. More people now grew fruit and vegetables that they sold in the local markets. As a result, Zhao said, the villagers' income had doubled in fifteen years. It didn't sound exceptional over such a long period, but it came with additional benefits. Zhao explained that since 2006, villagers had received a government stipend after turning sixty years of age, which allowed them to retire for a minimal annual fee.

Farmers who stayed in the village or returned after a stint outside have turned entrepreneurial. In Xinzhou, Zhao told me that a fifth of the land is now farmed by Big Households. A Wuhan-based company just planted a 300-acre kiwifruit orchard under modern greenhouses.

As Zhao and I arrived at Village Number 10, I spotted Old Xia. Standing among six other party executives from nearby villages, his dark intense eyes on me, he waited silently for our cohort to get out of our cars and settle in the spartan meeting room at the village's government office. He was shorter than all his colleagues, but his neatly-ironed white shirt reflected two terms Doug often used to describe him: crisp and disciplined.

As everyone proceeded with the first polite exchanges, I notice that Xia preferred to let his colleagues answer my questions about recent developments in the area. I quickly realized that his Mandarin wasn't good enough to communicate directly with me. I could guess what he said, but I needed someone to help translate from the local dialect.

"Doug's input about fertilizer was really valuable," he said, when I pressed him about what Doug's stint in Xinzhou had brought to the community. "We used to only apply nitrogen, but he introduced compound fertilizers that were much more effective."

"But Doug was stubborn too," he added. "He wanted to follow a rigid irrigation program even on days like today, when rain was sure to come." All the officials nodded in agreement, looking out the window at the gray sky.

It was clear that Xia was guarded in front of his colleagues. His answers were concise, but lacked the emotion I was hoping he would share about his relationship with Doug. "So that's it?" I thought. "Fertilizer and irrigation?"

After a quick lunch, I asked Xia to go out for a stroll in nearby village #7, hoping for a less formal conversation. One of his colleagues accompanied us and helped with translation in Mandarin. The village was like many I saw back during Doug's time; it hadn't changed much. The houses were still made of brick, and poor-quality paint peeled away everywhere. But the streets were paved and clean, and they looked more orderly. Unlike before, there was no litter in sight. On a small public square brightened by a ray of sunshine that managed to break through the clouds, Xia showed me colorful exercise equipment being fitted out for public use.

"People here don't need much. With the basic pension and the cash they get from leasing their land out, they have enough. But all of them watch satellite TV and some even travel regularly to other provinces," he said, "so they've become more demanding about a cleaner environment."

He too had ambitions. His son, who used to play with Doug outside their home, recently graduated from Wuhan Agriculture University with a degree in automation. "I wanted him to go for a PhD, but he's decided to take a job in Guangzhou," he said, disappointed. "I bought an apartment in Wuhan for him and hope he'll return, but there is not much I can say."

At the corner of a block, I counted three tractors. "We have twenty of those altogether," Xia said. "A group of local farmers bought them and lease them out at the time of cultivation."

Then for the first time he smiled at me. "It's all thanks to Dugelasi," he said, using Doug's Chinese name. "He was the one who first came up with the idea of using a tractor."

Later Old Xia proudly pointed at several sprayers. The tanks were plastic and were bought from a local equipment maker, but they were similar to the one Doug built so painstakingly out of stainless steel a decade ago.

On my way back to the airport, with Yao once again at the wheel, I was quieter, trying to make sense of what I had seen and heard. To the untrained eye, the region hadn't changed much. But I was impressed. One difference was the level of mechanization. It was still true that Chinese farms were too small to use equipment like that used in the U.S. and that the machines they did use were only partially automated to keep costs down. But the move toward some level of mechanization was a good sign. With more villagers moving to small towns like Yangluo, was getting harder and costlier to find farm workers. And mechanized solutions that work in China will likely work in other developing countries too.

It was also interesting to hear Xia talk about the increased attention to fertilizer and to soil amendments in general. Back when Doug talked about plowing deeper, nobody wanted to have anything to do with it. I was happy that locals listened to at least some of what he had said and applied it in ways they knew to be best.

When Doug called people out about the empty chemical packs that he saw near the aquaculture ponds, peasants stared at him uncomprehendingly. Today, consumers like Yao who favor more natural ways and the emergence of more professional farmers like big households are forcing changes in local agriculture practices. I have recently started to see people fishing in canals around Shanghai that used to be heavily polluted.

The scale of China's agriculture and its problems remain so large that they defy easy predictions. But as my story shows, progress is possible. And change is essential. The lives and livelihoods of real people are at stake.

In Hubei, the rickety shuttle bus was still tumbling down the highway when the first drops of water interrupted my reflections. It was a day of rain for Hubei—exactly as Old Xia had predicted.

EPILOGUE

MOST FOREIGN businesspeople who engage with China pay lip
service to the truth that the country's scale, complexity and culture
make for a different environment than they are used to operating
in. But many executives I have advised struggle to genuinely
grasp the implications of that. I think that, subconsciously,
they still believe that as China develops economically, it will
become more Western. And this leads them to repeat some of the
mistakes I made in Creative Food's early days. My bagged salads
failed because I ignored longstanding culinary traditions and
views on health, and the Chinese preference for fresh vegetables
from local wet markets over giant Western-style supermarkets'
alternatives.

In many respects, China is more likely to be a global trend-
setter than a follower. For example, in 2020 Chinese consumers
used electronic payments at a rate 60 times higher than in the
United States. Twenty five percent of them ordered groceries
online versus less than 4% in the United States. Those percentages
have grown for the U.S. because of the COVID-19's effects on
consumer behavior there, but China is growing even faster.

Lin Gang, a 36-year-old orange grower in Qinglong village in
Sichuan province, regards me via WeChat video, one of the few
ways of meeting in a time of global pandemic. I am in my home
office in Oakland, California, seeking a few more nuggets of

insight from one on the front lines of agriculture in China today. Lin beams at me from behind round spectacles. His two-year-old son battles to climb onto his lap as he tells me his story.

He grew up in a hilly region in southwestern China, roughly 150 km by car southeast of Chengdu, at a time when it took up to four hours to reach the provincial capital by train. With his parents working in faraway coastal towns, he spent long stretches of time away from his family, boarding with friends in a nearby town. "Being far away from my parents, seeing them once a year only, weighed on me as a student," he says. "One day I called my mom from a street phone. But I couldn't say a word. I just choked (on sobs) while she repeated my name."

In his late teens, he went to Beijing to study agronomy at the prestigious China Agriculture University. He worked hard, spent a decade as a technician on an industrial farm in the northwest region of Xinjiang, and then returned home to be with his retired parents. That was in 2017. He married a local girl and fathered two children. Since then, he has successfully applied new sustainable growing practices to his family's crop and harvests fruit that can fetch three times the average market price. "I came back to my village to take over the family farm and changed the way we grow and market our wonderful local blood oranges," he says.

In 2020, he went one step further: He pulled in a few neighbors who had been following some of his practices and formed a small cooperative. "This allows us to group purchase the fertilizer, equipment and pesticides that we need to grow and to invest in our own online WeChat store," he explains. "We hope to bring more villagers into our group so everyone can benefit."

As with the broccoli and lettuce growers I worked with at Creative Food, orcharding families including Lin's once sold their produce to local wholesalers who bought oranges from them for as little as a dime per pound, then moved the fruits through long chains of intermediaries ending in a wet market or on the shelves of a supermarket in an urban neighborhood a thousand miles away. Farmers kept up with the growing demand by throwing more fertilizer and pesticides at their crops, saturating their soils with chemicals along the way. Years of food scandals stemming from these practices resulted in a corrosion of consumer confidence. In reaction, end-customers — especially moms like my friends Xu and Li in Shanghai — organized with neighbors and schoolmates to buy directly from producers they trusted. But these early efforts still lacked the necessary scale to really change the way Chinese bought their foods.

Now everything has changed.

Lin and other young farmers like him, wanting to win those customers' trust (and their business), drew on their education and entrepreneurial spirit and changed the way their foods are grown. But in doing so, they also tapped into the giant online ecosystems that have revolutionized the way consumers purchase goods in China.

In Lin's marketing video on WeChat, classical guitar plays in the background while an invisible hand draws characters forming the name of his cooperative: "Good farmers. Food from the Terroir." It goes on to show pristine orange groves on hillsides and a pastoral scene of young men and women sitting at a long communal table shaded from the sun, tasting a selection of oranges. The WeChat store is now an important channel for selling the cooperative's produce and interacting with those who buy it. "I get messages from consumers who tell me what we did right — and where we can improve," he says with a smile.

As Lin speaks, I think back to my conversation with Lu, the broccoli grower in Shanghai who argued with me in his fields against focusing on quality rather than size because that was not what local farmers were used to. Lin represents a new breed of farmers who know who their consumers are and what they want and are willing to change local farming practices thoughtfully — and to share their knowledge to benefit their communities as well as themselves and their customers.

The evolution from Lu's attitude to Lin's and from the Chinese food consumers of the past to today's growing demand for quality, transparency, and clean food parallels the modernization of China's food sector, a modernization that is in many ways uniquely Chinese but has big implications. Just as I learned that in order to thrive as a foreigner in business in China, I needed to listen to my local managers and workers and respect the country's rich culture and agricultural past, so Western businesses seeking to profit from China's vast potential must understand how differently China's food sector is changing.

Observing carefully and acknowledging differences requires real openness. The reality is that I truly grew my business only once I let go of my arrogance. My managers' insights weren't always displayed in elegant Power Point slides. Some struggled to articulate their views in a way I understood, and language sometimes felt like an insurmountable barrier. But none of that mattered. It was building of trust in their judgment that transformed my business.

China's leading role in the digital grocery space also reinforces another lesson I learned at Creative Food: consumer retail in China is not going to follow the U.S. model. With big supermarket chains like Wal-Mart struggling to offer consumers in China the safe foods they now expect, digital ecosystems like Alibaba, WeChat, JD.com and others have entered the fray to offer platforms that connect hundreds of millions of farmers like Lin with hundreds of millions of consumers. Through these platforms, the farmers and consumers have created what amounts to a digital village.

Best agriculture practices and technical information spread easily and rapidly among farmers across huge distances in a way that I could never have imagined twenty years ago. Through the same platforms, as Lin noted, consumers rate quality and hold farmers accountable. Middlemen posing as farmers get caught, penalized or delisted when consumers complain. And farmers earn a better profit.

For a long time, I saw the country's 700 million farmers as a huge hurdle to China's agricultural modernization. Now I see them as the gatekeepers of this very different agricultural model. Even when urbanization reaches a mature rate of 70%, perhaps 20 or 30 years from now, China will likely still have hundreds of millions of relatively small family farms. Certainly, there is more scale than in the past, and some sectors are industrializing more than others. A significant part of the dairy sector, for example, is industrialized and operating at global standards of efficiency. But I now believe that the family-based farm will continue to be the foundation of China's agricultural system for decades to come – and that this is a good thing for both agriculture and the country itself.

Lin's generation represents the emergence of larger, more professional family farms made possible by the fifteen million villagers who have been migrating to the cities every year over the past two decades. "My family doesn't have a lot of land," says Lin, "but the cooperative can lease land from people who left for the city. We get to keep the harvest, and they keep access to their family plot for when they want to come back and retire in the village."

All this also means that a "foodie" culture has returned to China, where culinary traditions, as I noted, have been important for centuries. Today's Chinese consumer continues to access the wide variety of foods they traditionally purchased from

XAVIER NAVILLE

neighborhood markets while also reviving breeds and varieties that had faded away. Free-range black pig meat from the Zhejiang hills near Shanghai can now be delivered in twenty-nine minutes to most Shanghai residents—and a QR code on the packaging connects to a website showing live images of the farm's animals.

Again, all this puts China ahead of the West in some ways. In the U.S., for example, farmers markets and community supported agriculture initiatives have surged. But while they have expanded, they still largely serve consumers who can afford to pay, say, $1 for an egg—a price that only an aspirational elite can afford. In China, what is now called *community group purchasing* offers fast deliveries and affordable prices on high-quality foods to tens of millions of average urban households.

This represents tremendous opportunities for foreign business and entrepreneurs with eyes on the giant Chinese market. But I advise all my clients to understand that we don't know better than the locals and that we should learn from them. Listen, listen, listen and be willing to adjust your model. In today's China, it's unlikely that a Frenchman who doesn't speak the language would be able to carve out a niche serving lettuce to restaurant chains across the country. There are many local operators now capable of delivering the same quality, faster and cheaper than I did. I just did it earlier and built a business that benefits from being larger than all its competitors. It is my strong belief that tomorrow's winners will come to China with products and services that competitors can't easily replicate and they will tailor their business models to fit China's specific operating environment, whether that means intellectual property that is actually defensible or access to food supplies that China doesn't have.

In our conversation today, Lin is proud to say that the other two families in his cooperative now earn a profit of about $15,000 annually, much more than the average rural income in Sichuan province. He himself was able to rebuild his traditional rammed-earth home into a modern concrete building with electricity and a sewage system.

He is also proud that he reunited his family after all those years away from home and that his parents are enjoying retirement. Most afternoons, his dad plays Mahjong with old friends. In the evening, his mom practices square dancing with other villagers. A new high-speed train station will soon connect their village to Chengdu in less than 30 minutes. "I can imagine my children studying and working away from home, but they'll be able to visit us," he says with satisfaction, adding, "Maybe one day, they will want to return to the village for good like I did."

He hopes the positive changes he helped bring to local farming practices will pay off for others beyond his own family. "Since I studied under experts at university, I've been fascinated by how I could improve China's soils. Today, I am proud that people here benefit from that experience," he says. "My hope is that when the soils recover and become healthy, the village itself will be healthy."

ACKNOWLEDGEMENTS

There is only one name on the book cover, but none of this would have been possible without the loyalty and dedication of an army of friends and colleagues who all contributed at various levels to creating the Creative Food story.

There wouldn't be a story without my adored wife, Jane Lanhee Lee's, savvy and unconditional support over two decades since I met her. When I woke up with a knot in my stomach, she found the words to get me into the right mindset for the day. When I waivered, she asked tough questions, without ever entertaining the idea that Creative Food wouldn't succeed. Then, it's Jane again who felt that my stories needed to be shared with a wider audience. And once I started to write, she lit a fire under me by making it clear that she would never look at me the same if I didn't complete this project.

When Jane's editing became too much for our relationship- she one day picked three colored markers to underline all the parts where I repeated myself — Leslie T Chang intervened. I remember her sitting in our living room in Shanghai on a promotion trip for the Chinese translation of her book "Factory Girls", looking at us bickering. She took me under her wing, introduced me to a wonderful editor and master-edited the book over five years, writing tens of pages of comments. To her "good enough" was never an option. Thank you, Leslie, for your brilliant reads, broad vision and for believing in me. I can't imagine how you did it all. The late nights spent editing my manuscript, the hours on the plane you spent working on my document while reporting for your own book and taking care of your family—I will never be able to thank you enough. You're a true and genuine friend and the best teacher one can hope for.

Terzah Becker had the ungrateful task of turning my prose into something coherent. She invested far beyond the normal call of duty, working on week-ends to send me feedback on a timely basis, riding the ups and downs with me, and always ready to find appeasing words when I got frustrated with the whole process. Writing this book brought me a new friend.

France Naville essentially grew up with this book. Joining me in my little office on Xinguo Road near her Elementary school in Shanghai to do her homework while I wrote. As of this moment, she is a bright high school sophomore proofreading the pre-publishing copy with a level of scrutiny and speed that I would be incapable of. From an interested watcher, she has turned into an invaluable partner.

I still talk to Mike Chen nearly every day, for many of our consulting projects, causing my family to chant "Mikeu, Mikeu" each time his Wechat handle appears on my phone. For twenty years, France's godfather has remained a loyal friend and an invaluable asset in my quest to understand China and its people in a more nuanced way. These months away from each other during the Covid pandemic have reminded me how much I miss traveling with him, sharing dinner in remote hotels around the China countryside.

Einar Gustafsson and Agust Gudmundsson's trust in me never wavered, proving time after time that their word and commitment to Creative Food was infallible. I am proud that they have now turned my rickety enterprise into a massive business known across China for its professionalism.

Graham Earnshaw, my publisher, had the foresight to see in

this book the opportunity to communicate a nuanced perspective of China and the ways it is changing to the world.

At the worst time for Creative Food, Roger Marshall tapped into his connections to help save the company, staying true to his word that he believed in the business. He was the most constant supporter for an aspiring leader. He assembled a group of intelligent investors and directors who never failed to express their enthusiasm for Creative Food's achievements. Lewis Rutherfurd, Hang Wah Man, Bernard Pouliot, Frank Fletcher, Ricky Wong, thank you for staying on beam while everything else seemed to ask for a change.

My forever counsel and friend, Frank Rocco, made sure I remained sane at all times. He and his wife May Lam provided me with a home to stay on my occasional trips to Hong Kong. I am proud to count them as close friends.

Denis and Isabelle Andre hosted me countless times in their homes in my first years in Shanghai, providing comfort and cultural familiarity at a time when there wasn't any.

I am forever grateful to Creative Food's managers who gave it all to make Creative Food a success and continued to help in the reporting of this book: Xu Shen, Yang Zhongcheng, Sun Guoqiang, Su Hong, Qiu Wei, Kevin Zhong, Tiger Wang, Tracy Wu, Fang Yijie.

Mike DeNoma built the platform that allowed me to start Creative. He was kind and generous with his time when helping me with the reporting of Asiafoods' early days.

David Landers, whom I replaced as Finance Director in Asiafoods, provided guidance, advice and friendship over the past two decades.

My partner at Vision Management Consultants, Frank Gibson, has lived with this book as long as I have, providing advice, exchanging ideas and sharing his intelligent views on

China's unique path to modernization.

Fred Crosetto helped with contacts and his own experience of running a business in China. Michael Dunne shared his experience of writing "American Wheels Chinese Roads, the story of General Motors in China". Rob Robson from One Harvest in Australia brought me into his family, providing solace for Jane and I when things got rough.

Eric Rosenblum introduced me to Jane and for that I'll be eternally grateful.

My sister Dorothee Naville, has been such an amazing contributor, taking on the duties of being a daughter and a son to my parents when I was living overseas. She never held a grudge, allowing me to grow a life far away from home without feeling like I had abandoned everyone.

Nearly three years after the day my dad bid his farewell to this world, I'm still learning about him. Dad, you taught me to respect all individuals, and to look for the details that make everyone special. I miss you every day.

Mom, your unconditional love and high expectations instilled the necessary self-esteem that carried me through this adventure. I love you.

About The Author

Xavier was born in France and in 1997 moved to China where he built Creative Food, which is today a key supplier to major restaurant chains across the country including McDonald's, KFC and Starbucks. He sold the company to Bakkavor Group PLC from the UK in 2007 and continued to run the business until 2011. Xavier is now a principal at Vision Management Consultants and works on strategy and M&A projects in the food sector for multinationals in China. He is also a Strategy & Execution coach for CEOs and their leadership teams. He currently lives in Oakland, California, and divides his time between there and China.